RACE,
RELIGION,
and the
CONTINUING
AMERICAN DILEMMA

Also by C. Eric Lincoln

The Black Muslims in America

My Face Is Black

Sounds of the Struggle: Persons and Perspectives in Civil Rights

The Negro Pilgrimage in America

A Pictorial History of the Negro in America (with Langston Hughes and Milton Meltzer)

Is Anybody Listening to Black America?

The Black Church Since Frazier

The Black Experience in Religion (editor)

Martin Luther King, Jr.: A Profile (editor)

This Road Since Freedom

The Avenue, Clayton City

The Black Church in the African American Experience (with Lawrence Mamiya)

Coming Through the Fire: Surviving Race and Place in America

RACE, RELIGION, and the CONTINUING AMERICAN DILEMMA

Revised Edition

C. Eric Lincoln

HILL and WANG
A division of Farrar, Straus and Giroux
New York

A portion of Chapter 4, "Black Ethnicity and Religious Nationalism," is adapted
from the author's work *The Black Church Since Frazier,* © 1974 by Schocken
Books, Inc., and is used by permission of Schocken Books. Other parts of this book
are adapted from articles that first appeared in *Soundings, Review and Expositor,
Democrat and Chronicle, Religion in Life, Religious Education,* and *The Journal of
the Interdenominational Theological Center*; and in *The Muslim Community in
North America,* Earle H. Waugh, editor, published by the University of Alberta
Press.

Library of Congress Cataloging in Publication Data
Lincoln, C. Eric (Charles Eric), 1924–
    Race, religion, and the continuing American dilemma / C. Eric
Lincoln.— Rev. ed.
        p. cm.
    Includes bibliographical references and index.
    ISBN 0-8090-1623-0 (alk. paper)
        1. United States—Race relations.   2. United States—Race
relations—Religious aspects.   3. Racism—United States.   4. Afro-
Americans—Religion.   5. United States—Church history.   I. Title.
E185.61.L572   1999
305.8′00973—dc21   98-33377

For H. SHELTON SMITH

> Professor of Religion Emeritus, Duke University, whose work and whose life were an insistent reminder to the church he loved and celebrated that "image" is not enough

and for
RASHANA, RUNAKO, TAURUS, KENAN, AND NYASHA

> children of my children, whose fledgling investment in the faith is still innocent of its national expression

Contents

Prologue: The Social Greening of America[1]

WE Americans, whatever our color, need to rethink the principles and presuppositions which structure our conditional approach to living with each other. We must learn to accept each other with appreciation for what we are and for what we can become, while daring to hope and to believe that we ourselves will be so accepted. It will not be easily accomplished. Too much history, and too much that masquerades as history, gets in the way. But history, real or imagined, is always what is past and can only be justified in context. So must our own determinations be made in context, lest the incoherence in the history we leave compound the dilemma bequeathed by the history we received. Blacks know, for example, that not all the devils in the world are blue-eyed white males. It is time to say that. We do not enhance the principle of personal culpability by branding all those of a class of cohorts as ipso facto a class of culpables.

By the same logic, all of our social misfits are not young black studs hunting in packs and rapping out the frustrations their daddies brought back from 'Nam and the Persian Gulf in jungle rhythms punctuated with obscenities. In 'Nam and in the Gulf there was no black or white, just buddy-buddy. Brothers-in-arms, sometimes in the very arms of death. Back at home, it is a pale horse of a different color, but it is still death, and if you don't like it, you can at least rap about it. Somebody may get the message eventually.

The prevailing American tradition damns all blacks with the

same tar brush and baptizes all whites in the same bucket of white-wash, irrespective of merit or consent. Stifled between these blankets of blame and blessing, an undetermined number of self-conscious individuals reject the dubious endowments of conventional wisdom in favor of being free to be themselves on their own terms. In the challenge ahead, we will need to identify these moral mavericks, for they will have prominent roles to play in the social greening of the world that is on its way. We sense that they are there, but we do not always know who they are. What we do know is that black people and white people alike range from degeneracy to heroism, but they are all people, mere people, substantially like ourselves.

This society will take a quantum leap forward when we learn to look for and to celebrate the many positives that spangle our long travail together. It is not disloyal to the cause, however that cause is defined, to recognize through all the murkiness of self-interest the uniqueness of the human endowment when it is performing at its best. The supreme disloyalty is not to a bell that has tolled itself into silence, but to the bell that has yet to ring. In our contemporary struggle for self-affirmation through the appreciation of others, we could, for example, remember with profit the patient, caring black women who over countless generations of the Anglo-African odyssey nurtured and cared for the sons and daughters of white Americans, often to the neglect of their own. Surely these women were a national treasure, as were those selfless white women who forfeited fame, fortune, marriage, and leisure to plant the liberating torch of literacy and education in the stygian darkness so lately punctured by "emancipation." The civil rights movement was made up of inspired and intrepid coalitions of Blacks-and-whites-together, who ignored the fickle lines of race and gender and religion and marched through the gates of hell to redeem the soul of America. We have all that to build on, and that spirit, though bruised and muted, is not dead. We must not forfeit by default what cost so much to wring out of our own recalcitrance. There are white people and black people next door and across town who know that the future is here and are prepared to endorse it, if they can hear a word of encouragement or see a gesture of support. But there is still risk in ignoring convention, in being out of step with the agents of panic and the gurus of political correctness. It is time now to reach for the hand that is reaching for tomorrow, whatever color that hand may be. The evening of today is already far spent.

We must get on with the future of our country and our world. It will be a future in which the claims of race and place will be denied and rebuffed until they die for want of nurture, or it will be no future at all. The world has grown too small for bigotry, too tired for casuistry, and too uncertain for temporizing. People everywhere are seriously reevaluating what it means to live, and what conditions of living are unacceptable for the human imprimatur wherever it may be found.

By any estimate, we have a lot going for us here in America. We live in the world's greatest democracy; we are the world's most advanced humanitarian society; our nation is the world's most renowned and effective citadel of freedom. We exceed the rest of the world in technological proficiency and genius and creativity. We have unfathomable reservoirs of self-confidence and inexhaustible fountains of optimism.

We are all colors, all creeds, all nationalities. We are Americans, the people of the Dream. Such is our self-perception. We can be more than that when we learn to use our singular advantages and achievements in the true humanizing of the social order, and in the creation of a truly responsible society. Americans have deep wellsprings of self-reliance, and we are not readily given to admissions of failure or self-doubt. Yet we know, if only because we are too American not to know, that we can be better than we are. We can excel in whatever we undertake with conviction.

The record speaks for itself! In science and technology, in medicine and communications, in the mapping of space and the production of energy, ad so on, ad infinitum, the record speaks most eloquently. We have won enough Nobel Prizes to consider that achievement a national property. Yet the signs and the symbols of our dismal record in coming to terms with our humanity wink back at us with silent accusation like frozen stars in a firmament of moral expectation. We can be better than we are. Our failures fly in the face of an ethical commitment that is stated or implicit in all of the critical foundations of the culture: religion, law, citizenship, and all the rest. In America, the right to be human is the right to participate in all of the common ventures afforded by a just and humane society.

Now we must prepare for a new society that gives full honor to what we profess. We do not have much time, for the new order for which we must prepare is already here in prospect and expectation. We must not let the lingering haze of the smoldering fires of yesterday obscure the possibilities inherent in tomorrow. If we do not learn to trust each other, we cannot truly trust ourselves. The stresses of contemporary civilization are multifarious and multiplying. But one thing claims attention above all the rest. It seems that all over the world, in the words of Omar Khayyam, "Men want dug up again," which is to say that faceless and long-abused people are demanding and dying for the right to be human and to be so recognized—to have life with dignity, creativity, and responsibility. That, it seems to me, is neither unreasonable nor impossible. We all belong in the circle of human enfranchisement. That is the least we can do for our country; that is the most we can do for each other; that is the best we can do for ourselves and for our posterity. That is the ultimate meaning of survival, and the only strategy that will work. I call it no-fault reconciliation—the recognition that we are all of a kind, with the same vulnerabilities, the same possibilities, and the same needs for God and each other.

C. Eric Lincoln
July 1998

Introduction

The problem of the Twentieth Century is the problem of the color line. . . .

The Nation has not yet found peace from its sins; the freedman has not yet found peace in his promised land. . . .

Christianity is contrary to the spirit of caste—spiritual kinship transcends all other relations. The race problem will be solved when Christianity gains control of the innate wickedness of the human heart, and men learn to apply in dealing with their fellows the simple principles of the Golden Rule and the Sermon on the Mount. . . .

W.E.B. Du Bois[1]

TIME has a fugitive quality to it, and the twentieth century, which was once heralded as a bright new occasion for human ennoblement, is coming to a close. It is no longer bright, and it is no longer new. We still have not found peace from our sins; nor is the evidence that we entertain a serious commitment to the principles of the Golden Rule one of the compelling features of our generation. Prominent among our problems remains the perennial problem Du Bois complained of when the twentieth century was still in its infancy. That problem persists despite the cosmetics of countless "political solutions" and "gentlemen's agreements" which promised change without changing anything, and despite the tortured strategies of those good Americans whose consciences are always agonized but whose convenience remains rooted firmly in the *status quo ante*. It is still a problem of the color line, and that problem ramifies in all of our more critical relations, polluting the environment and straining the parameters of credibility in which the democratic ideal is somehow expected to function.

Wherever important human interests happen to lie, there the problem seems to lurk. It is not, as is so often urged by simplistic thinking, merely a matter of economics, for in America the economic condition functions as the first line of determination for most worthwhile values and opportunities. For example, when race and economics are so conjoined that one implies the other, millions of bona fide Americans find their opportunities for participation in America reduced to nothing palpable at all. They have "rights without lights," which is to say that they have no means whatever of going where they have a *right* to go, or the *will* to go. As far as meaningful participation in America is concerned, they are functionally disqualified. Shut out. A people thus handicapped, reasoned Dr. Du Bois, cannot reasonably be asked to compete with those who are free of such impediments. But then, reason is not immune to torture, as any reading of the American approach to racial justice will quickly illustrate.

There have been some changes, and some of them were significant enough to blunt temporarily the jagged edges of the black struggle for true freedom and equal justice. But America was never even close to the realization of equivalence for all Americans with valid claims and expectations under the canopy of equal citizenship.

In 1968 the government-sponsored Kerner Report spelled out our failure to stay the course of legal and moral rehabilitation. America, the Kerner Commission discovered, is "two societies: separate and unequal." But the Kerner Report was barely noted, and duly filed away, and retrenchment and retreat (which came to be known as "slipback") moved into the vacuum left by the languishing civil rights movement. By the mid-seventies, efforts to negate or reduce some of the gains won from the American conscience at such appalling costs were both organized and unremitting, and in some instances openly revanchist.

Our strange dilemma is that the human values we hold as individuals are routinely eviscerated by the inhuman systems we create to negate them in our consuming passion to distinguish and separate humans from other humans. It was to such a system, for example, that former Interior Secretary James Watt unconsciously appealed when he absently alluded to his advisory panel as "a Black . . . a woman, two Jews and a cripple." America was outraged, of course, and President Reagan was obliged to find a new Secretary. But the outrage was more because Mr. Watt embarrassed us by "going public" with some of our most deeply held private sentiments than because we honestly objected to the substance of his gaffe. We care about the poor, the disadvantaged, the handicapped, etc., in the abstract, because there is always the possibility that any of us as individuals could someday encounter poverty or disadvantage. But the fact that we create and defend with such vigor the very systems which produce and perpetuate poverty and disadvantage gives a decidedly hollow ring to our protestations against calling them to public attention.

The deluge of suits against affirmative action filed over the last several years reveals even more about the confused state of American values. Some of the cases argued before the Supreme Court, such as *Bakke vs. Regents of the University of California, United Steelworkers vs. Weber,* and *Fullilove vs. Klutznick,* for example, illustrate the ease and the cynicism with which the prior issues of human rights and simple justice get lost in the tortuous labyrinth of specious counterclaims which would effectively nullify even that minimum gesture of moral concern that affirmative action is supposed to represent. Affirmative action was conceived as a remedial approach to accumulated injustices and their long and tragic train of consequences. It is the official, belated recognition that America has a Problem, but the problem with the Problem is that we have approached it so tardily, so tentatively, so testily, and without grace or moral conviction.

Affirmative action was intended to mitigate the general exclusion of disadvantaged "minorities" from a broad range of opportunities ranging from employment to admission to prestigious universities and professional schools. However, affirmative action was interpreted by some opponents as reverse discrimination, or as a covert means of "qualifying" Blacks for college admissions or jobs for which they were less qualified than whites competing for the same openings. Others objected to the implications of a quota system they believed they saw in the reservations of limited percentages, or "set-asides," for minorities (and women) in specified employment and admission policies. The original intent of the program— to stimulate entry-level opportunities for a very limited number of minority citizens who had been seriously maimed and disadvantaged by our historical social and racial insensitivities—was lost in the backswing of the pendulum of adjustment. Some individual white males who felt that opportunities they deserved were being sacrificed in favor of social policy raised their objections in a continuing series of lawsuits and political strategies. Such objections gathered momentum as America appeared to back away from its fleeting but turbulent commitment to an equal society.

It was in such an atmosphere that President William Jefferson "Bill" Clinton addressed the graduating seniors at the University of California, San Diego, in 1997. The President had chosen California as a logical place to begin what would quickly be labeled his racial reconciliation initiative. California seemed to reflect more intensely the inflammable sensitivity of American racial intolerance. The brutal beating of black Rodney King by white policemen, caught on camera in March of 1991, caused retaliating riots which destroyed millions of dollars in property and set the city of Los Angeles on edge. The Rodney King incident was followed by the O. J. Simpson trial. In 1996 California passed Proposition 209, which ended that state's observance of all affirmative-action requirements. Ironically, 209 was championed by University of California regent Wardell Connerly, a self-admittedly reluctant African American who subsequently sought to export similar initiatives to other western states. Following the banning of affirmative action, the admission of black law students at UCLA dropped by eighty percent. The decline was even higher—eighty-one percent—at Berkeley. The University of California, Davis, declined twenty-six percent in African-American admissions, while admissions of Latinos declined from about twenty-nine to fifty percent at the same institutions.

California may or may not be a bellwether, but it is certainly not the only state with symptoms of escalating racial tensions. Between 1995 and 1997, more than 260 churches have been firebombed or burned. The vast majority of them housed black congregations and were clearly the objects of racial hatred, although no organized conspiracy has as yet been uncovered. In 1997, unemployment was twice as high for black males as for their white counterparts, and African Americans were eight times more likely to go to prison than other Americans. This situation is exacerbated by the routine attribution of white criminal behavior to anonymous blacks, thus reinforcing the stigma of criminality so often assigned to the whole black race. Occasionally such imaginary racial attributions are uncovered, as in the 1989 case in Boston where a white man attributed his premeditated murder of his wife to a fictitious "black man." Following closely was a 1994 case in South Carolina, where a young white woman involved in an extramarital affair with a white male drowned her two small boys and inflamed the community by accusing another fictitious "black man" of the double murder. No one knows how many such crimes are paid for by innocent people, but the climate for justice is poisoned by suspicion that the weight of significant public opinion and subsequent law enforcement falls disproportionately upon the backs of black Americans, and they become fair game for whatever strategies the law can provide for securing the rest of America against crime.

Most of these "strategies" take the form of bigger and better jails and more rigidly enforced islands of reservation in the jobless, drug-ridden, dead-end ghettos called the "inner city." No-nonsense "law enforcement," often exposed as police brutality, is another. In New York City, where the black population is many times the national average, the police force is overwhelmingly white. And in New York City in August of 1997, four white policemen were charged with severely beating a black man in a precinct station. They then allegedly sodomized him with the wooden handle of a toilet plunger and knocked out his front teeth as they forced the feces-smeared stick into his mouth.

Our racial xenophobia is deep-rooted and pervasive. But Americans are not unaware of their failure to be what they claim to be.

George Bernard Shaw once said of the American people that "to rouse their eager interest, their distinguished consideration and their undying devotion, all that is necessary is to hold them up to the ridicule of the rest of the universe." Shaw's acerbities notwithstanding, it is not hard to make a case for something closely resembling national masochism when we review some American postures and policies of the recent past. But if we do in fact have a masochistic bent, it is more likely to derive from an unconscious need for friendly censure and chastisement than from a real desire for international ridicule. We are a young nation, still raw in many of our cultural affectations; and we have a subliminal awareness that the approval we covet, particularly from "the Continent," which we perceive to be our standard of reference, is often claimed prematurely when measured against our cultural performance. In short, despite our public posture of indomitable self-assurance, there is a strong element of uncertainty buried in our private reckoning.

The American Dilemma

Americans as a people are not given to admissions of failure or of doubt, but it seems that the more loudly we proclaim our perfection, the more insistent seems to be our need for corroboration from significant others. Even in the formative years of this Republic, when an exuberant, unchastened idealism committed us to the notion of a perfect society here in the West, we were so certain, but still we longed to be told just how right we were and how well we were doing. However, when Alexis de Tocqueville offered his appraisal of American democracy after its first half century, America may have been titillated by the attention of the distinguished Frenchman, but there is no evidence that his criticisms of our racial practices were taken to heart. A hundred years later, still in search of some external confirmation of our national self-image, we invited Gunnar Myrdal, the Swedish social scientist, to appraise our progress and tell us how far we had come. After an exhaustive study, Myrdal offered an assessment we were hardly prepared to receive. He said America had a dilemma; and the dilemma derived from the conflict between the high-sounding Christian concepts embodied in the American creed and the way Americans really behaved.[2] That dilemma is still with us, and it ramifies in every aspect of contemporary American behavior and ideology. Once again, it is the apparent inability to extrapolate the schedule of values with which we seek to confirm self-identity into behavior that would give substance to the moral fantasies we are wont to indulge. The American dilemma Myrdal discovered on the eve of World War II is not new, nor was it new at the time he brought it to the attention of the American people. It is the same dilemma that produced the Black Church, which shared the birth of our nation; and it continues as the dilemma that still plagues church and society alike to this day.

It would be an irresponsible overstatement of a serious case to pretend that the American dilemma, in the form of racism, is all that troubles contemporary America. Such is not the case. But the dilemma does reflect a cluster of social and moral problems which, because of their early institutionalization, have gained a pseudo-respectability with a great degree of tacit social approval. Such problems are difficult to deal with. In recent years the law has been our most effective weapon, but the law can get at only that part of the dilemma which deals with "illegal" behavior. It cannot deal with the moral issues or the inconsistencies between precept and reality. Ultimately, that must be the task of the church: black, white, or the two together. In the meantime, we are beset with other challenges.

In the course of his 1978 commencement address at Harvard University, Alexander Solzhenitsyn, the celebrated Russian novelist, spoke of the American dilemma in terms even less complimentary than Tocqueville or Myrdal, although he did not (as they did) speak specifically to the issue of our racial hypocrisy. But Solzhenitsyn did chide America for glorified technological achievements which do not redeem our moral poverty; and he accused us of a preoccupation with the worship of man and his material needs while our sense of responsibility to God and society grows progressively less pronounced. He referred to America as an "abyss of human decadence," against which we seem to have no defense. We are characterized, he said, by the "misuse of liberty," having prostituted our vaunted freedom for cheap satisfactions. We were warned that courage is in decline and that the stage is set for the triumph of mediocrity. Whatever its validity, Solzhenitsyn's address constitutes a rather dour appraisal of a nation that was confidently bidding to become a "righteous empire" a mere two centuries ago. What is particularly troublesome is that, though cast in different language, the dilemma pictured by Alexander Solzhenitsyn is essentially the same American dilemma described by Gunnar Myrdal in the heyday of American power and prestige a half century ago. But the power, the prestige, and the self-assurance have all wavered. Courage has no stomach for decadence.

We are living in the third century of our national sovereignty, and we move ever more fitfully toward the American rendezvous with history. Almost from our beginnings as a nation, we referred to our cultural and political and economic pretensions as manifest destiny, but today our destiny is considerably less "manifest" than it once seemed to be. There is a pervasive erosion of confidence in American leadership, and perhaps in the American Dream itself. Our national purpose is fragmented and confused, and the symptoms of our cultural malaise are everywhere apparent. We seem incapable of learning from the past or planning effectively for the future. It was not very long ago that racism expressed in differential housing, black unemployment, segregation in education, and most other practical aspects of our common existence caused our cities to be laid waste and our schools to become battlegrounds, and forced on us the official, belated recognition that the American dilemma was still intact. But in spite of the hard lessons of the sixties, we still managed to profess surprise and shock when racial violence erupted in Miami in the seventies—even though the misery in the black ghettos was more pronounced than ever; even though the Ku Klux Klan was resurgent all over the country; and even though the North had managed to outdo the South in devising ever-new stratagems for maintaining segregation in the public schools.

The Prism of Faith

What is new in racial justice in America is so often what is old: a somber tale that has been too long in the telling; a weary variation on a theme that never seems to find retirement. We cannot avoid the conclusion that few of the changes we hoped for have been truly accomplished, even though the cosmetics of progress are always being paraded before us with cynical reassurance. But true reassurance comes hard, because the most convincing data are read not from the charts and the graphs, but in the faces of the hopeless legions of the battered, the jobless, and the dispossessed who people the back streets of affluent America.

Two centuries ago, despite the moving rhetoric of the revolutionary impulse, and despite the fact that thousands of black patriots fought and died for the cause of American freedom, the American commonwealth "conceived in liberty" for some was born in slavery for others. The stage was set then for the strange dilemma which today mocks our cultural pretensions, enervates our national purpose, and challenges the moral commitments implicit in our claim to be a nation under God.

We have an avowed national passion for political and cultural simplicity, but America is probably one of the most complex societies in the long history of human experience. Americans love it, hate it, tout it, tolerate it, defend it, and struggle to change it. But few truly comprehend it. As a nation, we were conceived in the most patent of political contradictions: we asserted that all men are created equal, with certain inalienable rights, as we casually stripped vast numbers of Africans of every vestige of their rights, both human and political. We were holding men in abject slavery, and we were remarkably oblivious of the moral and rational incompatibility of what we were saying with what we were doing. At that moment our national dilemma was born, and because of it, the Declaration, which launched what we chose to hail as a noble experiment in human freedom, managed to achieve a certain innocuousness. Its prescription for the democratic ordering of human affairs was vacant with respect to the ugly chancre of human debasement that was already growing on the American experiment before it was fairly born.

In spite of our persistence in the distortion of our own ideals, God has been both gracious and patient, and America has become a mighty power in the world. America counts her bathtubs and television sets in the millions; her war machine is sufficient to deter any aggressor, real or imagined. We have negotiated outer space and sent men to the moon; and the Coca-Cola sign and the golden arches of McDonald's promise lighthearted refreshment in the most remote hamlets of this terrestrial globe. But there are people in America who are dying for want of bread. And there are people in America whose principal struggle is to retain a last clutch on dignity.

In our effort to make sense of our racial enigma, perhaps we could profit by a look at some of the major institutions contributing to the shaping and the definition of that phenomenon. Religion is one such institution, and it is of fundamental importance. There are others, to be sure, but it is from an urgent religious commitment that this nation traces its first beginnings; and it was the recognition that God created men equal as an expression of his own moral nature that justified the American revolt against British sovereignty, which had chosen to ignore that divine expression. That is why we must look at America through the prism of religion, for religion was the efficient cause by means of which this nation came into being.

The American Context

In the larger sense, this is a book about America, a self-perceived "nation under God": the exemplary Christian society the Founding Fathers hoped would be a showcase for the world to see and emulate. In a more intimate sense, it is about a perplexing American phenomenon: the strange rapprochement between church and society which continues to embarrass the faith, vitiate the society, and saddle both with a burdensome dilemma that seems to persist despite the fervor of our religion or the ardor with which we pursue our commitment to democracy. A principal focus of our interest will be on black religion, for the black experience in religion is a critical aspect of American history and development. Black religion is a unique cultural precipitate, born of the peculiar American interpretation of the faith and the Blackamerican response to the anomalous schedule of exigencies that interpretation entails. But it is not really possible to talk meaningfully about black religion and the Black Church without reference, implicit or explicit, to white religion and the White Church, for, in the context of American Christianity, one implies the other. Nevertheless, it is the black fraction who are the principal victims of our spiritual and cultural schizophrenia, and in consequence, it is black religion and the Black Church upon which the principal onus of dealing with that malady has fallen by default. So, while the mainstream church, by whatever name—the American Church, or the Established Church, or the White Church—figures prominently in our scenario of the continuing American dilemma, it is essentially a point of reference, a backdrop, as it were, to the more singular phenomenon we wish to set in high relief.

Black Religion

Whatever its denominational or cultic expression, Christianity always implies at minimum a recognition of a relationship with the Divine that transcends all human accidents and considerations. Black religion is no different, and the Black Church is the response of a distinctive body of Christians to the divine initiative which reaches out to all who would believe. But black religion, like every other, has a cultural context. It is set in human history; and while its critical reference is to God, it reflects the peculiar experience, concerns, and exigencies of the human condition. In consequence, any religion of Blacks in America which did not in some fundamental way address the prevailing issues of racialism would be improbable, if not grotesque. The critical concerns of life and death are the principal concerns of religion. In America, such fundamental teachings of the faith as love, brotherhood, and altruistic responsibility have always been shadowed by cultural adhesions which act to qualify Christian response in the presence of racial difference. This reluctance to accept an ethic that is fundamental, clear, and unqualified has introduced into American religion a kind of black exceptionalism, unique in Western Christianity except for the Dutch Boers' blatant abuse of Reformed Calvinism in their calculated rape of South Africa.

In the wake of the social confusion and frustration engendered by our laissez-faire morality, many Americans have learned to rely less on secular means of problem-solving and more on the security religion has to offer. But others become increasingly impatient with religion and demand evidence of what the church is doing to resolve the problems of society in exchange for its prerogatives. Such antagonisms are intensified when dreams fall apart and there is no apparent rescue available through any ordinary human agency, or when there are no logical explanations for human failure. Perhaps there is indeed a vestigial confusion of religion with magic to which people may succumb when the secular institutions to which we entrust the principal values and interests of our lives fail to deliver. In any case, religion figures predominantly in the critical considerations of every generation that experiences the stress of war, the terror of economic uncertainty, the dehumanization of racial oppression.

For African Americans, a people whose total experience has been a sustained condition of multiform stress, religion is never far from the threshold of consciousness, for whether it is embraced with fervor or rejected with disdain, it is the focal element of the black experience. It was religion which sent the American Founding Fathers on their initial "errand into the wilderness," an event that subsequently required the involuntary relocation of millions of Africans to make that errand viable. It was religion that suggested the convenient notion that the benighted Africans could unlearn their heathenism through continuous labor for a white Christian civilization whose God-ordained burden was to be their "masters" and "mistresses" forever. And it was religion that supplied the principal narcotics of dependency and control once the Blacks were broken and reduced to chattel. Religion made them the designated "sons of Ham," cursed to be hewers of wood and drawers of water in perpetual expiation of an alleged ancestral indiscretion. But it was also religion that gave them the stamina to survive, the occasion to resist, the will to pursue their liberation. And it was religion that gave them the humility and the grace to seek coexistence in peace and forgiveness, whenever they were permitted, with the very oppressors who had denied their humanity and taken away their freedom in the name of religion in the first place.

Black religion, then, attempts to deal with the implications of racial perception and counterperception. At stake is considerably more than where one sits on the public bus or who is welcome at the local church. More significant is whether the human condition is racially inclusive, and whether the divine imperative is unconditional and capable of realization. In a society where three centuries of racial prerogatives are institutionalized in pejorative attitudes and behavior long since considered natural and normative, if the Black Church did not exist, it would probably be necessary to invent it.

The alternative would seem to be the tacit ratification of an idolatrous chauvinism which makes questionable the impartiality of God no less than the equivalence of all God's children. Worship, which is the grateful recognition of human contingency, implies a sense of perspective: all humans need to know not only that God is, but what God is like. Conversely, we need to have some authentic notions about our proper relationship to other selves, and our worthiness to be included in the peculiar concern God reserves for those in his own image. In a society where significant truths and values are racially determined, such issues are painfully clouded and frequently compromised. But in the Black Church, the normative presuppositions which gave American society its racist cast are disregarded, and the equal worth of all races is affirmed as a necessary inference of the common fatherhood of God. The imputation of pariahism, the assumption of privilege, and the demands of prerogative based on racial identity are all rejected. The Black Church perceives itself as an expression of the divine intent that, however nefarious the strategies of evil, the faith will not be rendered destitute and the righteousness of God will not be left without a witness. If the established oracles are silent or unreliable, then lo, a voice cries forth from the wilderness.

RACE,
RELIGION,
and the
CONTINUING
AMERICAN DILEMMA

The American Dilemma
in Perspective

THE same fetters that bind the captive bind the captor, and the American people are captives of their own myths, woven so cleverly and so imperceptibly into the fabric of our national experience. When a serious candidate for President of the United States can testify candidly, as did Ronald Reagan in his debate with Jimmy Carter in 1980, that when he was growing up "this country didn't even know it had a racial problem," then the candor of selective ignorance has swung full circle to reemerge as the casuistry of presumptive innocence. Thus the Great American Myth perpetuates itself through all the accidents of our imperfect understanding, so marvelously convenient to what we do understand and affirm.

If the American people ever take seriously the political rhetoric of innocence by ignorance, the erosion of our credibility for world leadership will be even greater than it is at present. Mr. Reagan's posturing was recognized, of course, for what it was—a classic instance of the way in which our systems of anti-values function to protect us from unpleasant realities we do not want to know about. Nevertheless, if we ever get through the mist and the murk of our self-willed naïveté, we will discover that our moral values have long since been corroded, that the democratic ideal has been corrupted, and we have allowed ourselves to be transported by dreams that never were to a Shangri La we know does not exist.

That is our dilemma. After the dreaming is done, there has to be an awakening, and the reality of our imperfections must be addressed. Sooner or later the dreams that enrapture us and the tales that regale us must make way for the truth which alone can make us free. All of us. That is our prospect and that is the sobering reality that White Church and Black Church are called to address in the common interest of the faith we share and the fate we must define for ourselves.

Violence

The most obvious feature of contemporary American life is violence. Violence stalks us all: the old, the young, the unborn, the rich, the poor, black and white. The high incidence of social aggression which characterizes America and makes us unique among "developed" civilizations is scarcely incidental. It is the inevitable harvest of the political and the moral laissez faire which has strangled the American character for so long that we are hard pushed to distinguish the American Dream from the de facto American tradition. Crime in the streets is warp to the woof of the Watergates and other political crimes which define and shape our contemporary society, and our continual crises in blood are the natural progeny of our crisis in moral values.

Americans like to imagine themselves affronted by the murder of political leaders like the brothers Kennedy or of spiritual leaders like Martin Luther King, Jr. But there is cynicism and hypocrisy implicit in our willingness to be shocked by such violence, for violence has long been an integral part of our way of life. It began with the effort to exterminate the Indian; it was confirmed as a way of life in our protracted effort to dehumanize the African. Neither human life nor human dignity is characteristically sacred to us, and the political overtones of the frequent assaults on public officials suggest that life in general is cheap in America. Black life is cheapest of all. It has always been bought and sold with impunity, whether at the slave-auction block, or in the courtrooms, or through a thousand and one sophisticated stratagems designed to exploit whatever values the white man recognized in the black condition—economic, sexual, political, military, psychological, and so on, ad infinitum. Black life is still cheap. And it continues to be a paradoxical aspect of the ecological structure of American civilization.

Life is cheap but violence is not always reliable. The madness that killed the Kennedys; that cut down Martin Luther King, Malcolm X, and countless others of recent memory; that struck at Governor George Wallace and President Ronald Reagan is but a logical extension of an implied license to kill *if the killing is selective*. Official killing is routinely justified if the killer is in uniform and acting under cover of law on behalf of society. It is only when the killing becomes personal that it becomes intolerable. But then it is too late. What this society somehow refuses to grasp is that what happens tomorrow is in part determined by what was accepted yesterday. Who is next is in part already determined by what we have already done or failed to do about who was last. The violence which racks our cities and kills our leaders is a violence America institutionalized in practice, accepted in principle, and acquiesced in by default.

The poor, the black, and the faceless have never been free of the shadow of violence, whether under pretense of law or through tacit consensus. The rivers and bayous of the rural South, like the streets and alleys of the black ghettos which pockmark urban America, have a long, sad tale to tell about violence and about the social, political, and economic forces which converge in the selection of its principal victims. But there is little comfort and less security to be derived from the statistics which make that violence a phenomenon of the ghetto, for there are no physical boundaries for hatred or indifference, and the violence they engender is neither self-regulated nor self-contained. Human sensitivity is narcotized by the implied license for selective aggression, and whenever such violence is permitted or urged upon an approved subject, sooner or later the lines become blurred and one subject becomes as potential as another. It is madness to believe that the forces we have loosed in this society against the black, the poor, the disinherited will retain the power of discrimination. A dog gone mad knows no master— only the taste of blood.

Too many American cities have become camps of hostility. Too many American children have been taught to hate rather than to appreciate. Somewhere the American Dream has gone wrong. What happened to the moral glue, the vaunted ethical principles we relied upon to preserve the integrity of the Dream while we got on with the dreaming?

Power and Responsibility

In the seventeenth century, Thomas Hobbes in trying to rationalize the existence of human society deduced that men organized themselves into social entities for their mutual protection and for the greater enhancement of those qualities of human existence which they as individuals, and collectively, find by experience to be gratifying, or to have value. The alternative to an organized society, reasoned Hobbes, is a "state of nature," a dismal and unrewarding existence characterized by unlimited aggression and counteraggression; an existence in which every individual is a law unto himself, in which there is no definition of morality, and in which force and fraud are the respected instruments for the realization of self-interest, which, in the state of nature, is the sole factor of human motivation.

Men organized themselves into societies because, in the state of nature, life was "solitary, mean, nasty, brutish and short." To remedy such an unattractive existence, each man relinquished a degree of personal, natural autonomy—i.e., the liberty of every man to do what seemed best to him to promote his own interests and to preserve his own existence. The hope was that all men together, *society, the confraternity of those who agree to live under the rule of law,* might through the resulting collective of power so regulate behavior and the distribution of scarce values as to refine human existence and to broaden somewhat the scope of human motivation.

It is not important that we accept Hobbes's theory as an adequate explanation of social existence. It is important to recognize that the de facto existence of any social entity suggests that it exists for some reason; that that reason must somehow encompass the general *and* the individual welfare; and that when a society ceases to function in the common interests for which men modify their pursuit of self-interest and accept law and order, then such a society has probably outlived its purpose and its usefulness. In short, a society in which large numbers of people find life to be solitary, nasty, mean, brutish and short is already in reversion toward a state of nature, however it may be styled. When the power which belongs to the people is by whatever artifice arrogated and manipulated in the preservation and extension of selective interests, what stake have the distressed and the oppressed in the responsible maintenance of that society? They have all of the responsibilities of citizens and none of the power needed to fulfill those responsibilities.

Responsibility without power is slavery. Power without responsibility is tyranny. If the interests of the oppressed are not protected, if the power they relinquish is used against them capriciously, if solitariness is exchanged for alienation, meanness for poverty, brutishness for perpetual anxiety, what then is such a society except a sophisticated state of nature? If some are always preselected as the pieces and never the players in the game, for them the game may not be worth the candle. Such is the typical experience of the black and the poor in America, and of such are the contradictions of the American dilemma by which their participation in our common values is conditioned. The ready array of official statistics which tell the hungry how well fed they are, and the magic charts with the inevitably cheerful projections which promise miracle reversals to the derelict and the destitute, provide no satisfactions of substance. Poverty and ignorance are not necessarily the same, and America must beware, lest in our smugness we underestimate the power of the poor to act on their own behalf.

The Power in City Hall

The prime prerequisite of any organized society is power. The corollary of power is responsibility. The logical consequence of legitimate power responsibly exercised is peace, order, and a reasonable participation in the common values of the society. The irresponsible exercise of power is the invitation to anarchy and the prelude to revolution—a proposition to which we have not always given responsible attention. The ultimate expression of power is control, direct or indirect, manifest or covert. The most sophisticated expression of power is control over decisions and the decision-making process. Who participates in the *real* decision-making process in America? That is an issue for Americans to ponder. And redress.

Life in America is manipulated through the instrumentality of decisions made or avoided. Men who sit in boardrooms remote from the scene make the decisions which control the life circumstances of millions they have not seen, will never see, and do not want to see. When City Hall was lily-white, the procuration of the black ghetto was a national scandal. The power which manipulated the lives and the life chances of millions of Blackamericans was neither benevolent nor benign. It was sinister; and it was programmed to continue indefinitely a black supporting cast for the ego and status needs of the white overculture. As a consequence, the black community lost a little more hope, a little more faith, and a little more commitment to peaceful protest with each new disclosure of abuse. Each morning all over America the great American tragedy was reenacted each time a black man looked at himself in the mirror as he shaved, and each time a black woman put on the face she would wear in her efforts to find bread for her family in the kitchens of the elegant houses far from the decaying flats and tenements of the racial compound to which she was assigned. What each saw in the looking glass was a cipher citizen—an American who would have no serious input in any of the decisions which would determine the quality of his or her significant experiences for that day, or any day; whose life chances had already been programmed with sinister predictability by persons unknown, or, even if known, unavailable and unconcerned.

Wherever the life chances of some are consistently manipulated by others, freedom is in contest and the struggle to redress is inevitable. Where freedom has been long withheld, people who have never experienced it may not know what it is precisely, but they are nevertheless sensitive to the absence of some vital quality which leaves their lives bereft of meaningful participation in the significant experiences of the human enterprise. Conversely, those who distrain freedom from others equate it with privilege— privilege to which they alone are entitled. That is why it is possible that America misread Martin Luther King. Certainly, not many Americans had King's full dream in mind, even though, black and white together, they locked arms and marched through the South with such apparent purpose. But the South was only the *symbol*, not the problem. The problem was attitudinal, not regional. What Dr. King wanted was not merely to reform the South but to make *all* America safe for the kind of democracy that could accept full participation of all her citizens, regardless of color. But when the Black Panthers operating outside the South let it be known that they, too, were determined to overcome, and "by any means necessary," their startling assertion of an unconditional commitment to freedom was rejected as the ultimate profanation of the consensual racial understanding thought to be operative in the civil rights movement. While most white Americans cannot visualize a qualified freedom for themselves and their children, the notion that freedom is important enough to black people for them to want to pursue it on its own terms was unthinkable and untenable.

Freedom implies power—*the power to be responsible*. Such power was unthinkable because black responsibility lay well beyond what liberal white America envisioned when it endorsed the black mission to overcome. The power that shaped life in the black ghetto was not, and is not, of course, black power. It does not originate in the ghetto. It is power from the outside. It is alien power, with many faces. It is the nonresident merchants who come into the ghetto with the sun in the morning, and who leave with the sun in the evening, taking with them the day's toll for their visitation. It is also the vexatious blue presence—that alien, anonymous, contemptuous phalanx known as "the law," but more often than not considered an army of occupation pursuing its own private system of spoils. It is the ubiquitous presence of alien schoolteachers, case workers, process servers, rent collectors, repossessors, bailiffs, political hustlers, and assorted functionaries and racketeers whose economic stakes in the black ghetto require their temporary and grudging presence imposed upon a community they detest and which detests them in return. It is clearly not a question of the right of people from outside the ghetto to live, or work, or maintain businesses there, but the reciprocation of that right is startlingly difficult to demonstrate in suburbia.

It will be argued that City Hall is no longer lily-white; that in fact some of America's largest cities and scores of smaller towns have black mayors and other black elected officials. This observation deserves the closest attention. But in 1983 Blacks still constituted scarcely more than one percent of all elected officials. Meanwhile, black income was only fifty-six percent of whites', *down* five percent from its best showing in 1970, and while seventy-four percent of all black men over sixteen were employed in 1960, only fifty-five percent were employed in 1983. Other indicators of the economic status of Blacks are consistent. What they say in sum is that, no matter who sits in the mayor's office, the economics of being black are not substantially improved. Not yet. Black mayors win and retain their offices through coalitions with established power, and the significant interests of such power are seldom coordinate with those of the people confined to the ghetto. The black mayor is a symbol, a hopeful sign of the potential power of the black electorate. But if that power were miraculously doubled or even tripled, it would still be potential and there would be no dramatic improvement in the life of the masses who inhabit the ghetto. When the available patronage has been divided and dispensed, the Blacks who benefit substantially will be few in number and the black masses, whose circumstances are the most desolate and the most desperate, will generally remain beyond the effective reach of the most conscientious black mayor. The Irish Catholics of Boston have "run" that city for decades, but the *economic power* in Boston is not Irish Catholic, a fact with which every Irish mayor has had to come to terms in the structure of his administration and its programs. Who, then, runs the runners while the runners are running the city? Or, to put it another way, what is the power behind the political power that keeps things the way they were? The Blacks in City Hall are an important development toward America's political maturation. Their presence is the best evidence of the political direction the struggle for full freedom must take. But that struggle must ultimately receive ratification from those sources which operate above and beyond the sound and the fury of politics, and from which most politicians are required to take their cues.

Power as Consensus

It is the opinion of some that power is possessed by individuals and that, as a result, only individuals may be held responsible for its abuse. That may be true as far as it goes, but it does not go far enough, for no abstract value can be more dependent upon group response than power. Ultimately, all real power is social and consensual. One man may dominate another by brute force, but if he wishes to extend his domination, cooperation and consensus from like-minded others must be available.

In a complex society like ours, no individual acquires power until he discovers a body of sentiment which can be mobilized in support of his intentions. A Hitler or Stalin "rises to power" because he is canny enough to know where to look for conformable sentiment, ambitious enough to mine it, and callous enough to make instruments of the people whose private susceptibilities are available for supportive exploitation. There are, for example, no solitary racists of consequence. For racism to flourish with the vigor it enjoys in America, there must be an extensive climate of acceptance and participation by large numbers of people who constitute its power base. It is the consensus of private persons that gives racism its derivative power. For all his ugliness and bombast, the isolated racist is a toothless tiger, for, to be effective, racism must have responsible approval and reliable nurture. Social nurture. The power of racism is the power conceded by those respectable citizens who by their action or inaction communicate the consensus which directs and empowers the overt bigot to act on their behalf. The lessons of the Ku Klux Klan are illustrative. Wherever the Klan has been met with firm, public opposition of the white gentry on whose behalf it claims to be acting, its threats to its intended targets have fizzled, and it has withdrawn from the scene in embarrassment and defeat.

The Racial Patrimony

In the late sixties the reaction to the Kerner Report's* charge that white racism is the prevailing sentiment in America, and that its ramifications touch critical aspects of life and liberty with a deadly corrosiveness, was immediate and distressed, for Americans seldom perceive themselves as racists. It is therefore all the more tragic that whether one is personally a racist or not becomes increasingly inconsequential, because the silent consensus which institutionalizes the racist ideology makes it normative to the whole culture and entraps us all. The white nonracist is hardly more free to be his better self than is the oppressed Black who is the conventional target of racism. Social acceptability, economic security, and even personal safety may all be contingent upon one's public conformity to the prescribed patterns of behavior which dictate and condition racial intercourse.

During the heat of the civil rights struggle, young Blacks agonized over whether it was incautious to depend on their rebellious white counterparts to provide major leadership for what they conceived as a *black* revolution. Many felt that black people needed to learn to do for themselves, and that the ex-

---

* Report of a commission appointed by President Lyndon B. Johnson, headed by Father Theodore Hesburgh, president of Notre Dame. The commission was charged with the investigation of racial disorder in America.

perience of leadership under fire was crucial. It was argued that, however earnest they were, the young white dissidents were not necessarily the answer to the black future merely because they were not for the moment preoccupied with being white. As white youth they were still the heirs to the white establishment, and although the establishment tradition requires the dutiful toleration if not the willful indulgence of the unconventional behavior of its progeny for a time, the day comes inevitably when the sons and daughters of privilege are called home to mind the store from which privilege derives.

The goldfish swallowers of the thirties, the flagpole sitters of the forties, the panty-raiders of the fifties, the hippies, yippies, and assorted protest-prone social revolutionaries of the sixties, all addressed themselves, wittingly or unwittingly, to the traditional expectations of a doting society of middle-class Moms and Dads who professed not to understand them but who would have been alarmed and disappointed with a generation of youth they did understand. The truth is that this society demands youthful unrestraint as evidence of a properly developing capacity for independence and self-assertion, and it has created an elaborate network of facilities for its protection and containment. Unconventional self-expression is a legitimate and valued aspect of learning, of growing up, even when it is of doubtful immediate practicality. It is one of the more critical rites of passage. In this regard, a primary function of the traditional college has been to provide a temporary sanctuary for nonconformism. Youth must be served, and campus permissiveness, the license to experiment, to experience life outside the conventional patterns of approved behavior, is an accepted process of socialization. In the main, it has produced predictable results. After four years or so of indulgence, the serious candidate for success, i.e., for establishment status and approval, is ready to put away childish things and enter the ranks of his compeers. The wildest campus radical has characteristically emerged from his college extravagances as the most conservative pillar of the community, and his erstwhile determination to bring down the system is forgotten in his new determination to make it more secure. The young white visionaries who marched and sang in the black struggle, and the young white radicals who repudiated the System and vowed to bring it down in the sixties, edged toward conformity in the seventies. By the early eighties they had duly accepted the responsibilities of their patrimony and were home managing the family interests. It is from these same interests that the Blacks are still trying to extricate themselves.

Power and Morality

The common experience of black people is that the formidable conglomerates of power which structure American society conspire to insure their retention in an excluded caste at the bottom of the racial and ethnic heap, and farthest from the realization of the benefits normally to be derived from being American. There is a deep suspicion among Blacks that the power which informs America is at best morally indifferent, and that despite conventional protestations to the contrary, America as a society has come perilously close to abandoning the notion that justice is possible, or even desirable, or that morality is a factor of consequence in either social relations or individual well-being. Our prime commitment seems to be to expedience, and since neither justice nor morality lends itself to mere opportunism, what is right seems increasingly to be equated with whatever comes out of the ebb and flow of human intercourse. Justice, like the price of pork bellies, becomes a function of the market, and morality is whatever it takes to keep the market active.

Our distorted sense of justice at home often sends us rushing off to settle the world's problems in the style in which we still imagine best exemplifies our national image. But the national image we cherish so much at home and want so desperately to export to the world is unfortunately at serious odds with the way we are perceived abroad. To much of the world we are "the ugly Americans." The toll we are required to pay for the privilege of being hated is astronomical, and it increases with every world crisis we undertake to resolve in the "American way." There are some people on earth who simply do not want our democracy, or our presence, or our interference, a lesson we seem loath to take to heart. And there are some who challenge the sincerity of our efforts to insure the establishment of democratic principles and values in remote corners of the globe when our own camp is in such serious disarray.

Stations of Security

Social stress and social disorganization offer a difficult challenge to organized religion. When secular values are at great odds with what the faith alleges to be God's will for man and society, the church is expected to address the tension with appropriate leadership. The problem is exacerbated when the church confuses its ministry of moral precept and spiritual superintendence with the demands made upon it to ratify the popular sentiments of the moment. But the church cannot with impunity shift with every breeze that blows across the social landscape. The church is, and must be, a conservator of values—an archive of those experiences and relationships which characterize and exemplify those enduring truths by which human effort is to be illuminated and measured. The church is charged with the larger view, a more comprehensive perspective than the self-interest of individuals, or the specious agendas of ad hoc factions which impugn its relevance but covet its prestige.

Religious values are stations of security in a world in which everything else is in flux. Man has to have something to hold on to as familiar ground keeps slipping from under him. Religion serves this need, and because it does, the human investment in it is replicated in no other institution. Its promise is the pearl of great price before which all other values pale into relative insignificance.

After the Bolshevik Revolution, the Russians outlawed religion and turned their churches into palaces of culture. The Communists ridiculed the idea of God and imposed severe penalties on believers who persisted in their spiritual decadence. They defaced the religious paintings, smashed the icons, destroyed the sacred literature, and substituted political interests for spiritual values. But religion survived because the felt need for it was not destroyed with its physical paraphernalia. In spite of the awesome pressure of the state and the Communist Party, religion prevailed because the innate sense of human contingency is far more pervasive and meaningful than any earth-born fear, and the satisfactions of the faith are beyond the competition of any human emolument or political honor.

The New Moral Management

Given the function of religion, our problems derive principally from a willful confusion of the values which ought to distinguish it from the expectations of the secular mode. Christianity holds that its cardinal values are primal and immutable because they are consistent with the revealed character of God. While lesser values may be subject to modification or refinement, what God has ordained for man must not be profaned. Christian morality is a matter of recognizing which values are immutable, which are derivative and subsidiary, and choosing accordingly. Some things must change; some things must persist through change, or change itself becomes the only value of significance.

How a society deals with change is its best index for meaningful survival, and to retreat from the implications of change rather than to help society find conciliance in the enduring moral structures to which civilizations owe their survival is to abandon responsibility for license. A primary weakness of the religious establishment in America has been its apparent unwillingness to confront the exigencies of change with integrity. Time and time again the church has confused the people by looking the other way when personal interests have been measured against those values fundamental to the faith. This has been especially true in racial matters. Certainly the character of the Divine and the divine intention for the human family are expressed quite clearly in the notion of a common father in whose image all humanity is cast. This would seem to be an immutable value impossible of modification so long as God is God and man comes in his likeness. And no less certain is the fact that racial preferment, however strongly it may be felt, is a derivative value, a *learned* response quite obviously at odds with the notion of brotherhood and the commandment to love. Hence, it can have no claim whatever to Divine approval or sanction.

Nor can there be effective absolution in the abdication of personal morality to popular opinion or to the self-appointed arbiters of our social conscience. Too often, professional brokers to whom we entrust our moral investments are not themselves the best evidence of serious commitment. The result is that the moral leadership of our seminal institutions is frequently quite shallow and unconvincing. Government, religion, communications, education, entertainment, et cetera are susceptible and suspect, and the confidence we once had in the "American way" has been seriously eroded by sustained disappointment and defeat.

Moral management by consignment or by consensus is reconstructing our moral patterning through the casual, almost subliminal introduction of so-called alternative values designed to erase the age-old distinctions between up and down, right and wrong, the beautiful and the monstrous. Today we are invited to believe that the only real responsibility man has is to himself and his own gratifications, and that all moral alternatives are equally valid since they have no meaningful reference beyond the self. Cloaked in the casuistry of such dubious sophistication, this convenient nonsense is no less destructive for all its cleverness. And it is no less vulgar for all the notables who endorse it through fear, or by default, or merely because in a moment of weakness they prostitute themselves to the cheap opportunism the retreat from responsibility seems to engender. But it *is* confusing, for we live in a time when the issues of personal and social intercourse are exceedingly complex, and the parameters of personal and social responsibility grow more indistinct with each new problem we are called upon to confront. In less than a generation the enduring problem of racism has been joined by such formidable issues as abortion, euthanasia, biogenetics, nuclear energy, technocracy, and the arms race. Ironically, these are all of a piece. They are all new expressions of our troubled understanding

about the value of human life and the inalienable rights which
inure to it.

Civilized Decadence

If Americans are confused, our confusion must not be counted
incidental. The price of freedom is always the risk that it may be
corrupted or taken away by perverse ideologies which claim
shelter under its protection. The decline of great civilizations is
characteristically initiated by internal assaults on their systems
of value. If the eternal verities by which men live can be put at
issue, and if the conventions by which society is ordered can be
questioned—if the good, the true, and the beautiful can be
challenged openly and without fear—that is democracy. But if
that which is patently and inherently evil and degrading can be
successfully masqueraded as a reasonable "alternative" to that
which affirms human life, human dignity, and human responsibility, we need not worry about armies of invasion. The civilization where this can happen is already committed to its own
dissolution and demise.

We have never come close to realizing the notion of righteous
empire which excited our Puritan founders, but we now seem
further from that ideal than ever before. The moral and spiritual
impetus which gave leadership and direction to the birth of this
nation was in substantial default from the beginning, but our
initial deficit was not so much a lack of vision as it was a lack of
courage. Today we appear to lack both. Our minds are keener,
our perceptions are more acute, our information is more prodigious, but our selfish inconsistency disarms our determination
to succeed. Those we have traditionally looked to as guardians of
our more civilized efforts—those whom Solzhenitsyn calls "the
ruling elite"—have too often chosen silence or dissimulation rather
than lose face with the cult to which they look for approval and
validation.

Somehow, we have managed to survive a full generation of
domestic tension and turmoil. The schoolhouse door has lost its
attraction for political posturing. The cattle prods are sheathed;

the snarling attack dogs have been leashed; the church bombers have cached their dynamite; and the storm troopers have put away their dark glasses and scraped the gore from their billy clubs. Reproved by the world for this savagery, we have tried with doubtful success to blot out the reality that troubles us. But reality will not go away, and to recognize reality is to return to responsibility. Before we can have tomorrow, we must first get through today. There is no compromise, and that, in brief, is the crux of our dilemma. We will never create the bright new world we dream about until we confront the world we have made.

We still have time to relearn, if we have the will, that there is evil in the world, and that to compromise with evil in any of its guises is to be destroyed by it. When the beast walks among us, either we restrain it and deny it or it will hold us captive in our own houses. A system of values without consistency and without constraint cannot be trusted with the ordering of any society worthy of the name. And if our commitment is merely to be narcotized rather than to earn the tranquillity to which we hold ourselves entitled, then we must be prepared for the delirium and the agony that come when the fix has lost its magic and the morning after has arrived.

If it is to the established church we look for rescue, we will not be especially cheered by its accomplishments to date, for the American church has consistently failed to take to heart the ancient indictment that racism is a corruption and a denial of those immutable values which are critical to human dignity. More than that, it has been reluctant to resist with the vigor of conviction the contemporary onslaught of narcissistic hedonism, in a variety of guises, which further jeopardizes that dignity by idolizing the individual self as the center of all values, and demanding that all other values be bent into conformance. As a result, American religion finds itself increasingly pushed into the role of being either an adversary to its own conscience or preoccupied with the busyness and bustle triviality requires for the illusion of respectability.

Why has the initial dream of a city to be set on a hill as a beacon, and as an example of Christian virtue at its best, been downgraded? What happened to the moral conviction that made us strong, the spiritual certitude that made us invincible, the energetic determination that kept us creative as we contemplated the New Jerusalem we were to build, and the American Dream that was our destiny? The New Jerusalem perished aborning in the travail of slavery, and we aborted the Dream in the effort to make it racially exclusive.

Countless billions of dollars and untold quantums of time and energy have been poured into a continuing patchwork of strategies designed to reserve for some what belongs to all; and millions of lives have been shortchanged or corrupted in the process. Our racial madness has exacted an enormous toll of the American potential in the form of poverty, ignorance, race hatred, self-hatred, high mortality, low morality, insecurity, ethical compromise, and selective exclusion from the pursuit of the ordinary common values we all helped to create. We shall never know what potential genius, black and white, has been sacrificed to the racial Moloch which designated some of us as keepers and others to be kept. But the possibilities stagger the imagination. What great music was never written; what miracles of medicine remain undiscovered; what strategies for peace and understanding among the nations of the world have never been developed because we have been preoccupied with building fences and closing the doors which eliminate the kept and enervate the keepers, to the inconvenience of everybody, and to the impairment of our common capacity to get on with the Dream we once dared to believe in?

The toll of racialism is devastating for Blackamericans, but in the long run its costs may be even higher for white America. Beyond the extraordinary cost in dollars, the inconvenience and the inherent danger of trying to suppress a whole race of people, white America has lost its self-respect and its moral authority. A scarcely camouflaged sense of guilt pervades the church and the society-at-large, and the abuse of power, sex, drugs, and people is the prevailing alternative to responsible interaction. The frantic pursuit of momentary escape from the nagging realization that there is a dilemma, an open chasm between what we claim to be and what we are, dominates our private agendas, colors our national character, and subjects us to international blackmail and ridicule. Our principal allies suffer our eager support, even as they castigate our policies and our postures and impatiently await the comeuppance they privately wish for us. And the protégé nations we have appointed ourselves to save reflect uniformly our own inclinations through the repression of their own exploited classes in the interests of their own privileged elite.

Such are the tragedies we have opted to live with, an enormous price to pay for the doubtful privileges of color. But the greater tragedy is the wasted witness we might have paid to the majesty of God and to the possibilities we hold for a more perfect rendering of his image.

Improbable Deliverance

The suggestion that the Black Church could be destined for a pivotal role in the future of Western Christianity has usually been met with polite derision. But the peremptory dismissal of such a possibility flies in the face of innumerable instances in which the direction of religious and cultural history has been significantly determined by improbable forces and institutions prematurely dismissed as inconsequential. Reality comes in two forms. There is that which is *truly* real and independent of all subjective interpretations. And there is a *perceived* reality which may be no more than a projection of all those conventions and convictions which derive from selective experience. But selective experience is not an infallible index of the real, however satisfying it may be, for it is by definition resistant to any truth contrary to what it already prefers to believe. In consequence, the Black Church is not a likely institution for future significance in the forecast of mainstream American religion, because neither the Black Church nor the black experience from which it derives has ever been a matter of serious consequence in the catalogue of social facts from which the American perception of reality is drawn. The official interpretation of the black experience was laid down long ago in the celebrated doctrine of natural white superiority and inherent black incapacity, and it was institutionalized with intended finality in all of the sources Americans rely on to read our cultural catalogue with proper understanding. It is an integral part of the Great American Myth, and it was protected by an elaborate system of cultural taboos reinforced by legal and religious proscriptions for three and a half centuries. This awesome icon of racist whimsy was buttressed as well with a clever and invidious folklore designed to give credence and respectability to what was patently incredible and unrespectable. And it was romanticized in literature and art, sanctified by convention, and justified by the doctrine of the white man's responsibility for black uplift.

The problem is that the same perceptions and emotional responses which hark back to an era that is mercifully behind us find continued expression in attitudes and behaviors which refuse to let what is past be done with. It is against this continuing agony that the mission of the Black Church, however little known and appreciated beyond its traditional constituency, finds a compelling reason for the projection of its ministry to America.

2

The Racial Factor in the Shaping of Religion in America

The African Antecedents

WHEN Zedekiah, the last King of Judah, delivered Jeremiah up to the nervous rabble of his decaying establishment, those so-called princes, too cowardly to murder the prophet outright, dumped him into an abandoned well and waited for nature to take its course. Tradition has it that Ebedmelech the African rescued Jeremiah and was rewarded by God's promise that in the impending destruction of Jerusalem and the Babylonian captivity he, Ebedmelech, would not be delivered into the hands of strangers (Jeremiah 38:1–13; 39:15–18).[1] There is another tradition that six centuries later another African, whose name was Simon, helped Jesus struggle up Mount Calvary under the burden of the cross (Mark 15:21),* which was to become the symbol of a New Jerusalem. Somewhere between Jeremiah and Jesus, between God's promise to Ebedmelech and Simon's travail on the way to Golgotha, Jewish nationhood reached its nadir, and Christian tradition began its remarkable ascendancy. The ramifications of that tradition are with us now, two thousand years later. At stake is the religious commitment and the religious identity of millions of Blackamericans whose identification with white American Christianity is distorted by the unfortunate history of racial dissonance within the organized structures of

---

* There is a heretical tradition that Simon the African was crucified instead of Jesus.

the faith. In consequence, many black Christians sensitive to the more subtle implications of a religion often construed as a legacy of their bondage are determined to reclaim that ancient biblical heritage which avoids the embarrassments of brotherly denigration in America, and reestablish their connection with the faith at its inception.

For those uncomfortable with more recent and less sanguine exposures to the faith, Pentecost takes on new meaning. For among those "devout men from every nation under heaven" (Acts 2:5) who heard Peter proclaim the promise to them and to their children (Acts 2:39) were men from Africa (Acts 2:10). But as if to underscore divine intention that *black*[2] Africa (which first touched the destiny of Israel when Abraham came out of Ur and settled in Egypt, and continued through all the centuries thereafter) should be a direct and unequivocal heir to that promise, after Pentecost, the divine imperative came to the evangelist Philip, directing him toward a rendezvous which made inequitable the inclusion of black Africans among the charter members of the faith. "Take the desert road that leads toward Gaza," Philip was told. Waiting for him on that road with a copy of the Book of Isaiah in his hand was an African nobleman, treasurer to Her Majesty Candace, Queen of Ethiopia. He invited Philip to join him in his chariot, received the good news from his lips, and accepted baptism at his hand (Acts 8:26–39), all of which symbolizes from the beginning the African involvement in the new faith that was to spread throughout the world.

This must be reckoned a momentous event in the history of Christianity, but whether it has probable significance for the present mood of black American Christians needs closer examination. At minimum, there is the indisputable fact that Christianity experienced an early and fruitful establishment in North Africa, in Egypt, and in Ethiopia; and that the church in Africa gave back to the Church Universal an extraordinary interest on its investment. During the three hundred years from the third through the fifth century, when the church wrestled with its most critical theological formulations, of the eighteen or twenty most prominent leaders, no fewer than nine were African:

Clement, Origen, Tertullian, Cyprian, Dionysius, Athanasius, Didymus, Augustine, and Cyril. Cyprian and Augustine were the great intellectuals who worked out the basic political and theological doctrines of the Western church. How ironic it is that so much light should come from an allegedly "dark continent," and that it should eventuate in a civilization called the Christian West. Or that in time the Christian West, goaded by an insatiable economic self-interest, would turn again to Africa, not to bless her, but to suck her blood. But such are the inexplicables of human history. Neither the light of reason nor the illumination of the spirit is a sure hedge to the predaciousness that seems ever the corollary of power, irrespective of race, geography, or nationality. As fate would have it, the men who caught men (or bought them), and the men who were caught (or bought), were destined to play out their respective generations against the backdrop of the faith they were to share in a new world. But it was to be a world informed by latter-day apostles whose understanding of that faith was clouded by an incipient racism, a degraded economics, and an illusion of manifest destiny.

I have said that Africa knew the Hebrew nation in its infancy, from Abraham even; and the civilizations of Africa were ancient even then. Still, it is sometimes necessary to remind Christians in the West that Egypt is in Africa, and that Egyptians are Africans, despite the desperate efforts of our race-conscious latter-day historians to deny Africa a place of significance in the history of civilization. More than that, the Egyptians themselves are racial hybrids, representing a fusion of black peoples from the south with lighter-skinned races from the north. Even today the most casual observer is impressed by the strong physical resemblance between contemporary Egyptians and the so-called Negroid Africans of the sub-Sahara regions. As a case in point, the late Egyptian President Anwar Sadat would have been comfortably inconspicuous in any black church gathering until he prostrated himself for prayer. But the racial composition of the Egyptian people is for our present purposes somewhat beside the point, except that the peculiar convergence of events which brought Africans and American Christianity into a strange concubinage for three and a half centuries made it imperative to deny the African's role in the development of Egyptian civilization, in keeping with the conventional fiction of black cultural insignificance. This perspective has been promoted by practically all Western scholarship through a concerted pedagogical effort to separate Egypt as a cultural entity from the rest of Africa. But Egypt *was* and *is* African, and is quite likely to remain so, and the black experience in Egypt is hardly a matter of speculation wherever intellectual objectivity can be mustered.

One wonders why most Western historians have put themselves to such pains. The Blacks who were brought to America as slaves came from the coastal states of West Africa for the most part, not from Egypt. But the black presence in Egypt was established long before the white man came to Africa, whether to conquer, as did the Greeks and the Romans, or to deal in flesh, as did most of the rest of Western Europe. Despite the frustration it poses for scholars with such compelling needs to deny, or to reduce to insignificance, the black African's capacity for cultural relevance, the data of history simply refuse to be silent. In the final analysis, relevance itself is a matter of perspective. Perspective is an aspect of culture, and culture is by definition committed to values deriving from its own body of experience. One may redact the data of history in the interest of an alternative *theory*, but one cannot redact the facts of history and create an alternative *reality*. Whatever *was*, was indeed; and whatever *is*, is incontrovertible, a self-evident principle, it would seem. It is not our present task to seek to validate the relevance of the black experience in Egypt. My commitment is to another aspect of history which begins with the desecration of black Africa by the world's most advanced and enlightened white cultures, all of whose values were anchored in Christian perspectives. More particularly, our concern is America, where those perspectives continue to produce conflict between black and white Christians to this day. But we must begin with Africa, the motherland of the Black Diaspora, from which the sea captains of Europe and America took, in the course of four centuries, unnumbered tons of gold, uncounted shiploads of ivory, and millions upon millions of black men and women. To the plunderers, Africa was the "Gold Coast," the "Ivory Coast," the "Slave Coast." But it was never a community of people deserving Christian recognition and concern.

From 638, the Christian influence in Africa declined before the vast hegemony of Islam. In consequence, history was compelled to wait for Prince Henry the Navigator, that half-English, half-Portuguese Grand Master of the Order of Christ, to open up the so-called dark continent for Christ and commerce; and to see the slave trade established in medieval Europe fifty years before Columbus would discover a new Europe, where slavery was to become the major instrument of economic and social aggrandizement[3] for almost three centuries. But Portuguese Christianity was not alone in introducing black slavery to Europe, for, under Enrique III of Castile, gold and slaves from Africa were marketed in Seville in the last decade of the fifteenth century, and although good Queen Isabella, that canny and daring patron of Columbus, sought unsuccessfully to kill the practice before it was well rooted, she failed. She failed because the prevailing sentiment of the church was that it was better for a "heathen" to have his body bound and his soul free, than vice versa. So, by 1501, it was possible and profitable for the Spanish Crown to issue an edict permitting not only "freshly caught" Africans but those born in Christianity as well to be sold in America. At first the notion seemed to be that Christianized Blacks could better convert the Indians, although it was never quite clear why "savages" and "heathens" should promise greater success in the conversion enterprise than Christians boasting the spiritual seasoning of centuries. Perhaps the fact that slaves from Guinea brought four times as much in the American market as Indian slaves was not altogether irrelevant.

Impressed by the Spanish success, by the end of the fifteenth century Portugal had developed a voracious parasitism which she was to continue to indulge until she was dislodged by the freedom struggles that convulsed Africa after our most recent world war, leaving only the oppressive regime of the white South Africans to await some final Armageddon of liberation. With Africa as an inexhaustible source of supply for free black labor, Portugal contracted with Spain in the early days of the slave trade to provide the Spaniards with slaves for markets Spain had developed in the New World. By this arrangement the Portuguese hoped to maintain a monopoly on her very profitable procurements from the villages and towns of West Africa. But the neighboring states of Western Europe were not to be denied their share in this commerce, and the Portuguese monopoly was soon broken by Spanish, English, French, Dutch, and American competition. In the New World, labor was short and the market was aggressive. As a result, there were 500,000 slaves in the American colonies by the time of the Revolution—an embarrassing statistic patently inconsonant with the brave rhetoric of the Founding Fathers and the moral principles of an avowedly Christian nation.

Since no records were kept, we have no way of knowing how many, if any, of the slaves brought into the English colonies were Christian, although there were substantial numbers of black Christians with the Spanish adventurers in South and Central America, in Mexico, and in the Spanish settlements in Florida from the very beginning of the Spanish explorations in the New World. Some of them were slaves, some were not. Black Pedro Alonzo was captain of Columbus's flagship, the *Niña*. Another Black whose name was Estevanico, who with Cabeza de Vaca explored parts of Mexico and the Southwest, led an expedition into what is now New Mexico and Arizona, where he discovered the Zuni Indians. Estevanico is said to have planted the first wheat crop in America, in 1539. In the slave trade itself, the Catholic Portuguese and Spaniards were generally anxious to see their slaves baptized; the Anglo-Saxon Protestants were not. The Catholics, it seemed, gave a first consideration, however perfunctory, to the demands of the church. We are told that the Portuguese

> sold the performers of heathen rites and gave the proceeds to the poor. The numbers were so great that the slaver depended on the missionary to complete his cargo. Merolla sold a slave for a flask of wine for the sacraments. Even if Negroes had been

baptized, the [Catholic] missionary saw no sin in enslaving them. In reality, however, baptism encouraged and sanctioned slavery for it made the Negro a Christian and a man *nolens volens*, while the Christian slave trade was a beneficent agency to bring black barbarians into Christian civilization. Only, let not the slave be sold to heretics, for then he would be doubly damned.[4]

This was representative Catholicism at work in the slave trade: a bow toward Rome and on with the business at hand, being careful only to have no dealing with the heathen Mohammedans lest the poor souls, already damned for being black, be damned again for falling into the ways of Islam. The Protestants ignored Rome and bowed instead to an incipient racism which, ere long, would develop a ponderous psychology of justification that would burden both church and society in the West for generations. The Englishman considered *himself* first, above all. And when he contemplated his own perfection, he saw the alleged heathenism of the Africans as but one aspect of a generalized disparity. They were beings apart. They were not merely black, they were black *and* heathen. Historian Winthrop Jordan declares:

Heathenism was from the Anglo-Saxon's point of view not so much a specifically religious defect, but was one manifestation of a general refusal to measure up to proper standards, as a failure to be English. . . . Being Christian was not merely a matter of subscribing to certain doctrines; it was a quality inherent in oneself and one's society. It was interconnected with all the other attributes of normal and proper men.[5]

It was all a matter of the black man's depraved condition. Since he was not an Englishman, his importance and his place in the Englishman's scheme of things was predetermined. From such a perspective the Anglo-Saxon could scarcely be expected to develop a warm appreciation of the African's humanity, his native religion, or his capacity to benefit from Christian instruction.

If the Anglo-Saxon's racial and cultural arrogance had been less consummate, it is possible that he could have learned something from the African which might have given him cause for reflection. The Africans he dismissed arbitrarily as heathens did,

as a matter of fact, believe in one supreme God. Above the intermediary gods and spirits which so distressed the white man was
always the One God who was the giver and sustainer of life.
What the white man dismissed as African ancestor worship was
a highly sophisticated expression of family integrity and continuity, an observation strangely and unaccountably lost on a
people so irrevocably committed to the institutionalization of
family relationships as were the English. What is more, the
African moral codes were consistent with the notion of One God
of all people, a notion which has not always been honored in the
breech in the West. The slave trader saw none of this. He understood less than he saw, and cared about less than he understood.
After all, "the English errand in Africa was not [the search for]
a new or perfect community, but a business trip."[6] The great
civilizations the Africans had raised at Ghana, at Mele, at Jenné,
Songhay, and Timbuktu, their art, their religion, their culture
meant nothing to the men who came bringing Bibles, trinkets,
and chains.

As slavery went, the English were probably no worse than the
worst and certainly no better than the best, and the line that
separated the one from the other is scarcely discernible from any
perspective of human responsibility. Whether Anglo-Saxon,
Spaniard, or Dane, Portuguese, Dutch, or American, the men
who wasted Africa decimated her towns and villages, corrupted
her politics, destroyed her economy, and hauled her people away
wholesale to distant lands where those who survived were reduced to submission and servility. It is not a question of whether
the Anglo-Saxon was better or worse. What is important is that
America is the place where white Christians and Blacks still
confront each other in the continuing conflicts of culture, morality, and religion we call the American dilemma.

Chained neck to neck, wrist to wrist, and ankle to ankle, and
shipped off into a new kind of Babylonian captivity in Christian
America, the Africans left their gods but not their God. Muslim
and heathen alike, and possibly some Christians as well, chained
body to body between decks four feet high; if they survived the
darkness, the filth, the horror, and the degradation of the "middle

passage," they would arrive by and by in the land of the American Christians: the Congregationalists, the Presbyterians, the Roman Catholics, the Quakers, the Lutherans, the Baptists, the Methodists, and, of course, the Anglicans—once removed. There they would eventually meet the white man's God.

The Gospel through the Windows

There was a fleeting moment in our history when some denominations sought to commit their churches to do what our Founding Fathers had elected not to do; namely, to give de facto recognition to the principle that *all* men stand before God equal in their nakedness and need. But in the end the churches failed to rescue what the statesmen decided to overlook. Bigotry seeped through the restraints of the faith to join the undertow already sucking at the political foundations of the new nation. Black Christians, despairing of the peculiar spiritual mentality which confined them to the back pews and "nigger heavens" in the white churches, eventually withdrew and founded independent communions.

If there had been no racism in America, there would be no racial churches. As it is, we have white churches and black churches; white denominations and black denominations; American Christianity and black religion. Although there was no concerted effort at black conversion until the early eighteenth century, American Christianity was even then in a quandary about what to do about black Christians. The problem became acute once the number of Blacks who opted for Christ began to grow. The minutes of the Presbyterian Synod of South Carolina and Georgia meeting in 1834 disclose the vexations typically faced by the white churches:

> The gospel, as things are now, can never be preached to the two classes successfully in conjunction. The galleries or the back seats on the lower floors of white churches are generally appropriated to the Negroes, when it can be done without inconvenience to the whites. When it cannot be done conveniently, the Negroes must catch the gospel as it escapes through the doors and windows.[7]

It was evident that the black worshipper wanted somewhat more than the white man's convenience would allow, for "when the Negro worshipper gained conscious self-respect he grew tired of the back pews and upper galleries of the white churches, and sought places of worship more compatible with his sense of freedom and dignity."[8] However, the only place in which a black Christian was able to worship with dignity was in a black church. But black churches were considered dangerous to established white interests, and in every Southern state they were forbidden, suppressed, or severely regulated by law until the Civil War settled for all time the black Christian's right to independent worship. Even under the most benign circumstances, the black-church-within-the-white-church arrangement had never been a completely satisfying arrangement for either Blacks or whites. The peculiar conditions imposed upon Blacks to protect the white man's sense of uniqueness humiliated the one and posed a continuing moral contradiction for the other. This was no less true in the highly selective sermons preached for the Blacks than in the segregated arrangements for their worship. But the black Christians were no more blind to the abuse of the faith than to the abuse of themselves as human beings and fellow Christians. Accordingly, when the chasm of credibility could no longer be bridged by patience and humility, they determined to be free of what they could not accept. The remarks of ex-slave Lunsford Lane are revealing:

> There was one kind-hearted clergyman I used often to hear; he was very popular among the colored people. But after he had preached a sermon to us in which he urged from the Bible that it was the will of heaven . . . that we should be slaves, and our masters our owners, Many of us left him, considering like the doubting disciple of old, 'This is a hard saying; Who can hear it?'[9]

There were many Blacks who, like Lunsford Lane, could not be reconciled to their status in the white church, and since they often found the doctrine preached to them there to be without comfort, their spiritual unrest must have increased with each occasion for doubt. They had their own thoughts about their bodies and their souls and their destinies, but it was extremely impolitic not to accept the white man's arrangements, for the white man represented the sum total of temporal power within the universe of the black experience in America. So in the white man's church they sat wherever his pleasure indicated they should, and waited. They stifled the urge to scream and to shout and to raise their arms to heaven; and they strangled the sobs and the moans that welled up inside and made their bodies shake and tremble like leaves in a storm. Only their tears could not be stayed—tears of sorrow and distress, so often mistaken for tears of joy for having the privilege of confronting God in the presence of the slavemaster.

With Fear and Trembling . . . as unto Christ

Often, when the white man's worship service was over, the black man's might truly begin, for neither his heart nor his private membership was in the white church, where he was scorned and demeaned. There was that *other* church, that *invisible institution* which met in the swamps and the bayous, and which joined all black believers in a common experience at a single level of human and spiritual recognition. Deep in the woods and safely out of sight of the critical, disapproving eyes of the master and the overseer, the shouts rolled up—and out. The agony so long suppressed burdened the air with sobs and screams and rhythmic moans. God's praises were sung. His mercy enjoined. His justice invoked. There in the Invisible Church the black Christian met God on his own terms and in his own way without the white intermediary. That invisible communion was the beginning of the Black Church, the seminal institution which spans most of the history of the black experience. It offers the most accessible key to the complexity and the genius of the black subculture, and it reflects both a vision of the tragedy and an aspect of hope of the continuing American dilemma.

Perhaps more than any other people since the Israelites were enslaved in Egypt, the Blackamerican has been shaped and characterized by the unique place religion has occupied in his personal life and in the common destiny of the race. His American experience is inseparable from his religious heritage because for much of that history there was little else to offer meaning to existence, or to fall back upon for strength to confront the exigencies of his distressed condition.

But Christianity in America had already been accommodated to black pacification and control in the interest of the most abominable institution ever to challenge Christian morality. In consequence, that version of Christianity urged upon the slaves bore no "good news" beyond a legacy of toil, and no hope for rescue this side of Jordan. It was a religion that called them to work and to die for the doubtful aggrandizement of self-appointed Christian masters whose calculated manipulation of the faith was intended to so confuse the slave as to make his dehumanization seem reasonable and inevitable. Was not the African the accursed son of Ham? *(Albeit he was not a Hebrew!)* Was not his blackness a sign of his degradation at God's hand? *(Although he was made in God's own image!)* And did not the Apostle Paul admonish the slave who wanted to join his fellowship of Christians that he must first return to his master, thereby proving for all times that there was no incompatibility between the faith and human bondage? Unrequited toil was the inevitable lot, the God-ordained lot, the *proper* lot of the black man and his progeny forever. It was the penalty for his sins, even as his blackness was the sign of his depravity. And this by divine decree. He must labor in the fields for his earthly master whom God had set over him, "from can-to-can't," i.e., from "can see to can't see"—from daylight until dark, all of his life, and for all time. He must not complain, for all that he was or ever would be depended upon his white master. *It was God's will!* To run away would be to commit an unforgivable sin—the theft of his master's God-given property, viz., himself! To kill himself would be to destroy property not his own. A slave who committed suicide could receive no rites of the church, and was destined to burn in hell forever. But if he bore his lot with love and patience, being at all times loyal and obedient to the masters set over him in this world, he would be properly rewarded in the world to come.

It was God's will, and it was the white man's Christian duty, indeed, the white man's burden, to see that will fulfilled.

> Servants, be obedient to them that are your masters . . . with fear and trembling . . . as unto Christ. . . . Remember, God required this of you. . . . There is something so becoming and engaging in the modest, cheerful, good natured behavior that a little work done in that manner seems better done. . . . It also gains the goodwill and love of those you belong to. . . . Besides . . . your murmuring and grumbling is against God who hath placed you in their service.[10]

Such were the teachings of the white man's church as they were offered to the African who found himself involuntarily resident in America.

In the South

Those who laid claim to the black man's body, his labor, his children born and unborn, were Christians, and the strange claims these white Christians made upon their fellow Christians who were black were supported by a system of law anxious to accommodate the claims of property but insensitive to the claims of persons who happened to be black. This unfortunate priority of interests might well have been predicted in the larger context of the developing American self-perception. There was a world to be won, an empire to be built, and the notion that the Africans were provided by a benign providence to be the instruments of the white man's destiny seemed increasingly logical and circumspect. Empire building requires prodigious quantities of cheap labor. Slave labor seemed indispensable, and *African* slave labor appeared to be ideal. Indian slaves had proved to be impractical, indenture too clumsy, and the flood-tide of Eastern and Southern European immigration was far into a future yet to be created.*

---

* The high mortality rate among Indians confined in slavery was exacerbated by the relative ease (and frequency) with which they vanished into the familiar forests—and home. Some whites were enslaved through illegal extensions of indenture contracts and by other questionable stratagems. However, the prospect of trouble with the Crown made such practices hazardous. No such impediments stood in the way of African slavery.

Into the furnace of expediency the Africans were thrust, and the question of their claims as persons was dismissed as academic and irrelevant.

Sooner or later the question of black humanity would have to be dealt with, of course, but for the moment it was simply not an issue of compelling significance. It could wait. In the meantime, the once tentative notions about the black man's "difference" would develop into inflexible ideologies, with all of the fervor and assurance that vested interests could muster. Both God and reason would be called to bear witness as the rationalizations of moral justification took on the encrustations of immutable truth. Peter Kalm, a Swedish observer traveling in America in 1748, struck by the indifference of the Americans concerning the spiritual condition of the Africans they enslaved, reported that the whites

> are partly led by the conceit of its being shameful, to have a spiritual brother or sister among so despicable a people, partly thinking that they would not be able to keep their Negroes so meanly afterwards; and partly through fear of the Negroes growing too proud, on seeing themselves upon a level with their masters in religious matters.[11]

The notion of sharing a brotherhood in Christ with Africans, in this world or any other, was certainly not a popular one. A typical response to so incredible a suggestion was said to have been: "What, such as they? What, those black dogs be made Christians? What, shall they be like us?" "Is it possible," one distraught Christian lady wanted to know, "that any of my slaves could go to heaven, and must I see them there?"[12]

In the South the essential factor at work was a racial tribalism which militated against sharing a common experience with Blacks as equals under any circumstances, religious or otherwise. Social distance must not be breeched by the ordinary amenities of common worship. Three hundred years later the churches of America would still be in scandalous agitation over the same issue. There would be kneel-ins and lockouts, and black caucuses and demands for reparations, and a variety of other forms of behavior which, in a Christian democracy, must have appeared to be bizarre to the most tolerant of observers. But the precedents were in place even before the issues were born. A convocation of Anglican ministers meeting at Oxford, Maryland, in 1731 revealed a sad lack of interest in the spiritual well-being of black people. Here is the record:

> Mr. Fletcher said his parishioners were generally so brutish that they would not suffer their Negroes to be instructed, catechized, or baptized. . . .

> Mr. Airey finds the people of his parish very inclined to have their Negroes instructed, but they will not be at any pains and trouble of it. . . .

> Mr. Manadier has often pressed on his people their obligation to instruct their Negroes, but yet they are very remiss and neglectful.

> Mr. Nicholas says . . . he has from the pulpit and in conversation been Instant with his Parishioners to instruct their Negroes, in order to their being made Christians; but that the best answer he can get, even from the best people is that they are very sorry, and lament that they cannot comply with it.

> Mr. Cox has urged the necessity of instructing the Negroes, but 'tho his Parishioners allow it to be a good thing, yet they generally excuse themselves as thinking it to be impractical.[13]

Father John Carroll, a distinguished Catholic clergyman, and later Archbishop of Baltimore and signatory to the Declaration of Independence, was sensitive to the fact that the Blacks were " 'kept so constantly at work' that their spiritual nurture was neglected, with the result that they were 'very dull in faith and depraved in morals.' " But the sensitivity of the good bishop, like that of many of his Protestant counterparts, was apparently dulled by self-interest, for despite their dullness and depravity he owned, and presumably "kept constantly at work," several of these poor creatures himself.

If the experiences of these clergymen were typical of the colonial spirit, and the evidence suggests this to be the case, then the popular notion of that day that American slavery was pre-eminently, or even initially, an altruistic endeavor to save the heathen Africans from the consequences of black sin would hardly stand critical review. It is true that the Catholics in America were themselves suppressed, which ought to have made them more sensitive to the plight of the Blacks. But American Catholicism has traditionally been preoccupied with other interests, and the plight of black people in or outside the church has apparently never been an item of high priority for American Catholics. The Catholic Church had less spiritual impact upon the black experience during the developing years of the Republic than any other major communion with the exception of Judaism. But while both Catholics and Jews were themselves suspect in the eyes of the Protestant establishment, and neither communion was prepared to contribute to its own jeopardy by identifying with the interests of black people, the Jews became in time the principal advocates and participants in the black struggle for freedom.

The Anglicans were the "established" church in the five Southern colonies, but the institutional weakness of Anglicanism during the colonial period, coupled with the vested interests of its controlling factions, made that church an unlikely haven for the black dispossessed. Anglicanism was the preferred bracelet of the Southern aristocracy, which is to say the planter class. The Bishop of London could (and did) issue whatever pronouncements he thought wise, but the real control of the parish churches was in the hands of the vestrymen, who in most cases turned out to be the principal slaveholders. The strong sentiment for Christianizing the slaves which emerged in eighteenth-century England was simply not shared in America, where the principal issues had already congealed in terms of race rather than circumstance. Hence, the English suggestion that Blacks not only be allowed to become "brothers in Christ" to the colonists but be encouraged to become free men through hard work and faithful service only showed how vast the gap was between English and American thinking. To the English, slavery was a matter of happenstance—of fortune; and fortune could be changed if one could manage the cultural requirements of English civilization, of which Christianity was a cardinal example. But to the Americans it was a matter of race, and race was immutable and forever.

In the North

The situation in New England was dishearteningly similar in effect to that prevailing in the South. In 1701 the Society for the Propagation of the Gospel began sending missionaries from England to bring the faith to the Blacks. This was almost a hundred years after the Africans were introduced to Jamestown in 1619. Blacks arrived in Boston in 1638, and while life in Puritan New England was never as harsh as it was in the Anglican South, for one whose face was black—whether Christian, pagan, infidel, slave, or free—life was a struggle beyond imagination, and dignity was an anticipation for some other world. For most of the colonial period Christianity was effectively reserved for the elite, and its benefits were preempted by the elect. But in the context of prevailing circumstances men who were black were neither elite nor elect. They were the legion of the accursed and the damned. They were Africans. They had been separated from the roots of their ancient religions and forbidden to practice their alleged paganism in Christian America. They were damned, not by God, but by those same Christians who welcomed their bodies but denied their souls, and who turned them away from their churches. Like their brothers in the South, the Puritans chose to believe that Blacks and Indians were inferior beings who were a part of a divine inheritance God had set aside for them and their benefit! In that light, it is hardly astonishing that so little was done to minister to the Blacks' spiritual requirements when the existence of those requirements was not generally recognized. As late as 1680, Governor Bradstreet could inform the British Committee of Trade and Plantations that of the Blacks in Massachusetts there had been none baptized there as far as he knew.[14] History will forgive the governor for being incompletely informed about an event which was indeed rare—having occurred only once. But there was in fact a black woman in the household of a Reverend Stoughton of Dorchester who, "being well approved . . . for sound knowledge and true godliness," was baptized and admitted to the church in 1641.[15]

But the souls of black men and women in Puritan New England were not at a premium, to say the least. As a matter of fact, whether or not Blacks *had* souls was a popular subject of sporting debate among the most learned divines and theologians of the day. Dean Berkeley of Rhode Island let it be known in 1731 that his parishioners "consider the Blacks as creatures of another species, who [had] no right to be admitted to the sacraments. . . . Such," he added, was "the main obstacle to the conversion of those poor people."[16] Cotton Mather, in a celebrated work called *The Negro Christianized,* published in 1743, defended the black man's soul with consuming passion, and even suggested (blasphemy of blasphemies) that the Blacks just might be "the Elect of God" sent among the Puritans by Divine Providence! But Dr. Mather's arguments may well have derived from other interests. Whatever he may have thought about Blacks being elect, he urged the conversion of Blacks as a matter of great practical benefit to the masters. Enraptured by the possibilities inherent in black conversion, he exclaimed:

> Oh that our neighbors would consider the incomparable Benefits that would follow upon your Endeavors to Christianize your Negroes. . . . Oh the consolation that will belong to you! . . . Your Negroes are immediately raised unto an astonishing felicity. . . . They are become amiable spectacles such as the Angels of God would repair to the windows of heaven to look down upon. Tho' they remain your servants, yet they become the children of God. Tho' they are to enjoy no Earthly Goods, but the small allowance that your Justice and Bounty shall see proper for them. . . . Tho' they are your vassals, and must with a profound subject wait upon you, yet the Angels of God now take them under their Guardianship. Oh what you have done for them. Happy Masters . . . it will not be long before you and they come . . . together in the Heavenly City . . . and [you] hear them forever blessing the gracious God for the Day when He first made them your servants.[17]

But Mather's arguments fell mostly on deaf ears. The Society for the Propagation of the Gospel in Foreign Parts, after a very meager harvest in its efforts to bring the Indians to Christ, eventually turned its attention to the Blacks. But the Puritans were more wary of the Anglican-based SPG than they were of whatever devils might be resident in the soul-less Africans among them. They kept the Blacks away from the missionaries, with telling results. The records of the society reveal that in 1729 their agent in Boston, one Dr. Cutler, harvested only one black convert, a slave. Twenty-one years later, in 1750, he could boast of having baptized "five Negro children, one of whom was a slave," during the seven months preceding his report. The society's laborers in neighboring Connecticut fared little better. The Reverend Samuel Seabury of New London noted in his report of November 12, 1739, that in the latter half of that year he had added to Christ's meager company of Blacks in America one mulatto servant and one Negro child.[18]

The Logic of Exclusion

We may safely conclude, then, that for the first hundred years of the American experiment the Christian church took no more official notice of black people than did the British Crown. Indeed, not as much, for as they were units of production to be bought and sold, the Crown had a vast economic stake in the granting of charters for the procurement and sale of Blacks in the interest of an uninterrupted labor supply for its growing dominions in America and the West Indies.

The interests of the church in America were more exclusive. At first the church was content merely to ignore whatever spiritual needs or potentials the African might have, despite the fact that an important rationale for slavery was that it was designed to provide for the moral and spiritual uplift of the benighted Africans. Later, when the economic blessings of slavery became more evident, the Christian slavemasters would hold themselves to be the very instruments of the divine plan for bringing the

savage African to Christ, albeit via the slave block. He was the
white man's burden, to be sure, but since he would reap great
spiritual benefit from his lowly but disciplined sojourn among
God's elect, his presence was to be tolerated as a Christian duty.
Nonetheless, for the better part of a century the active proselytiz-
ing of these involuntary servants the settlers had brought among
themselves with such solicitude was everywhere discouraged; and
the penalties for instructing them in the Christian religion were
severe enough to dampen the ardor of spiritual outreach for most
Christian ministers who may have been troubled by the summary
exclusion of Blacks from the churches. In consequence, it did
come to pass that for all black people the American commonwealth so proudly conceived as a free, Christian nation was
curiously un-Christian and demonstrably unfree as well.

Virginia and Massachusetts were the principal centers of the
early colonial establishment, but as we have seen, lack of interest
in the Christianization of Blacks was quite general. For the most
part, the exclusion of Blacks from Christian concern was seldom
a matter requiring comment or explanation. From the beginning,
the Anglo-Americans considered the Blacks among them as beings
of a lower order who, if they were human at all, were not human
in the same sense that white men were human. Hence, neither
the blessings of liberty nor the comforts of heaven were considered to have any reference to Blacks. It was simply understood
that "men" meant *white* men, whether the context was social,
political, religious, or general. In short, the American mind-set
was such as to effectively exclude Blacks from any frame of
reference dealing with what could be considered normative
human interests or relations.

In those colonies where slaves were considered indispensable
to the plantation economy, the economic investment in human
bodies was enormous, and the planters were suspicious of any
tampering with their property rights. "Talk to a planter about
the soul of a Negro," commented a writer in a popular colonial
journal, "and he'll be apt to tell you that the body of one Negro
may be worth 20 pounds, but the souls of a hundred of them
would not yield him one farthing."[19] There was also much concern

that the religious enterprise required *time* for worship, and for being instructed or catechized, and that time would be lost to production. In America, the maxim that time is money and that money requires no apology has a long history and a popular application. Sunday was the day the slaves were expected to devote to raising their own food and recouping their strength as best they could against the inevitability of the week ahead. The slave system was geared to the premise that black labor was a perishable commodity, and that its extraction should be at a steady, continuous rate, to be interfered with only under the most compelling circumstances. "Negroes . . . were bought for the purpose of performing labor. What fact could be more obvious and natural, or less demanding of explanation?"[20] In a system which routinely expected a slave mother to be back at her plow the same day she "dropped" (i.e., gave birth to) a child, "church-time," including time spent at instruction, prayer, or other religious endeavors, was thought of as time squandered at the master's expense.

But the main objection to the spiritual enlightenment of the Blacks derived from the fear that a slave who became a Christian might somehow claim freedom on that account. This was in itself enough to discourage absolutely any attempt at their conversion in the plantation country, although in New England, where full political rights could be held only by church members, the opportunities for Blacks to become Christians were hardly more favorable. The threat implied in social equality was a factor of consequence in both North and South. It was thought that the Blacks would become "uppity" or "impudent" by reason of their association with whites in religious services, and they would "not so readily keep their places" thereafter if they were admitted to fellowship with whites. Long before Crispus Attucks ran away from slavery to become the first American to die for this country's independence, the Corporation of Harvard College was bitterly protesting the seating of a Negro even in the gallery of the First Parish Church in Cambridge.

Aside from motives deriving from economic interest and conceit, there was also a real fear that slaves meeting under cover of religious worship would plot insurrection or revolt. These apprehensions proved to be well founded, for in the decades following the American Revolution, when it became clear to the black patriots that their political rights were totally unaffected by their patriotism or their valor, they were not reluctant to use whatever cover or pretext was available to strike more directly for their freedom. Indeed, having been bereft of all rights whatever by those for whose independence they had struggled, it was a sad revelation to learn that the cause of American independence for which they had fought was not a cause which recognized the right of freedom for anyone who happened to be black. Although information concerning insurrections, escape, sabotage, gentricide, and the like was commonly suppressed in the effort to avoid contagion, no segment of the slave era was free from the concerted acts of black people resisting their subjugation.

So it was that from the beginning the American Nation under God showed no serious concern for either the spiritual or the political needs of the black wards fetched from Africa. Left to their own resources, the vast majority of Blacks practiced whatever fragments of African religions they could remember, modified by the singular exigencies of life on the plantation. Most religious practices were secret, for while the slavemaster reserved Christianity for himself and his kind, he had no sympathy and less appreciation for other religions he did not understand or care to learn about. The "heathen rituals" of the Africans were generally dismissed as childish superstitions much given to the gibberish and frenzy indicative of a low order of intelligence which required continuous and white control. In consequence, all expressions of African religion were forbidden; and whenever possible, Africans with the same tribal or language affiliation were split up and sold off to widely separated plantations.

Opening the Doors

When the Society for the Propagation of the Gospel launched its campaign to have Blacks conditionally admitted to the select circle of American Christendom, it did so under the shadow of colonial legislation that had been passed by Maryland in 1664 and by Virginia in 1667 guaranteeing that a slave's status was unaffected by the circumstance of baptism. By 1706, four additional colonies had made a similar determination, and these laws were then given religious sanction by an edict from the Bishop of London in 1727. The edict assured the planters that conversion "does not make the least alteration in Civil property . . . but continues Persons in the same state as it found them. . . ."[21] The society's missionary activities were in some respects a curious turn of history, for the African involvement in Christianity was centuries old long before the English had given up some pagan practices very similar to those from which they now decided the Africans ought to be rescued. But, as we have already observed, the most difficult obstacle faced by the SPG was the white resistance to sharing the faith with Blacks. This antipathy was deeply embedded in custom and convention and fortified by law. As early as 1715, a North Carolina law provided a heavy fine "if any master or owner of Negroes, or slaves . . . shall permit or suffer any Negro or Negroes to build . . . on their lands . . . any house under pretense of meeting-house upon account of worship . . . and shall not suppress or hinder them. . . ." In 1800 a law in South Carolina made it illegal for "any number of slaves, free Negroes, mulattoes or mestizoes, even in the company of white persons to . . . assemble for the purpose of . . . religious worship, either before the rising of the sun, or the going down of the same."[22]

In North Carolina no slave or free Black could legally preach or exhort "in any prayer meeting or other association for worship where slaves of different families were collected together."[23] Other laws required the presence of whites—from five or six to a majority—at any meeting or worship service Blacks could attend. Some of the harsher proscriptions were in response to the slave insurrections of Toussaint L'Ouverture in Haiti, and Nat Turner and Denmark Vesey in Virginia, but the determination to limit and to direct the black religious experience was well established a hundred years before there was a major black resurrection to agitate the planters. There were other reasons born of more subtle imaginings, for, in America, Christianity was considered as unconditionally the white man's exclusive entitlement as any of the other cultural ensigns put forward as distinguishing the Anglo-Saxon heritage.

The Great Awakening

It was not until the first Great Awakening, that tumultuous series of outdoor revivals and camp meetings that swept the country around 1740, that the Christian religion became reasonably accessible to the black masses. The cold, impersonal churches of Puritan New England, where dispassionate, abstract theological arguments were offered from the lofty pulpits in lieu of preaching, had little appeal to Blacks, whose doctrinal views were anchored in a cheerless reality no learned argument could alleviate. In the South, the staid formalism of the Episcopal Church with its Latin liturgy and esoteric symbolism was hardly more attractive or comforting. The black condition demanded a God with *feelings*, a God the distressed could talk to! Only when it moved out of the established churches and into the groves and brush arbors, leaving behind the private pews, the nigger heavens, and the other demeaning trappings of class and race, did the white man's religion begin to take on real significance for black people. Fiery exhorters—some of whom were black— who could *"preach the Bible real,"* supported by fervent singing and praying and testifying, gave the Black Diaspora a perspective on the faith that bore promise of true spiritual utility.

In New England, despite the salubrious spirit of the Awakening, there was no immediate rush among Blacks to become Christians merely because the more onerous barriers to the faith had been temporarily relaxed. Normative Christian nurture still required a cultus, a fellowship, which in turn implied church membership, a status not easily attained by either the poor or the black. Despite the ardent efforts of the Society for the Propagation of the Gospel, if there was hungering and thirsting for the white man's religion, that yearning was scarcely reflected in the pews of the churches by the close of the Revolutionary War. The Reverend Samuel Hopkins of Newport attributed the absence of the Blacks to "the deepest prejudices against the Christian religion."[24]

The story was quite different in the South, where the Methodists and Baptists had gathered thousands of Blacks into their churches before the end of the eighteenth century.[25] When the Methodist Church was formally organized in 1784, fully one-fifth of its membership was black; and by the turn of the century, Blacks in the Methodist and Baptist churches were numbered in the tens of thousands. Presbyterians were a distant third, with smaller numbers of Blacks scattered among the other major denominations.

But that is not the whole story. The Episcopal Church, dominant in the states where Blacks were most populous, failed altogether to attract a significant black constituency. The Presbyterians and the Quakers, both more benign denominations in their attitudes toward Blacks, had little more success than the Congregationalists of New England, who considered themselves the principal friends of the Blacks.

The Great Awakening aroused in thousands of Americans, white and black, a new spiritual consciousness which culminated, in many cases, in church affiliation—mainly with Baptists and Methodists. Popular theory advanced to account for the black attraction to the faith at this peculiar moment in American history suggests that while New England Calvinism was too cold and reasoned for the African mind, Catholicism and Episcopalianism were "too symbolic and ritualistic," the Quakers "too meditative" and "too reflective." The burden of this argument, of course, rests upon the conventional presupposition that black people are "exuberant" and "emotional" *by nature*, impatient with symbolism and abstraction, and not much given to reflection. But, from the beginning, conventional Western perception conceived the African world as essentially a world of the senses, not a world of the mind. The practical effects of this condition explained the African's spiritual retardation and postponed his significant religious investment. The Great Awakening, with its spiritual boisterousness, uncomplicated preaching, and vivid stories, coupled with the opportunity for substantial personal participation through singing, praying, and testifying, struck a responsive chord in the African he had never before experienced in America. All this was thought to replicate to some degree traditional African religion, while elevating the African experience to increasingly higher planes of spiritual involvement. A major objection to this theory is that it strains too hard at the gnat of African emotionalism while overlooking the obvious: what the Africans found in the camp meetings of the Great Awakening was *acceptance and involvement as human beings*. However tentative his reception, and however transitory the occasion, the camp meetings became a sanctuary to which the African could escape for an interlude of peace and dignity from the humdrum horror of slavery. Under the brush arbors, the black slave was a servant among servants and a seeker among seekers, all terrified, sanctified, and exultant together. It was the only moment in his life that his color and his station were not the absolute conditioners of his humanity.

The camp meetings were a serious deviation from conventional norms of religious behavior, and the practices of the Great Awakening came under fire from the traditionalists of the day. The behavior of the Blacks was particularly cited as evidence of the alleged degenerate nature of revivalism. A prominent New England minister complained:

> So great has been the enthusiasm created by Wesley and White-field and Tennant . . . the very Servants and Slaves pretend to extraordinary inspiration, and under veil thereof cherish their idle dispositions, and in lieu of minding their respective businesses run rambling about to utter enthusiastic nonsense.[26]

Whether it was the religious style of the Great Awakening or the relaxation of social constraints that was decisive for black involvement, that involvement was furthered by the suspension of conventional procedures which required converts to go through a period of instruction before full admission to Christian fellowship. Because most white Christians held firmly to the belief that Blacks were incapable of receiving instruction, and incapable of fulfilling the moral obligations which were a part of that instruction, the practical result was to keep Blacks out of the churches because of these alleged inadequacies. In New England, where church membership and citizenship were closely linked, this linkage alone was effective in the exclusion of Blacks from the churches. In the South, the worrisome problem of the legal status of Christian slaves was a formidable deterrent to black evangelization, as was the great fear that social distance between Blacks and whites would be jeopardized. As it turned out, the Great Awakening not only was the wedge which opened the faith to the Blacks; it was also the first serious breach in the forbidding fortress of religious formalism which contributed to the effective maintenance of barriers between social classes as well as to the racial-caste arrangement. But the most notable accomplishment of the Awakening was the legitimation of the spiritual quest at the level of felt need rather than at the level of privilege, so that the common man of whatever race was provided a less cumbersome access to the faith.

By the time Thomas Jefferson came to draft the Declaration of Independence, black Christians were a substantial segment of the church. The overwhelming majority of them were slaves, for they remained slaves after conversion, just as they remained slaves after the War for Independence had raised their hopes and claimed their blood. For all that, religion did make a difference in their lives, and it has continued to modify the black experience and its impingement upon America ever since.

Attracted by the informality and the excitement of the Awakening, Blacks accepted Christianity not so much because they could give vent to their alleged natural exuberance or native fervor but because it was suddenly available on terms they could live with. The rules which had kept them on the plantations and out of the churches were relaxed momentarily in the informality of the brush arbors, and the opportunities to enter into new kinds of relationships with other human beings were at least tentatively present. The consequences of the black religious involvement were both immediate and far-reaching. First of all, the argument about the African's spiritual and moral capacity was made moot by the fact that thousands of Blacks accepted Christianity and were received as Christians. This was a *fait accompli*. Impossible as it was, it *was*. Second, while the religious test of the Awakening was based on religious experience rather than theological understanding, the acquisition of some modicum of instruction and information was inevitable in the process of Christian worship and fellowship. Third, any kind of Christian association, even that of master and slave, modified relationships to some degree and raised implicit questions in the minds of all parties about the morality of the slave system. Finally, Christianity provided an organizational and moral base for self-liberation which in time the Blacks were certain to exploit.

It is a reasonable conclusion, then, that despite distortions and limitations, sharing the same religion provided opportunities for the socialization of Blacks and for the humanization of the whites who held them in thrall. Few slaves, torn away as they were from their previous cultures, found anything to fill the cultural vacuum in the day-to-day existence which marked the slave system. The societies and tribal orders to which they belonged in Africa could not be replicated under the slavocracy in America. The drums were forbidden; the familiar languages were forbidden, as were the ancient rituals and ceremonies providing for identity and community. The established policy of separating slaves with a common tribal or language background was everywhere enforced. As a result, not only were the ties of cultural continuity with the motherland summarily severed by commercial deportation, but the opportunities for reasonable reconstruction after resettlement were effectively eliminated. The slave plantation had no room and less sympathy for an African counterpart of the Little Italys, or the barrios, or the Chinatowns which were later to become features of American ethnic pluralism. Instead, every effort was made to preclude the possibility of the Africans ever having effective cultural communion with each other, not to mention acceptance in the general American community. The vast majority of the slaves were confined to the fields from daylight until dark, and their participation in the culture of America was hardly any different from what it would have been had they remained in Africa. Whatever they may have remembered of their previous religious experiences could scarcely be replicated in the remote corners of the plantation, and could do little to enhance their life of bondage in America.

In spite of the dismal prospects for the religious needs of the Africans during their first hundred years in America, Christianity played a major part in the development of the new black subculture, for once it gained a foothold on the plantation, it became a meaningful substitute for many of the lost institutions which had been so important to tribal life in Africa. Common worship, communal singing, a common ritual, and common beliefs broke down the barriers of language and custom and brought men and women of many different tribal affiliations together in religious associations. Further, it is reasonable to assume that, despite the fact that white Christians could not seem to overcome the felt need to hold other Christians in bondage, Christian conscience regarding the practice was probably never completely at ease. In the long run, the very long run, perhaps, it is a reasonable speculation that the incongruity of enslaving one's brothers and sisters in Christ might have touched even the most unregenerate "masters," and that abominable "peculiar institution" would in time have capitulated to the ethics of the same faith in which it sought its justification. Indeed, had the Great Awakening occurred a hundred years earlier, slavery as an institution might not have survived the Revolution, for once Blacks became Christians in large numbers, the problem of justification and maintenance was exacerbated, and the system may well have fallen under its own weight in time. This is not to overlook the fact that some Blacks were undoubtedly more securely accommodated to their condition through religious involvement, for, as we have seen, the critical doctrines of the faith were not immune to distortion and manipulation. But the accommodation of some to a system of oppression is also a powerful factor in the determination of others to be free. In any case, religion became the primary occasion for a more humane contact with whites, and in consequence it was the most important instrument of black socialization. At minimum, their acceptance as Christians, however conditional, was an implied admission that they had souls and were persons of worth and responsibility, and therefore entitled to some recognition beyond that of mere brutes and chattels.

But American Christianity never did imply a presumption of racial equality for Blacks, whether social, political, or spiritual. Nor did it concede to them the mature sense of moral accountability all white Christians were presumed to have. Morally, the black Christian was simply expected to do the best he could with his limited capacity. God and society would forgive him his failures so long as he kept the place assigned him in the sociopolitical structure.

Since the white man's religion was not an effective shelter from the incidental effects of his secular inclinations, the black man's hopes for relief from pariahism through conversion to Christianity were quite vain. There is no record that conversion brought liberty to a single slave throughout the long history of slavery in America. But there seems to be substantial evidence that over the long run Christianity tends to reduce its disharmonies by grinding its ad hoc distortions of convenience into eventual conformation. If this is true, it is interesting to speculate that had the slaves identified themselves completely with the religion of the slavemaster and become adepts in the faith, neither the South nor the nation could thereafter have controlled the forces and counterforces that would have been loosed in contention for the truth. But truth, for all its magnificence, can be a long, long time in coming.

Black Religion and Its Cultus

If the matter had ended with fulfillment of the white man's intentions, the development of black religion would have been quite different. Unquestionably, three centuries or so of American religion have left their mark. There are black Christians who still yearn to have their blackness washed away at the magic fountain they were taught to believe flowed exclusively from the mysterious inner sanctum of the White Church. This is a lingering testimony about an era when the message of the faith was indistinguishable from the agenda of its sponsors. But the fact that black Christians were expected to accept uncritically the American version of the faith, and that they ran the risk of being humiliated by it, and of being spiritually stifled by its selective theology, could not, and did not, insure an abject spiritual under-class. For, despite the major role assigned religion in slave management, there was always a significant community of black Christians who had the grace and the spiritual acuity necessary to salvage value from the basic truths that underlay so much dross. Undoubtedly, both elements were inevitable features of the developing black experience, and the Black Church which finally emerged from that experience was destined to be racked by the differing perceptions of honest men and women in search of an expression of the faith which would transcend the vagaries of human manipulation, whatever their source.

Since religion required a *cultus*, i.e., a collectivity in com-munion with itself, there was no room in the White Church for the black Christians who needed to be persons as well as be-lievers. In consequence, even in the face of the formidable odds that would seek to suppress it, control it, or laugh it to scorn, the Black Church was as inevitable as religion itself. It was a unique institution, destined to leave an unmistakable mark on the religious and cultural history of America, for, from the very beginning, at least some discerned in the revived faith a beacon of freedom. As early as 1773, a black group in Boston petitioned the Massachusetts legislature that all slaves be freed on the grounds that obedience to God was not a viable option under slavery.

Such black revolutionaries as Nat Turner and Gabriel Prosser were devout Christians, but they saw their own enslavement as inconsistent with the freedom they believed the Christian life required. In 1800, in the course of his plans to liberate black Virginia, Prosser is said to have ordered his men to spare the Quakers and the Methodists (who were at the time considered anti-slavery). On the other hand, thirty-one years later, Nat Turner ravaged the Virginia countryside with a band of followers who cut down anything white on sight—men, women, and children. Turner is said to have had a vision during which he was told: "The serpent is loosed. Christ has laid down the Yoke. You must take it up again."[27] Before he and his men were finally routed, Nat Turner's retribution took the lives of sixty-one of his white brothers in Christ who had tormented him and his fellow black Christians with slavery. There were many revolts and minor insurrections which were not publicized for fear that the contagion of freedom would spread, but thousands who did not revolt liberated themselves by running away. Much of the strategy for escape via the Underground Railroad was contrived under cover of religious gatherings, and critical to the impulse for freedom was the notion that true religion and slavery were somehow inconsistent and incompatible. If a man cannot serve two masters, then it is clear that God must be preferable.

A countertheme in the deep faith which underscores black religion to this day is expressed in the absolute assurance that God will take care of his own. "Leaving it to God" has often been interpreted as a form of passivity which has at times slowed or impeded the black will to freedom. As a result, there is a substantial history of criticism of the Black Church's alleged willingness to let God do for them what Blacks should do for themselves. There is substance to this censure, but there is also a history of circumstances which accounts for it. Part of the problem derived from the slave's understanding of God and the meaning of faith. The God of black religion is inevitably the God of the Old Testament. He is an ever-present, *here-right-now God*; and more than that, he is a *fighting God*, a spiritual Paladin. Coupled with the warrior-God there is often the notion that true faith is the recognition of absolute contingency, i.e., the denial that man can of himself accomplish anything, and the unwillingness to compete with God, whose work and whose prerogative it is to deliver his own. It is still traditional among rural Blacks to cease all human activity when there is thunder or lightning or other indications that "the Lord is doing his work." The notion is that when God is at work, man's proper response is to be respectful and silent and out of the way. For those who laid the foundations of the Black Church, such an attitude was certainly not seen as the avoidance of self-help: it was the epitome of faith in a God who *needed* no help. Vengeance is mine, saith the Lord. One does not usurp that prerogative on impulse.

The misconceptions about black Christian passivity are of a piece with the misconceptions about black styles of worship. Ultimately, these misconceptions derive in both instances from differences in how God is perceived. Certainly a hero God "you can talk to" requires no symbolism and no esoterica. He is approachable, directly. Similarly, an all-powerful avenging God who is *here-right-now-and-ready-for-battle* may only require man to get out of the way so that he can act. Black religion embraces both notions of man's responsibility to work with God to accomplish his freedom, and man's responsibility to have consummate faith that God can handle the situation by himself. It must also be remembered that under slavery all members of the society were degraded by the system, and every human being was a potential enemy—a fact painfully illustrated by those slaves who turned out to be informers. There was no one to rely on with absolute confidence *except* God. This is the same unquestioning faith, born of dereliction and nurtured in the protracted agony of slavery, which, with the spirit of self-liberation, made black survival possible. Both readings of the faith were necessary, for in the absence of a strong religious conviction stabilized between extremes, the black experience in the context of American history would almost certainly have produced a different rendering.

Sources of the Black Experience in Religion

What were the sources of the religious experience of Blacks in America? There were at least two, and these were in conflict. The most obvious and the only official source of religious indoctrination for the slaves was the white preachers and exhorters who shared as a matter of course the prevailing presumptions of the slaveowners. The other source, which came to be called the Invisible Church, represented the slaves' effort to meet God on their own. Of the first source, historian Kenneth Stampp has said:

> Through religious instruction the bondsmen learned that slavery had divine sanction, that insolence was as much an offense against God as against the temporal master . . . servants should obey their masters . . . eternal salvation would be the reward for faithful service. . . .[28]

Professor Stampp is too modest. The essence of that version of Christianity taught to black people began with the injunction "Servants obey your master," and concluded with the warning: "He that knoweth the will of the master and doeth it not will be beaten with many stripes." But between the order and the threat was an elaborately conceived, universally promulgated theological doctrine which made the wisdom of God the agent and the reason for the black man's fall from grace into slavery. Black Christians were given to understand that slavery was God's will and his enactment. It was a consequence of black people's peculiar sinfulness and depravity that they should suffer, and that white men should be the agents of providential justice set over them. The proper response, indeed the only acceptable response, was complete submission, joyful acceptance, loyalty, and patience forever. Or, as black convention has it: "Sing and pray, live on hay; there'll be pie in the sky bye and bye when you die!" Such a doctrine was said to have been highly successful in teaching certain slaves "respect and obedience to their superiors"; it made them "more pleasant and profitable servants," and "aided the discipline of a plantation in a wonderful manner." So impressed were they with the salutary effects such a rendition of the faith had on their slaves that a distinguished group of South Carolinians published a pamphlet extolling "the practical working and wholesome effects of religious instruction when properly and judiciously imparted to our Negro peasantry."[29]

But the Negro peasantry wasn't necessarily buying all that was being sold. The black slave came early to the conclusion that religion as taught by the slavemasters or their representatives was not concerned with his salvation. The fact was that the religion he was offered was designed primarily to reduce the inherent hazards of slavekeeping to manageable proportions. By being made to function as a divine imperative in an enterprise that was patently Mephistophelian, it could insure the margin of security which extended slavekeeping long past its logical demise. In sum, it was a religious conspiracy designed to keep black people accommodated to an economic system in which they were compelled to be the uncompensated instruments of white Christian enrichment. In perpetuity. It was a sinister and presumptive enterprise, but one that has proven effective enough to blight three hundred and fifty years of Christian civilization in America. The consequences are everywhere apparent in the continuing American dilemma where the dehumanization of Christians by Christians with an eye for profit, or a yen for status, remains an accepted feature of the American scene. So blatant a strategy, even when attributed to the politics of God, was seen by the black slave for what it was from the very beginning. And it was rejected even then.

In 1787 two events of great historical significance took place in Philadelphia, the City of Brotherly Love. They were in stark contrast to each other in spirit and in their implications for the future of America. The delegates to the Philadelphia Convention gave their approval to the United States Constitution; and a little band of black Christians led by Richard Allen were pulled from their knees while praying in a segregated gallery in St. George's Methodist Episcopal Church.

In contrast to the Declaration of Independence, the construction of the Constitution provided little occasion for oratorical rhetoric. The men who gathered at Philadelphia for the Constitutional Convention were hard, practical men bent on preserving the prerogatives they had wrung from history, and intent on fully exploiting the incalculable promise of the new nation they were about to design. There were philosophers among them; and dreamers. But with the exception of a deist or two, they were men for whom Christianity in general, and Protestant Christianity in particular, represented the spiritual scaffolding upon which this nation under God should properly take form. Nonetheless, the suppression of liberty and the want of justice already in their midst were carefully ignored.

In the succeeding two hundred years of American history the spiritual and political energy spent in first trying to justify and then finally trying to undo what the Founding Fathers accomplished in their awesome moment of power has been of a magnitude unrivaled by any other interest. The price America has had to pay in dollars and in lives, in lost self-respect, and in human genius switched off to the low road of human perversity and hatred can be measured in terms of the present state of the nation's enduring racial dilemma. The Constitution, sadly profaned by three clauses protecting slavery, went on to become the law of the land. And Richard Allen and his intrepid band of black Christians went on to make a different kind of history by institutionalizing the Black Church in America.

The extraordinary genius of the Christian religion is exemplified in the fact that it has always managed to survive its distortions. For two thousand years the faith has been compromised by countless schisms and isms without succumbing to any of them. Popes, priests, preachers and parishioners, governments, and private interests have sought from the earliest times to subvert the authority and prestige of the church to private ends. None has enjoyed lasting success. Hence, the strategy of the slavocracy to use Christianity as the linchpin for the institutionalization of slavery and caste in America was ultimately doomed to failure, although the failure of the strategy cannot be credited to renouncements of it, early or late. It is not that there have been no prophetic voices in the American church, but at the critical junctures of American history those voices have always been muted by the racism with which we are afflicted. Hence, the tragedy of American religion is that it succumbed so early and so completely to the fetish of racism, so clearly in contradiction to the principles by which Christianity claims to be informed.

Capitulation to racial idolatry made God himself, not the African slaves, the principal adversary, for whatever the strategies man may devise to distrain the flesh, only God's lien may lie against the soul. The distraint of the African's body and the labor derived from its possession is a historical *fait accompli*. But the strategy of American Christianity failed in its effort to make black Christians a class of spiritual subordinates in concert. For, in accepting Christianity in America, the Africans were not necessarily accepting American Christianity. The God they addressed and the faith they knew transcended the American experience. If the white man's religion sacrificed its moral and spiritual validity to the Baal of white supremacy, the Black Church was born of the firm conviction that the racial Baal was a no-god.

3

The Black Response: The African Churches

Viable Religion

THE antecedent African religious experience is commonly overlooked in the conventional appraisal of the Anglo-African experience in America. Still, the issue and the identification of "African survivals," if any, remain controversial among Americans, who explain the phenomenon of black religion in terms of its alleged African origins and who passionately invoke their patron saints in anthropology and sociology to bear witness.* But the issue of antecedent survivals is substantially defused by larger factors which ultimately determine the nature and viability of *any* religion destined to survive in a hostile, alien environment.

First of all, a viable religion will be one which has a working reciprocity with the culture which produces it or with which it interacts. This is not to say that it needs to be a culture religion in the sense that the values of the society and those of the religion are indistinguishable. It is to suggest, however, that religion must be firmly rooted in the needs and the expectations

* W.E.B. Du Bois maintained that the religion of Africa accompanied the slaves to America, and that it was out of this "spiritual entity" that the Negro Church first arose. E. Franklin Frazier took quite the opposite position: that the culture of African slaves was so utterly disrupted as to preclude any significant continuity between African religion and the religion of Blacks in America. Dissenting from Frazier was Melville J. Herskovits, who argued that contemporary black religion continued to manifest African residuals in specific rituals and in general orientation to spiritual matters.

of the society which it both molds and reflects. Further, if a religion is to flourish, the needs and conditions, the fears, the anxieties, the hopes and aspirations to which it is addressed must be real in the experience of the believers. If it is not, the faith will never be more than an aberration, unless by some miracle the culture is itself modified to fit the faith.

The evidence of this would seem to be impressive. The missionary zeal of Western Christians in Africa and elsewhere in the "pagan" world produced few converts until other agents of socialization had accomplished their work. It was only when some critical segments of the native population had been sufficiently Westernized that Christianity began to make more sense in the new context than the traditional indigenous religions. For example, in a society where the supply of men is chronically short and there are no compensatory alternatives such as have been developed in Western cultures, a religion that teaches monogamy or the indistinction of sexual roles will have no significant appeal until those cultural values which have made monogamy and its attendant benefits viable are sufficiently institutionalized in the new culture. There is little that is incidental regarding the viability (or the structure) of a religion and its relation to the society which produces it or makes it its own. Christianity was swept out of North Africa by Islam after six centuries, not because Islam was a superior faith, but because Islam was more readily accommodated to the patterns of culture which antedated Christianity and its novel requirements by two thousand years or more. A viable religion will be a functional expression of the culture of which it is a part; or at the very least it will be a religion in which the expectations of the faith are not grossly incompatible with the existing norms, values, and social experience by which that culture is defined.

We may conclude, then, that whether any elements of African religion survived the dispersion of the African Diaspora in America is not necessarily a significant clue to the phenomenon of black religion. For almost a hundred years—from 1619, when the first Africans to become a part of an Anglo-American community were landed at Jamestown, Virginia, until 1701, when the Society for the Propagation of the Gospel in Foreign Parts turned its attention to the evangelization of Blacks—the Africans in America had little or no contact with Christianity. The arguments against the Christianization of Blacks, bond or free, South or North, were many and varied; but in sum they clearly illustrated the fact that American Christianity felt no compelling need to complicate prevailing social and theological conventions by extending the Gospel to black people. If black salvation was not outside the boundaries of God's grace (and even this was a matter of dispute), it was simply not within the boundaries of perceived American self-interest and responsibility. There the matter rested until the advantages of a Christian servant class were made explicit in the pulpit and protected by law.

What this adds up to is that the likelihood of significant survivals of African religion in America would be seriously diminished because of the hostility of the host society, and because the temper and the tone of the African religions were in obvious conflict with the prevailing religious conventions. This has nothing to do directly with the larger question of cultural transfer, but only with the nature of religion itself and the circumstances of its saliency. In places like Brazil and Haiti and Jamaica, a more benign religious climate, and a considerably less rigid social structure, was the rule. Even more important, in South America and the Caribbean, Africans of the same tribal or language groups were often permitted to maintain contact and some degree of affiliation, and something near the original cultus could be sustained or approximated. Under such circumstances, the transplantation of significant aspects of the African religious experience, or the Africanization of the host religion, was not absolutely precluded. But the Africans who were sold in America were summarily required to relinquish their principal cultural insignia, including religion, lest they challenge or inconvenience the total control demanded by the system of slavery. The slaves had two choices: they could resign themselves to their fate without struggle, or they could make a conscious effort at the redetermination of their destiny and their identity within the context of their developing body of Western experience. They

did both, and in the process they became a distinctive subculture, rooted in the African heritage, and developed in the
black experience in America. They became Blackamericans, and
as the first expression of their new identity, they created a Black
Church: spiritually, theologically, and idealistically independent
of any previous cultural commitment, and transcending the circumstances which called it into existence.

The establishment of the Black Church as an independent
institution provided dramatic evidence of the black capacity for
religious responsibility and the determination to achieve it. That
it came hard on the heels of the American thrust for political
independence was assigned no special significance at the time.
Indeed, it is still not a concept pursued with deep conviction in
America that Christian responsibility and personal freedom cannot be strangers to each other. But, for the black believer, the
Black Church was not only a symbol of God's intention that all
men should be free, it was also the instrument of God's continuing revelation of that intent. In the Black Church, while
God's love was unqualified, God's challenge was also unconditional, for he called every man to realize the highest potential
of his humanity by being a living testament of the divine image
in which he was cast. Since God himself was free, and man was
created free in his image, then man's struggle must ever be to
maintain or to recover the freedom with which he was endowed
by his Creator. Such is the first principle of Christian responsibility. God is the archetype and the first endorser of any struggle
for liberation.

Henry Highland Garnett, a black preacher and abolitionist,
assured the enslaved Christians who hesitated to shed the blood
of their Christian masters that God would smile upon every
effort they might make to disenthrall themselves. Tortured and
perplexed by the inconsistencies of slavery with the freedom God
required for Christian responsibility, Nathaniel Paul, another
black clergyman, cried out in anguish:

And oh Thou, immaculate God, be not angry with us while we
come into thy sanctuary and make bold inquiry . . . why it was

> that thou didst look with calm indifference . . . when thy holy law was violated, thy divine authority despised, and a portion of thine creatures reduced to a mere state of vassalage and misery.[1]

Thomas Fortune labeled the white man's religion "a living lie . . . fit only to be cast to the dogs." And David Walker in his celebrated appeal to revolution assured his brothers in bondage that God would deliver them if only they would but strike for their freedom:

> When that hour arrives and you move, be not afraid or dismayed; for be you assured that Jesus Christ the King of Heaven and of earth, who is the God of Justice . . . will surely go before you. And those enemies who have . . . stolen our rights, and kept us ignorant of Him . . . will remove. . . . Put every thing before us to death in order to gain our freedom which God has given us.[2]

Such sentiments bespoke the suppressed rage and sense of injury that every black Christian had to endure, and the Christian life on the white man's terms grew more onerous as time passed. An independent Black Church seemed to be the best answer to this predicament, and once the precedent of separate black congregations had been established, "African" churches sprang up wherever they were permitted. By the end of the Civil War, to belong to an African church was the clearest statement of how one felt about freedom and the free Christian's place in God's scheme of things.

The Birth of the African Churches

In 1778 Andrew Bryan became pastor of the First African Baptist Church in Savannah, Georgia, succeeding George Liele as leader of what was probably the first of the independent black churches. Liele had founded the church at Silver Bluffs, South Carolina, around 1773, and had managed to escape to Jamaica with the British during the Revolution. Bryan's church was under constant surveillance by the hated pattyrollers (i.e., slave patrols). His meetings were repeatedly broken up, and he and members of his congregation were whipped and thrown into prison. Finally, through the efforts of his master, he was released and permitted to continue his ministry in a barn set aside for his use on the plantation to which he was attached. He soon became well known throughout the area for his humble but effective ministry. When he died in 1812, so well respected had he come to be that in an unprecedented proceeding the white Baptist Association of Savannah issued a memorial statement noting his good works.

Farther north, in Philadelphia, a different religious scenario was being played out. On a fateful Sunday in November of 1787, a small group of black Methodists were pulled unceremoniously from their knees while inadvertently praying in a segregated section of a gallery in St. George's Methodist Church. Among the offenders were Richard Allen and Absalom Jones, both free Blacks known widely for their industry and Christian deportment. Informed of their unintended violation of St. George's racial policies, they were denied their request to be allowed to finish their prayers. After a brief consultation among themselves, the pioneer black Methodists "all went out . . . in a body and they were no more plagued with [them] in that church."[3] Though severely chastened by their bitter experience at St. George's, no one in the group so rudely and mindlessly rebuffed by the officers at St. George's left that white church with the intention of starting a new black church. It was only when it became clear that the moral and spiritual interests of their families were endangered by the absence of a full and regular church life that this intrepid little band of Methodist expatriates later moved to organize a fellowship they hoped would at least partially fill the spiritual void they had come to know since their departure from the church of their choice. On April 12, 1787, under the leadership of Richard Allen and Absalom Jones, a small group of black Philadelphians had formed themselves into the Free African Society, described as a "self-improvement association which was designed to provide mutual aid in times of misfortune, and to exercise a kind of moral oversight over its membership by visitation and prayer." The society was not a church, but in its organization and vision it showed remarkable insight into the peculiar schedule of needs common to the black condition. Gayraud Wilmore suggests:

> The suitability of the Free African Society pattern for meeting multiple needs in the Black community is amply demonstrated by the rapidity and enthusiasm by which it spread from Philadelphia to other cities. Wherever the Societies were organized they began as protests against white prejudice and neglect and with the objective of providing not only for religious needs, but for social service, mutual aid and solidarity among "people of African descent." . . . The African Societies did not only express the need for cultural unity and solidarity, but the protest and resistance of a persecuted people. . . .
>
> It created, therefore, the classic pattern for the Black Church in the United States. A pattern of religious commitment that has a double focus—the free and autonomous worship of God in the way Black people want to worship him, and the unity and social welfare of the Black community.[4]

As things turned out, the Free African Society, which was the first organization of and for Blacks in America, proved to be a very practical preparation for the Black Church that did in fact develop from its nurture. By 1790, to its agenda of mutual aid, abolition, the care of widows and orphans, and the moral circumspection of its membership, the society added sponsorship of regular religious services. This move was supported by certain influential white citizens including Benjamin Franklin, Bishop White, and Benjamin Rush among others, and the first formal worship was held on January 1, 1791. The Methodists at St. George's endeavored to suppress the project, but subscriptions from both black and white citizens encouraged the society to go on with its plans to organize a black church. It turned out that the prevailing sentiment within the society was for affiliation with the Church of England, and on July 17, 1794, the African Protestant Episcopal Church of St. Thomas was dedicated, with Absalom Jones as pastor. A few days later, on July 29, 1794, the remaining members of the society organized Bethel African Methodist Episcopal Church, under the leadership of

Richard Allen. Both churches were spawned by the Free African Society, but St. Thomas remained a black church within the Episcopal communion, while Bethel went on to become the mother church of the first black denomination. Soon after its dedication, Bethel issued a public statement with a preamble which read in part:

> Whereas, from time to time many inconveniences have arisen from white people and people of color mixing together in public assemblies, more particularly places of worship, we have thought it necessary to provide for ourselves a convenient house to assemble in, separate from our white brethren.

The statement then went on to list more particularly the reasons for the act of separation. They included the following:

> First, to prevent any offense being given to whites by their presence and their mingling with them in public worship; second, to prevent any of the colored people from taking offense at religion itself because of the partiality which was shown white worshippers on account of color. . . . and third, that they might "build each other up."[5]

After a protracted legal struggle with St. George's, which claimed spiritual and ecclesiastical oversight of the black congregation and moved to take over its property as well, Bethel eventually gained its complete independence. Richard Allen was ordained Deacon in 1799 and later became an elder. In the meantime, African Methodist churches were being organized along the Atlantic Coast as far south as Baltimore. In 1816, several of these churches met in conference in Philadelphia and the first national black denomination, the African Methodist Episcopal Church, was formed. Richard Allen became its first bishop. Thereafter, the denomination spread rapidly, with churches in Massachusetts, New York, Pittsburgh, and Charleston, South Carolina, where in 1812 the Reverend Morris Brown was pastor of a congregation in excess of three thousand.[*]

* Brown and his church were implicated in the plot charged to Denmark Vesey in 1822. Brown escaped to Philadelphia, but his church was closed.

The second of the African Methodist churches reached denominational status when the African Methodist Episcopal Zion Church elected James Varick to be its first bishop in 1822.[6] The Zionites, as they were called, had their origins in sentiments similar to those experienced by Richard Allen's Bethelites. In 1796 a group of black Christians led by Varick and Abraham Thompson withdrew from the John Street Methodist Church in New York to arrange for separate worship for black members of that church. There were no violent incidents, as there had been at St. George's. Indeed, it has been suggested that

> [the] Methodist Episcopal Church at the time Varick and his followers withdrew from it was a victim of circumstances. African slavery had produced its sickening effects all over the country, in Church and State. The Methodist Episcopal Church, like all other churches at the time, had been influenced by it. *They did not persecute their colored brethren, however, they simply denied them their rightful privileges.* . . . [italics supplied]. But this the colored brethren did not think they could stand and at the same time work out for themselves the high destiny which God holds out to all men who serve Him aright.[7]

The issue again was segregation and the demeaning treatment segregation implied. But it was more than the matter of inconvenience and injured pride: the notion that *people*, and most particularly *Christians*, who perceive themselves in the image of God, are simply not to be manipulated by human perfidy runs deep in the spiritual understanding of black religion. The white man's posturing, his arrogant gestures of superiority were not only offensive to Blacks; they were seen as offensive to the spirit of Christianity, and therefore to God himself. To submit willingly to such idolatry was to become an accessory to it. To what degree the white Methodists were themselves victims of circumstances, or whether they were simply morally and ethically remiss in the choices they made regarding their black brethren, is not a judgment to be made here. But it is nonetheless clear that what went on at St. George's and at John Street was not in any sense unusual. Theirs was the prevailing spirit in the American church in regard to black Christians, and the felt need of the Blacks to come out from among them became increasingly intense. Bishop W. J. Walls, one of the most respected historians of the African Church movement, describes the situation from which black Christians felt compelled to escape:

> [The Negro] was wanted in the church for the support he gave it, for the numbers he enabled sectarians to claim in exhibiting their strength, and with the minority, who were truly pious, he was wanted there for the good of his soul. For these and other reasons he was not kept entirely out of the church. But in the church he was hampered and regulated. His privileges were proscribed and limited; every possible effort was made to impress him with a sense of inferiority. Preachers were selected who delighted in discoursing upon such texts as 'Servants, obey your masters,' and who were adepts at impressing the Negro with inferiority in the most ingenious and least offensive way. . . . This state of things was not confined to any one particular branch of the American Church, but it was found in every denomination in every community in which there was any considerable number of the black race.[8]

It is not necessary to offer a detailed history of the several denominations which owe their origin to the movement for an independent Black Church symbolized in the break-away of the African Methodist churches. Over the course of two centuries, the AMEs and the AMEZs would be joined by yet another Methodist communion, the Christian Methodist Episcopal Church;* three major Baptist conventions;† one major pentecostal body;‡ and dozens of smaller sects. Together, the black Methodist churches, the three major Baptist conventions, and the Church of God in Christ make up the corpus of black religion in America, representing about ninety-five percent of the black Christians in the country today. The remainder are scattered

* Founded as the Colored Methodist Episcopal Church. The name was changed in 1954.
† The National Baptist Convention, Inc.; The National Baptist Convention of America; and the Progressive Baptist Convention.
‡ The Church of God in Christ.

among minor black churches, major white Protestant denominations, and the Roman Catholic Church.

A New Culture for the New Chosen

One of the values offered by Christian involvement was a ready-made culture with established traditions which could conceivably be instantly available to a people who had been brutally separated from their own. The Christian God was active in history and he involved himself in human affairs, and he delivered Israel from bondage. Were not the dispossessed Africans in the hands of the Western pharaohs, and would not God also deliver them? If God was just and if God was merciful, if God was on the side of the oppressed, then must not the long-suffering Blacks be the chosen people of God, even as Israel had been chosen in the days of her distress? Who else could better qualify? Such was the genesis of an idea destined for extended theological examination in the apologia of black religion three centuries later. But despite the encouragement of simplistic analogy, it was not the Hebrew tradition the Black Church sought to appropriate through Christian involvement. The Black Church is self-consciously an expression of the *black* experience, an altogether different stream of human events and relations than that illustrating Jewish history. Although the bondage of Israel was a compelling illustration of the love, the power, and the justice of God, the Black Diaspora in America never confused itself with biblical Israel. Black Christians knew themselves to be God's *black* chosen—a recognition and an affirmation of the illimitability of divine prerogative to save and to deliver. If God could choose once, God could choose again. God's concern for the oppressed is not exclusive to any one time or place or people.

Like the Jews, Blacks chose God and conceived themselves as chosen by God because of their understanding of the nature of his all-encompassing love and the character of his righteous justice. While black cults have occasionally found the efforts to appropriate a Jewish culture less anxiety-producing than the search for the legitimate black experience, mainstream black religion has pursued its own authentic heritage without the fantasies of cultural escapism. While most black Christians have a deep appreciation of the Jewish religion and Jewish culture, the Black Church has been content to see the Jewish heritage remain Jewish except for those universal principles which transcend Jewish culture and apply to all people. Black religion had its own reasons for being what it is; its own spiritual experience to draw upon; its own theological understanding as its surest counsel.

If black religion had no need to appropriate a culture, the Black Diaspora had even less need to have a culture thrust upon it, *noblesse oblige*, as it were, and in consequence, Blacks in America have been the despair of generations of Christians, academics, social scientists, political planners, and countless others who have felt compelled to reconstruct them in the idealized image of Euro-Americans. Overlooked is the obvious: although they were involuntarily severed from their own cultural roots, the African Diaspora did not come to America in search of a culture, European or otherwise. Once here, it was inevitable that from the treasures of the African heritage, and out of the survival learnings of the black experience in America, a new subculture would in fact evolve. But it is neither European nor African. It is *Blackamerican*. All cultures are syncretistic, which is the sure sign of a universal humanity. And all cultures are innovative, which is the unmistakable evidence of universal human genius. Hence, while the Blackamerican subculture is certainly affected for good or ill by the prevailing host culture which surrounds it, fosters, and borrows from it in return, and though it depends upon the wellsprings of its African heritage for identity and continuity, the black experience in America remains the primary source of its meaning and nurture. And the Black Church is the medium of its characteristic refraction.

Church and Culture

The Black Church, which is the formal institutionalization of black religion, has maintained a crucial social interest from the beginning. It was for much of its history an invisible system of relationships rather than a "place" or a physical entity. But it could be found in the bayous and the swamps and wherever the black faithful gathered in furtive, clandestine assemblage in search of a more satisfying truth than a segregated church could provide. It organized the energies and systematized the beliefs and practices of the slaves in such a way as to transcend the cultural vacuum created by the Blacks' estrangement from Africa. But, more than that, the Black Church was the unifying force which made of a scattered confusion of slaves a distinctive entity.

The church was the black man's government, his social club, his secret order, his espionage system, his political party, and his impetus to freedom and revolution. It provided the counterpart of the important social institutions which structured his *Weltanschauung* in the African culture from which he had been separated. Under its aegis were the rites of passage from puberty to adulthood, from singleness to marriage, from life to death. The church sponsored the communal meal, the ritual of sacrificial togetherness. When freedom came and the Invisible Church could be made manifest in wood and glass and stone, wherever there were black people, and whatever the exigencies of fortune, there they built a church house, a physical symbol of their faith in God's continuing deliverance and of their common bond in the black experience.

The church house was funded and raised as a community effort, and the church building became the community forum, the public school, the conservatory of music, the place where the elocutionary arts, the graphic arts, the literary arts, and the domestic arts were put on proud display. It was *lyceum* and *Gymnasium* as well as *sanctum sanctorum*. It was the prime developer of black leadership, a fact that is critical to the quality of the freedom every Blackamerican enjoys today. Historian W. J. Walls wrote of the AMEZ Church: "The African Methodist Episcopal Zion Church naturally . . . became to the Afro-American race what Faneuil Hall was to the Anglo-American—their cradle of liberty."[9] What Bishop Walls said of AMEZ can be reasonably said of the whole Black Church. It was indeed a cradle of liberty. It produced Nat Turner and it produced Martin Luther King, Jr. And ranged between their respective conceptualizations of Christian responsibility, the Black Church has been womb and mother to a vast spectrum of black leadership in every generation since its inception.

The Black Church is the most authentic representation of what it means to be black in America, for it is the one institution in which is crystallized the whole range of credits and debits, of genius and emotion, hope and fear, projection and recoil which characterize the random gathering of peoples of West Africa who were fused in the black experience in America. During the slave era the black churches were monitored by the white man, and not infrequently closed or destroyed if he considered them a threat to his interests or well-being. But the white man could not destroy the church itself. It was not flesh of his flesh, or substance of his substance. It was a witness against his rejection of the imperative of brotherhood, and since he could not destroy it, he eventually learned to let it alone. Amused by its style, confused by its meaning, sometimes a patron to its indigence, but always aloof from its fellowship, the white man kept counsel with his own spiritual kin and the Black Church was able to become itself without his spiritual taint. There would be occasions when some black church leaders would perjure themselves for the white man's approval, or corrupt themselves to invite his largesse. But perjurers there are in any church, and as for corruption, the very Author of the faith was himself sold out for thirty pieces of silver before the meaning of his efforts had even been reviewed. But the Black Church, like the living faith it represents, has managed for over two hundred years to survive obstruction within and without, and it still endures as the symbol of the hope and determination of the new black estate in America.

Over the long history of their extraordinary pilgrimage the Blacks were at times their own adversaries, and the white man had little to do to maintain his control except to fuel their divisiveness. Solidarity is always difficult under the onus of abject repression, and the slave experience in America produced its inevitable share of internal confusion and disagreement. When slavery was finally ended, some of the highly individualized postures of accommodation and resistance deriving from centuries of white dominion and black subservience were difficult to slough off until they had been loosened by new learnings and more self-confident experiences. But the white man was still in power, and from all available inferences he had always been in power, and would always be in power. It seemed to follow that the best strategy a black man could follow was to be as nearly "white" as he could manage.

This felt need to be white, or, more precisely, *like white,* was the rock on which the first real options for black solidarity foundered. Slavery was the common grist to which all Africans had been reduced, of course. But at the same time they were being leveled into one dimension of caste, the stage was set for intra-caste antagonisms which would greatly facilitate the critical task of external management. Before freedom became universal, there were four principal categories of differentiation which figured strongly in black-to-black relationships: legal status, role assignment, skin color, and church denomination. Legal status distinguished between Blacks who were free and those who were slaves. That distinction was scarcely marked, and life for slave and freeman was of essentially the same order. They shared similar restrictions of movement, social exclusion, economic contingency, nakedness before the bar, and, above all, the absence of power and the right to participate in meaningful decisions about themselves and the responsibilities to which they were subject.

While it is true that despite these common disabilities a few free Blacks did manage to distinguish themselves, it is also true that so, too, did some slaves. But the clue to such extraordinary accomplishment was obviously not in the matter of status, slave or free, but in the individuals themselves. There are always some who are born to fly, and fly they will, whatever their impediments. But the slave-free dichotomy, while being the most obvious fracture of the black community, was not the most devastating. Hundreds of free Blacks bought and freed their wives and children; others put their lives and their liberty in jeopardy as agents of the Underground Railroad. Few whites accepted the free Blacks as fellow citizens, or as legitimate participants in political or social life. Rather, the free people of color were generally despised by whites as "indigents" and "troublemakers." A well-thought-of slave of respectable ownership usually commanded far more respect and more leverage than most free Blacks, except possibly those "honorably retired" from slavery after a lifetime of faithful service; or those who had performed some extraordinary act that protected or preserved vested white interests. In the final analysis, of course, the issue of legal status was determined by the white man's practical response to black expectations. That response was spelled out quite forcefully in the Supreme Court decision, *Dred Scott vs. Sanford* in 1857, in which Chief Justice Roger B. Taney ruled that no Blacks, slave or free, were possessed of "any rights a white man was bound to respect." Justice Taney's ruling could hardly have been a shocking disclosure, for it was merely the legal ratification of conventional attitudes and practices.

A more serious source of community fracture among Blacks was role assignment. For the slave, the greatest status derived from being associated with the "master" or members of his family living in the Big House or manor. Valets, maids, cooks, "body servants," coachmen, etc., comprised an elite with certain privileges and opportunities not available to field hands. In fact, the field slaves rarely had any contact with any whites other than the despised overseer, who almost invariably was considered "poor white trash" by the patrician planters whose slaves they were hired to manage. But the house slaves not only had unique opportunities for acculturation; they often, by virtue of their responsibilities, became skilled artisans or professionals: chefs, nurses, wagonmakers, bricklayers, barbers, seamstresses, carpenters, gardeners, horse trainers, etc. Their duties often required intimate and prolonged association with "quality folks" of the patrician class, from whom they derived a kind of shadow status, which, coupled with the unusual privileges occasioned by their work, made them unusually vulnerable to conflicts of identity and crises of loyalty. Furthermore, once slavery was ended, the slaves who had been associated with the Big House were far better equipped for "freedom" than their counterparts who were trained only to the plow and the hoe. This was to be an important factor in the struggle for social mobility and economic advantage in the newly emergent subculture of Blackamerica.

The third agent of division was the most pernicious and the most tragic of all. It was skin color. Since masters were white and slaves were black by definition, within the black caste skin color became an important though contradictory index of personal worth. Like role assignments at the Big House, light skin was presumed by Blacks to be de facto evidence of superior status because it seemed a clear, if tacit, implication of the white man's personal, selective interest. And since the white man was the almost mystical symbol of the extraordinary power which defined the universe of black existence, it seemed a logical inference that to share the white man's blood was to participate in his power. Perhaps. But the canniest observers of the human experiment soon learn that logic has its limitations. There was a troublesome paradox which robbed the logical inferences of blood relationship of meaningful impact. While on some plantations there may have appeared to be a minor correlation between skin color and role assignment at the Big House, such a coincidence invariably represented the convenience of the master rather than a recognition by him or his class of any derivative rights of "blood," no matter how pronounced or unmistakable the evidence of consanguinity between master and slave. For the white man, "a darky" was a darky, no matter who his daddy was. In fact, a very clever legal disclaimer designed to quiet such issues before they arose was expressed quite early in the dictum that *the father of a slave is unknown.* Thus, in one simple clause, the moral questions implicit in the breakup and sale of slave families, and the troublesome implications of the rights of black children sired by the white master or his sons, were summarily put to rest.

If the color of a slave posed no problem for the white establishment, it became a problem of critical significance for the Blacks searching for whatever personal worth their tragic circumstances could afford. Color was one such indicator, even though it had no significance outside the black caste. In consequence, because the Black Church had the task of spiritual and cultural oversight of the black community, it was inevitable that the Black Church itself would at times be seriously threatened by the divisiveness of color and class. Very early in the new experience of freedom and culture-building, there were local churches in which only light-skinned Blacks of the Big House tradition were welcomed. Vestiges of this confused, self-deprecating mentality were still found in some older churches until quite recent times. While black churches attached to white denominations tended to be more color-conscious than others, the problem was not unknown in the authentic Black Church of independent tradition, although it was considerably less pronounced. The Black Church has borrowed its polity, its structure, and its ritual from the White Church intact, except for a few emendations here and there necessary to make clear an independent black proprietorship. But the Black Church added to the White Church polity and ritual its own unique interpretation and style, in consequence of which the peculiar concerns of the black subculture found inevitable expression. Born of the paranoia of a color-determined slave caste, the whimsical correlation of fair skin, power, and personal worth lingered on in the private reckonings of the black subculture until the phenomenon of independent states in black Africa, and the emergence of a new ethnic consciousness born of America's Black Revolution of the sixties and seventies, restored some measure of confidence to the brutalized psyche of the West African Diaspora. Suddenly black became beautiful and Black-americans had taken a giant step toward coming to terms with themselves.

Religion as a Factor of Separation

It is religion that provides the primary cohesiveness for the black community, and conversely, it is in religion that the fracture of the black community seems most prominently institutionalized. For the first hundred years of the black experience in America, religion was more an index of separation than of integration. When Richard Allen and his followers detached themselves from St. George's Methodist Church in Philadelphia because of the racial discrimination there, the Free African Society provided an opportunity to reflect about the direction their religious commitment should take next. When it was decided finally that the faithfulness and dignity of black people could best be preserved in a black church, the *kind* of black church, save that it would be African, was not an immediate issue. However, it was to become an issue of critical importance as the movement for a black church gathered momentum and the dream of religious independence began to take on the substance of reality.

Internal schism was to stalk the Black Church from its founding. It is to the credit of the Free African Society that it anticipated the problem and sought to avoid it, at least initially. Dr. Benjamin Rush, the Quaker who befriended the society, described these religious exiles as "the scattered appendages" of the churches of Philadelphia. He also noted that the emergent African Church had "drawn up articles and a plan of government so general as to embrace all, and yet so orthodox in cardinal points as to offend none."[10] Nevertheless, when in 1791 the society met to adopt a plan of government for its church, both Richard Allen and Absalom Jones wanted a Methodist polity, but, as we have seen, the majority of the Free African Society, perhaps still smarting from the memory of their treatment at the hands of the Methodists at St. George's, voted for the Church of England. In consequence, Absalom Jones deferred his preference and accepted the leadership role in the founding of the African Episcopal Church of St. Thomas. However, Richard Allen confessed that he "could not be anything but a Methodist." Accordingly, he decided that he "could go no further" with them and would "leave them in peace." He subsequently founded Bethel African Methodist Episcopal Church, and though he and Jones remained the closest of friends, the structural unity of the emergent Black Church had died aborning.

Sources of Black Church Proliferation

Religion derives from specific human needs and experiences, and it functions in the interests of helping man to cope with the more traumatic aspects of human existence. In consequence, we may expect a discernible relationship between the expression of religion and the cultural matrix from which it derives. This should mean that in a free society religious proliferation may be expected to reflect not only the intensiveness of human trauma, by which is meant those experiences which are the most challenging to human endurance and understanding, but also the capacity for cultural invention to shape or to modify the thrust of religion to make it more effective. For example, the Puritans who settled New England, the Baptists who came to Rhode Island, the Quakers in Pennsylvania, the Methodists on the frontier, the Anglicans along the South Atlantic seaboard, the Catholics in Maryland were all responding to certain cultural factors considered critical to the distinctive religious predispositions by which they were characterized. None of the creedal, theological, or ritual shibboleths which excited these communions were prominent among the reasons for sectarianism within the Black Church. Why, then, did the Black Church permit itself to be divided at its inception rather than take advantage of its political and theological innocence to unite all black Christians in a single communion?

While the Blacks were singularly free of the theological and political strictures which ostensibly determine white sectarianism, they were not at all free of the human and psychological factors which also influence religious preference. At the same time, although there are several black sectarian expressions, they are mainly limited to three distinctive traditions: Methodists, Baptists, and Pentecostals. Despite its demonstrated weakness in the face of the prevailing sentiment for slavery, the Methodist Church from time to time did evidence unusual solicitude toward Blacks. This tradition became an important part of the black experience. It is reflected vividly in Richard Allen's passionate confession of his own preference for Methodism, and even more dramatically in Gabriel Prosser's order that Methodists were to be spared in his anticipated slaughter of the slavemasters who tormented his people with bondage. The Baptists were somewhat less pronounced in their humanitarian concern for Blacks, but they, too, showed considerable solicitude for Blacks before the hardening of sentiments which brought on the Civil War.

The very first church built specifically for Blacks in America was a Baptist church built near Savannah, Georgia, around 1773. It was built in violation of the law and prevailing sentiment by a white slaveowner who was subsequently converted by the slave preacher who was its pastor. For the most part, the Anglicans and the Catholics were essentially indifferent to black spiritual needs, and the Quakers, who were the most solicitous of all for the humanitarian interests of the Blacks, made no special efforts to convert them to their understanding of the faith. More than that, since the Society of Friends did not have the kind of physical or organizational visibility which could be readily adapted to the unique conditions of the slaves, the attraction of that communion as a spiritual role model was never pronounced. Similar observations could be made of the Congregationalists, who maintained a very prominent interest in the education of the Blacks but showed little inclination for sharing their churches with them.

In brief, the Methodist and Baptist traditions became the primary forms of the black religious investment because those denominations were, on the whole, more responsive to black spiritual needs, and their rituals and worship patterns were more familiar. As a result, the movement across denominational lines between Methodist and Baptist communions within the Black Church has always been common and unimpeded. While there are de facto differences in ritual, creed, and polity which do distinguish the communions, the barriers to transferring from one denomination to the other have always been pro forma.

If sectarianism in the Black Church is not rooted in tradition, and if it is not substantially creedal or theological, what, then, are its causes? We find important clues in the social structure and its singular impingement upon the black experience. Consider the following, for example:

- The confusion of values and the subsequent desire to selectively replicate the white experience—e.g., if white people have many denominations, why should Blacks restrict themselves?
- The rejection of the leveling and homogenization implicit in the conventional caste arrangement—e.g., all Blacks are not the same. Blacks are capable of (and needful of) a variety of religious expressions.
- The dearth of leadership opportunities elsewhere in society. Leadership is a sign of status, and status is a scarce value. Since the Black Church is the largest and most viable black institution, it offers the best place to look for a following if one has an attractive cause, or a compelling call.
- The longing to be rid of the unremitting stress of living in a white-dominated world. For example, the black cult syndrome is decidedly insular and escapist. It is characterized by a marked impatience with the conventional coming kingdom which never seems to materialize, and is prepared to offer a kingdom which is more imminent and more tangible.

The African expatriates encountered a variety of religious traditions in the course of their cultural metamorphosis in the Western matrix. Although they brought with them no compelling traditions of Christian sectarianism, in the process of their acculturation they emerged identified with one or another established American religious tradition.

Religions are that precipitate of cultural experience which is characteristically expressed in creeds, moral requirements, and ritual practices. While it is usually the ultimate nature of the religious concern which first preoccupies the true believer, that preoccupation may be seriously challenged by such competing interests as ritual, governance, or theology which distinguish one communion from another. This phenomenon is more pronounced in a society where there is neither formal establishment nor proscription, and where religious expression short of the violation of public policy stirs little attention. Sectarian proliferation, then, is in some sense the institutionalization of the religious freedom Americans enjoy. Hence, there was certainly nothing anomalous about Richard Allen's allegiance to Methodism. On the other hand, if one considers the unique condition of Blacks when black religion was establishing itself as an independent communion, it could be argued that to found a black *Methodist* church in the light of Allen's demeaning experience with white Methodists does indeed constitute an anomaly. The sources of white sectarianism are historic, but with a creedal and theological *tabula rasa*, the emergent Black Church held for one specious moment the opportunity for *complete* religious independence, had it chosen to exploit it.

There was indeed an initial awareness of the advantages of a single black communion, but it was not fully developed. The primary impetus for a black church was not a felt need to be religiously unique, but to have the freedom necessary to responsibly fulfill the requirements of the conventional faith, and to escape the indignities of segregation. Blacks were not yet fully conscious of the sociopolitical power inherent in religious organization, because their organizational experience had always been carefully defined and closely monitored. Nonetheless, from the beginning, they were acutely sensitive to the need to control their own spiritual affairs. Richard Allen did attempt to persuade the black separatists from New York's John Street Methodist Church to affiliate with his fledgling African Methodist Episcopal communion. However, New York's black Methodists elected to pursue a separate destiny and founded AME Zion. Both the Bethelites and the Zionites were Methodist, but there was still a burgeoning company of independent black Baptists to consider. The ultimate question was not whether to be AME or AMEZ; nor was it to be either Methodist or Baptist, since those choices were all alike, merely addressed to the question of *which* of the white denominations they would pay a continuing spiritual fealty to. The alternative not seriously addressed was the creation of a truly distinctive black religion consciously designed for the peculiar needs and interests of the African Diaspora. But Richard Allen's personal predilections did not permit him to look beyond the familiar Christian faith as he had experienced it, and of what he knew best, he chose for his people. His own explanation was:

> I was confident there was no religious sect . . . [that] would suit the capacity of the colored people as well as the Methodist, for the plain and simple gospel suits best. . . . For the unlearned can understand, and the learned are sure to understand and the reason the Methodists are so successful in the awakening and conversion of the colored people is the plain doctrine and having a good discipline.[11]

There were many reasons why a Black Church qua Black Church was not a realistic option for Allen and his followers, including the great likelihood that it would simply not have been tolerated. But had it been possible, such a church would have become a fresh, new communion, free at its inception from the sectarian burdens inherited from the prevailing denominations and focused on the distinctive spectrum of black interests the realities of American life entailed. Such a church would have been designed to grow with the needs of its people, and to expand its horizons in consonance with their own. In the Caribbean and in South America, the African Diaspora was successful in the blending of certain African religions with selected Christian motifs. But this was not a real option in America, since, as we have noted, the policy of slave dispersal and suppression of religion left relatively little in the way of African religions for eclecticism to consider.

Another possibility might have been the summary abandonment of Christianity in favor of some other religion perceived as more conducive to the needs and aspirations of the black estate. After all, the black attachment to the white man's church was always tenuous at best and demeaning in any case; and the occasion for withdrawal from the white man's church might well have been sufficient occasion for being rid of the white man's religion. This was the least viable option. Although movement across sect or denominational lines may be relatively easy, religions are seldom, if ever, either embraced or abandoned en masse for rational considerations. Mass conversion from one religion to another has sometimes been decreed, as when Christianity became the official religion of Rome under Constantine in A.D. 313; and mass renunciation may on occasion have been a condition of liberty, or even life itself. But, in the absence of extraordinary duress, the motivations which impel men to separate themselves from one religion in favor of another are likely to be highly personal, individual, and particularistic. Reason may appear as a factor at some level of the process, but reason alone is seldom capable of exciting a mass reversal of religious sentiment.

There were even more formidable obstacles. For an essentially illiterate and captive people, there was simply no other religious precedent available except the remote, low profile of a mysterious and nonproselytizing Judaism. Islam, which was very much a part of the Afro-Hispanic experience of the fifteenth and sixteenth centuries, had retired from the continent with the conquistadors, and the native African religious heritage had been shattered by the exigencies of slavery. Christianity was what was avaliable. It was all these Fathers of the Black Church knew. It was their most singular cultural development, and it may yet prove the most fortuitous.

The early years of the African Churches were years of tumultuous competition. Both AMEs and AMEZs were aggressive (and sometimes uniquely resourceful) in devising ways to win individuals and established congregations to their respective "connections." Powerful black preachers and organizers followed in the wake of the Union armies, gathering in the bewildered hordes who found themselves suddenly free for the first time to make meaningful decisions about themselves. For the most part, these "anonymous appendages to the white churches" welcomed the jubilee that sent them at last to order their own spiritual destinies. The Southern Methodists (who had split away from the main Methodist body over the issue of slavery) were particularly vulnerable to the crusading African churches. Their black membership was probably larger than that of any other white communion, and in the uncertainty and disorganization brought by the war, they welcomed a formal petition from their rapidly eroding black membership to grant them permission to organize an independent black church. So it was that, with the official assistance and the good wishes of the parent Methodist Episcopal Church South, the Colored Methodist Episcopal Church was born at Jackson, Tennessee, in 1870. It was the third black Methodist communion. In the meantime, Blacks were also withdrawing from the white Baptist churches in ever increasing numbers and uniting in their own black conventions. The Presbyterians, Episcopalians, Congregationalists, and other mainline communions, having few black members to begin with, were less affected by the black crusade to free the thousands of black Christians from the ignominy of segregated worship and restore to them the dignity of God's image. By the end of the century the black denominational patterns were well set, but the scars of separation and its antecedent causes were deep. In consequence, albeit with some notable exceptions, the several denominations of the Black Church generally pursued their individual destinies without either expecting or receiving moral or material support from their erstwhile brothers and sisters in the white churches.

The new century brought wars, floods, crop failures, and immense shifts in population. As hundreds of thousands of Blacks left the agrarian life of the Southern plantations for an uncertain existence in the urban ghettos of the North, the Black Church could ill afford the fun-and-games approach that made church-mongering so characteristic of denominational competition in times past. The leadership of the New Black Jerusalem was in the hands of the Black Church, and the future of the whole black estate was troubled and uncertain. America's official intent to bind up its wounds and get on with its destiny seemed to deteriorate into a determined effort to expunge the troublesome memory of human slavery from its consciousness by abandoning the freedmen to the tender mercies of their erstwhile slave-masters. There were precarious times ahead. The Ku Klux Klan was once again unleashed, and in every section of the country its sinister influence was felt in political corruption and murder. The dislocations of the First World War fell ultimately on the poor and the black; there were race riots and counterriots. In the "Red Summer" of 1919 alone, hundreds of Americans were killed or injured in twenty-five racial confrontations. The Great Depression lay in the offing, and new waves of white immigrants from the war-battered states of Europe got the jobs and the attention that belonged to the Blackamericans, whose free blood and sweat had sustained the nation for three hundred years.

The challenge to the Black Church was formidable. There were schools and colleges to maintain and develop; political leaders to prepare and support; millions of people to sustain and encourage; civil rights organizations to staff and to nurture. There was a whole catalogue of social services to provide for all those Blacks forgotten or overlooked by the civil and social agencies. Above all, hope had to be kept alive, and a continuing assurance of divine love and justice was crucial for black survival and for public peace. In the meantime, the care of the sick, the burial of the dead, the comfort of the bereaved, and the spiritual and moral nurture of the church community must of course go on. And it did. The Black Church has been annealed by two hundred years of service to its constituency and to the nation. It came out of World War II with a new confidence born of maturation under stress, and with a new appreciation of its own competence. Now, chastened by an increasing awareness of the awesome responsibilities which lie ahead for the Christian church as a whole, it must prepare itself for those new horizons it must address on behalf of God and man.

4

Black Ethnicity and Religious Nationalism

THE acids of the American dilemma seep deep into the fabric of our culture, defacing the patterns and eroding the relationships we depend upon to reduce the abrasions of social intercourse. Because of its universal values, the Christian church has often been looked to as the principal hope for achieving reasonable tranquillity amid the currents and countercurrents of the human enterprise as we pursue the search for meaning and security in a world where both are increasingly difficult to achieve, or even to define. The church does in fact claim to have the answer, but whether it has the means has not been demonstrated convincingly, for, like any other institution, the credibility of the church is inseparable from its performance, and the quality of its pronounced intentions is not an infallible index of its reliability. The post-war efforts of the church to forge a union of its major Protestant divisions provide a case in point. Presumably, a united church could bring some impact to bear upon the vast, intricate machinery of racism. But performance in this quite critical matter of Christian concern has not been particularly encouraging. As a result, where black Christians were concerned, the hope for meaningful church union was already seriously undercut long before the efforts to achieve it got beyond the stage of debate.

Although the three major black Methodist denominations*

* These three denominations—the African Methodist Episcopal Church, the African Methodist Episcopal Zion Church, and the Christian Methodist Episcopal Church—had a combined membership of about 3.8 million in 1980.

were eventually committed to union after some elaborate concessions to protect them from discrimination had been offered by the white churches, conviction among the three black Baptist conventions* has been considerably more elusive in spite of protracted efforts at reassurance. The realities are that none of the black communions is truly comfortable with any prospects that would exchange their hard-won autonomy for the possible reinstitution of white control and direction.

In their own churches black Christians take for granted the dignity and freedom they fear they might well have to contend for in any formal association with their white brothers in Christ. The independent Black Church has created its own literature, established its own publishing houses, elected its own bishops, called its own pastors, founded its own colleges and seminaries, developed unique patterns of worship, and maintained successful oversight over millions whose circumstances placed them beyond the pale of white interest.

On the other hand, because Blacks have often been unsure of their own identity, and because the Black Church is itself a reflection of the cultural and spiritual ambivalence inherent in the American dilemma, even the Black Church has not in all instances been consistent in its understanding of what it is and why. At times it has seen itself as a less perfect counterpart of the White Church, striving for parity by pulling itself up by its own bootstraps. This self-denigration made some Negro churches more white in their ritual behavior and their social attitudes than some of the white churches they sought to emulate. The affectation of the language and gestures of "white preaching," the distribution of church offices and other emoluments on the basis of skin color, the effort to exclude from the worship services what has been defined as "black music" and "African emotionalism" have at times illustrated the uncertainty the Black Church has had about its role, its function, its clientele, and its identity.

But no matter what direction it has taken, the Black Church

* National Baptist Convention, USA, Inc., 6,300,000 members; National Baptist Convention of America, 2,500,000 members; Progressive Baptist Convention, Inc., 200,000 members. All figures are for 1980.

has been maligned for being black. Its deficiencies and short-comings have been catalogued again and again, but always with the implication that it could be magically rehabilitated by some-how getting rid of its blackness. If the Black Church could only be something other than itself, what a fine institution it would be! Its worship services would be more dignified and less exuberant. Its ministers would be better educated and more responsible. Its outreach would be more spiritual and less political, more practical and less otherworldly, more general and less particularized. It would be more efficiently administered, and white people would feel more comfortable when they came 'round to visit, if ever!

Black Ethnicity

The most crucial achievement of the World War II era was black ethnicity, and among the institutions most critically affected was the Black Church. It was not that the church itself needed the war experience to appreciate its peculiar role in the scheme of things, for it was the Black Church which first awakened the dispersed and demoralized Blacks to the possibilities of self-affirmation. The church could count some signal successes in spite of quite formidable odds. For three hundred years the African Diaspora had lived in essential isolation in an environment care-fully constructed to promote in them an enduring self-hatred and a belief in their own inadequacy. This notion was reinforced by every public and private institution, and by all the conventions by which the society was ordered. World War I provided the first tentative glimpses outside the closed cosmos the slaveholders made, and those Blacks who were so reluctantly sent overseas to fight for democracy returned home under an ominous pall of suspicion. Those who spread the word about their more benign experiences elsewhere in the world were silenced by violence. A prompt return to the old ways and the conventional insights was the price of a job; the price of being left alone. The price of staying alive.

The post-World War II return to normalcy was not so easily

managed. Far more Blacks were involved in our military dispersals around the globe than in the First World War, and they stayed longer. They saw more; they heard more; they experienced more. And they were better prepared to evaluate those experiences and to make informed judgments about what they saw and what they heard abroad in comparison to their common experiences at home. When the black soldiers came home again in 1945, they had enlightened new concepts about themselves in relation to others of whatever race, and they were not prepared to resume the pace and the place America had always reserved for them. They had discovered black ethnicity. For strength they turned toward each other, and the principal symbol of their inner strength was the Black Church, which had always been the reservoir of black togetherness and the affirmation of superlative value in being what God had designed them to be. Black ethnicity does not confuse blackness with ultimate value, or with racial supremacy, or with manifest destiny. But it does recognize that there are no values of the same order which *exceed* the value inherent in being black.

Ethnicity is a firm belief in the sufficiency of one's own cultural and racial heritage to permit the individual and the group to participate proudly as equals with all others in the common ventures of human experience. It does not apologize for being different, but finds in its own distinctiveness the identity which precludes anonymity. Identity is of enormous importance in establishing feelings of security and personal worth. In most ethnic groups it is simply taken for granted, having been effectively communicated by the body of myths, folklore, and tradition through which a culture ordinarily projects itself. It is the self-perceived image of who and what a people are. However, the peculiar circumstances of the black experience as a proscribed enclave within a dominant, hostile overculture made a positive identity for black people next to impossible. First of all, there was a fantastic body of myth, folklore, and conventional wisdom designed deliberately to confuse and obscure black identity, even for Blacks themselves. In consequence, the discovery of black ethnicity and concomitant self-approval could not occur until black people themselves could agree at least tentatively on who they were. There was no solid body of consensus. For generations, black people had struggled with such designations as "Niggers," "Nigras," "Darkies," "Black Anglo-Saxons," "Coloreds," "People of Color," "Negroes," "Afro-Americans," and "Afra-Americans." Some of the "names to go by" were self-designations; those considered to be "official" were gratuitous. They were also clear, simple, and telling in their import: black people, *however styled*, were *nobody* in particular, and most certainly they were nobody of consequence—not in the past; nor would they be in the future. So a "name to go by" was simply a convience to facilitate attention should they be needed; and one name was as good as another. Hence, darkies, niggers, Sam, George, boy, girl, whatever. Not infrequently just "You!"—with the right emphasis—was expected to get the desired results. But for the Blacks themselves, at issue was a matter far more critical than a mere name by which to be summoned, for how you are styled is in itself an important condition of who you are and who you perceive yourself to be. The real issue, of course, was how the black experience was to be read and interpreted. Only then could the people who had come through that experience be properly styled and evaluated.

Black Nationalism

Because black ethnicity and black identity are often expressed through black religion, black religion is often mistaken for black nationalism. They may, and often do, travel together, but the goals and interests of these two aspects of the black experience are not the same. Black nationalism is a political philosophy. Its goals, which are often amorphous by design, do not give primary consideration to man's spiritual quest, even though religion may appear as the focus of its activities. The distinction turns on whether ultimate value is assigned to the pragmatics of political interest, or whether it resides in the spiritual quest with which political intent may be closely associated. For the black masses, black religion and black nationalism are often one and the same, *in effect.* Both address the sources of their distress, and these require no labels. Those whose suffering seems most arbitrary are likely to be most impatient with fine distinctions, when in the fervor of black togetherness they finally confront the specter which stalks them all. As a result, black nationalism sometimes assumes the *character* of religion because it promises to the disinherited the swift and certain reversal of the circumstances of their oppression and suffering.

Double Consciousness and a Religion Apart

W.E.B. Du Bois made famous the theory of "double conscious-ness," a psychic phenomenon with which Blackamericans are affected through historical happenstance. They are part of two worlds, two cultures, living in and experiencing both, but for-ever frustrated in their struggle to reconcile the one to the other. It is one thing to be "American"; it is quite another to be a "Negro" in America. That is precisely why present-day Blacks reject the term "Negro." For them it has extremely pejorative connotations. Similarly, the simple goal of a black believer is to be Christian and regarded as such, but there is no precedent in the religious history of America which could provide real en-couragement for that notion. Being Christian and being black risks distortion by the racial prism through which black people are refracted. Hence, it may be less painful and more rewarding to the black believer to think of himself as belonging to a religion apart—one that is peculiarly his own, and not readily destroyed by white refraction. The genius of ethnicity is that it strengthens the ego of the group by rejecting the significance of whatever is beyond its spectrum of possibilities.

On the other hand, ethnicity may find value in precisely the ex-periences which have been belittled or devalued by others. For example, most black churchgoers want a rousing sermon with moving singing and fervent praying as a part of their worship. Some want to feel free to let the spirit enter their bodies as well as their souls and have its way with them. They may find the services of the typical white church cold and uninspiring. In this instance, black ethnicity denies the relevance of white styles of worship for black people and sanctions the ritual patterns developed in the churches of the black experience independent of white influence. These were the ritual styles derived from what was remembered of the African heritage and what grew out of the black experience in America. Together, these two discrete strands of cultural acquisition offer a distinctive pattern of worship which brings the greatest measure of fulfillment and satisfaction to those secure enough to look back to their own cultural experiences for strength and meaning. Hence, despite the sensitivity of some Blacks who confuse culture with accultura-tion, and who in consequence are uncomfortable in the presence of any expressions of their ethnic identification, black religion is obviously its own justification. It is true to its own heritage. And for that reason, if no other, it is to be valued as a distinctive cultural achievement.

The Scope of "Black Religion"

Our attention has been given primarily to those elements of the Black Church which best characterize it as the principal instru-mentality of black culture. While we have noted the principal black communions, our attention has been restricted mainly to those black denominations which became independent from white communions and developed separate churches. But black religion also includes the black Christians in white denominations because the overwhelming majority of these are in all-black local congregations, which, except for their sources of administra-tion and oversight, are rarely distinguishable from the autono-mous black churches.

It is different with the black cults, such as the Black Muslims, the Black Jews, and similar religious groups, for they are dis-tinctive by the very nature of their organization, structure, and beliefs. While some do not claim to be Christian, black ethnicity and religious nationalism are characteristic features of most black

cults. They exist as one kind of religious response to the difficulties of coping with the peculiar stresses of life in America,[1]
and as such, they are important facets of black religion.

The Black Church Today

One of the leading architects of the contemporary Black Church
was Martin Luther King, Jr. King's contributions to the moral
and political experience of America are enormous, and they transcend his more incidental involvements. Yet, in the context of
American tradition, King's relationship with the Black Church
could scarcely have been incidental. Recognition and commitment
eventually took him to the four corners of the world and gained
him admission to places and presences inaccessible to lesser men
of whatever color. Yet, when he first left Boston University to
offer himself to God and humanity, despite his excellent education
and preparation for the ministry, despite his eloquence, his high
moral character, and his promise, no doors were opened to him
except *black* doors. He belonged to the Black Church whether
he would or not, and when the Dexter Avenue Baptist Church of
Montgomery summoned him, Dexter was symbolically and pro-
phetically the Black Church summoning her own. Even a decade
later, when King had won the world's acclaim, including the
Nobel Peace Prize, and even as he was being hailed as a *héro
sans couleur*, a leader for all the people and for every cause, his
blackness, so far as American Christendom was concerned, was
not transcended even then. From Riverside Church in New York
City to St. Paul's in London, he spoke from the pulpits of many
famous churches and cathedrals, but he knew, and those who
invited him knew, that when the last amen was said, his brief
mission among them had been concluded. One of King's biographers writes that among the dozens of offers he received
following his successful leadership of the Montgomery boycott
was "the pastorship of a large Northern white church."[2] There is
no indication that King ever took such an invitation seriously, for
when he left the Dexter Street Church in Montgomery, it was to
return to Ebenezer Baptist in Atlanta, the black church in which

he was reared and nurtured. He belonged to the Black Church, and in it and for it he lived and died.

It was Martin Luther King who made the Black Church aware of its power to effect change, but King was not the first black clergyman to be a leader in social action. The history of black religion is replete with the names of such preacher-activists— from Nat Turner to Adam Clayton Powell, Jr., from Lemuel Haynes to Elijah Muhammad, from Henry McNeil Turner to Leon Sullivan. But King, as leader of the Montgomery Improvement Association, and later as founder and leader of the Southern Christian Leadership Conference, was the first to put together a *sustained coalition* of Christian clerical leadership. In Montgomery, as King himself put it, his task was to "be militant enough to keep [black] people aroused to positive action and yet moderate enough to keep this fervor within controllable and Christian bounds." His method was a strategy of Christian love and action:

> Love your enemies. . . . Let no man pull you so low as to make you hate him. . . . If you will protest courageously, and yet with dignity and Christian love, when the history books are written in future generations, the historians will have to pause to say "There lived a great people—a black people—who injected new meaning and dignity into the veins of civilization." This is our challenge and our overwhelming responsibility.[3]

While it must be left to history to determine how much dignity American civilization was able to retain after several years of Martin Luther King's revolutionary application of Christian love, the Black Church took on the dignity of leadership and the posture of martyrdom which is the traditional penalty for serious leadership in human rights. In Montgomery, the Black Church sought to convince a Christian society long committed to white supremacy and black subjugation that love and patience and sacrifice could effect a degree of social change, even in situations encrusted with prejudice and sanctified by tradition. Of far greater significance, the Black Church had convinced itself before the sixties were over that it had an attribute it never even suspected—*power.*

To understand the power of the Black Church, it must first be understood that there is no disjunction between the Black Church and the black community. The Church is the spiritual face of the black subculture, and whether one is a "church member" or not is beside the point. Because of the singular nature of the black experience and the centrality of institutionalized religion in the development of that experience, the credentials of personal identity, in times not too far past, depended primarily upon church affiliation. Thus, to belong to "Mt. Nebo Baptist" or to go to "Mason's Chapel Methodist" was the accepted way of establishing who one was and how he was to be regarded in the community.

In addition to traditional reliance on the local church for identity, recently education, vocational diversification, and new opportunities for secular occasions have supported the social identity of the Blackamerican. His pastor, his church, his office in the church, or merely his denomination are important indices of who *he* is. In the black community the Black Church is in a real sense a universal church, claiming and representing all Blacks out of a tradition that looks back to the time when there was *only* the Black Church to bear witness to "who" or "what" a black man was. The Black Church still accepts a broad responsibility for the black community inside and outside its formal communion. No one can die outside the Black Church if he is black. No matter how unsavory one's life may have been, the church claims its own at death, and with appropriate ceremony. The most colorful and protracted funerals in the black community are often those of persons without formal religious affiliation, who by the standards of other communions might be questionable candidates for the final rites of the church. But the refusal of a black pastor or congregation to give full ritual and spiritual attention to such a person would be unprecedented.

Because the church is still in an important sense the people, and because its leaders are still the people's representatives, the stature of the Black Church was immeasurably enhanced by the civil rights struggle in Montgomery. The desegregation of public transportation in that erstwhile capital of the Southern Confederacy represented a substantial victory over a long-entrenched bigotry which more than once threatened to drench the city in blood. But there was a larger victory. In winning the right to sit with other ordinary human beings in the front section of the bus, the black people of Montgomery also won for themselves and all other Blackamericans a final release from the deadly psychology that had immobilized generations of Blacks. The invincibility of the white man and the impeachability of his prerogatives, the incapacity of black people to follow black leadership or to hang together under the stress of white disapproval were deeply embedded in the conventions of black control. The great walk that lasted from December of 1955 to December of 1956 helped millions of Blacks all over the country to find themselves, accept their identity, and see more clearly the basic anatomy of white-black relations. What Blackamericans finally discovered at Montgomery was the structure of black control—how a formidable body of convention, myth, and taboo supported by the ready abuse of raw power spelled intimidation, fear, and accommodation for black people wherever they were. But Montgomery proved to be a turning point, for there black people learned to defy the conventions, to discount the myths, ignore the taboos, and deal with the terrorisms that had dogged them for a hundred years, with a new set of weapons —nonviolence, forgiveness, love, and determination. A new era in self-confidence and human dignity had come to America.

SCLC

It was inevitable that the lessons of Montgomery would be tested again and again and that each new encounter would produce a new body of experiences to be drawn upon for the refinement of strategy as the Black Church extended its commitment to justice and dignity. The first child of the Montgomery experience was SCLC, the Southern Christian Leadership Conference. SCLC was founded in 1957 at a meeting of some sixty churchmen, most of them ministers, at Atlanta's Ebenezer Baptist, whose pastor was Martin Luther King, Sr. The younger King was elected president, and SCLC remained his primary base of operations until his death. Martin Luther King, Jr.'s commitment to non-violence became the operating philosophy of SCLC, and address-ing itself to America's harassed and segregated Blacks, SCLC called upon them to

> live in full knowledge of its power to defy evil . . . to understand that non-violence is not a symbol of weakness or cowardice, but as Jesus demonstrated, non-violent resistance transforms weakness into strength and breeds courage in the face of danger.[4]

The nonviolent resistance movement was both instructive and embarrassing to the American religious establishment. It was a perfect example of elemental Christian ethics put into practice. But the practitioners were black, and their strategy of returning love for evil, and offering a nonviolent response in the face of indescribable provocation, was directed essentially at Christians who had always considered moral restraint to be the product of a racial heritage from which all Blacks were excluded by defini-tion. Worse than that, the unjust laws which the Blacks were refusing to accept were legislated and maintained by a Christian establishment proud to conceive of itself as a "nation under God," dedicated to "liberty and justice for all."

Many white clergymen who spoke in support of the programs of King and SCLC characteristically forfeited the understanding and cooperation of their parishioners, and often lost their pulpits. Others who "introduced tension" into their churches by trying to explain the goals of the civil rights movement as consistent with Christian ethics found themselves "too far ahead of the people" and quietly desisted in their efforts. Yet there were other white clergymen and some prominent laymen whose Christian con-science compelled them to support the thrust for the freedom and dignity of their black fellow Christians. They did so in spite of personal hazard by raising the money that helped keep the movement alive, and by joining the civil-disobedience demonstra-tions which were to rock the South for a decade after Mont-gomery. "Black and white together . . . we shall overcome . . . someday!" became institutionalized as the theme song of the movement. It was a moving reversal of history, and could its spirit and momentum have been maintained, the racial incubus that is the American dilemma might finally have been recognized for the evil that it is, and its stranglehold might have been broken altogether.

That achievement was not yet to be, but there were some important lessons learned from that brief excursion in Christian togetherness. Montgomery and SCLC showed the Black Church its potential power. A variety of strategies emerged, but there were differing opinions as to which programs and policies should be given priority, and which ones should be muted or abandoned. Then there was the problem of jurisdiction. The National Association for the Advancement of Colored People (NAACP) and the Urban League were long established as the primary institutions in the arena of civil rights. King himself had been careful not to appear in competition with the leadership of these groups, and SCLC was organized as "Southern" precisely to denote its regional emphasis, in deference to existing national organizations and leadership. It must not appear that black leadership was competing with itself or that there was confusion or discord in the ranks. The Southern Christian Leadership Conference projected itself as a kind of council of Southern clergymen who had taken on the responsibility of rallying the faithful more forcefully to the cause of freedom long championed by secular black leadership. SCLC was designed as the instrument for direct involvement of the black churches through its organized clergy, granting SCLC original jurisdiction wherever the need was indicated, but supporting and encouraging black secular leadership through its special access to the Black Church.

Despite the prominence of the Southern Christian Leadership Conference, the Black Church was not unanimous in either its spiritual or its ideological assessment of its proper role in "political" affairs. The principal opposition to SCLC ideology centered on Dr. J. H. Jackson, Chicago-based leader of the National Baptist Convention, USA, Incorporated. Jackson was convinced that the old schedule of virtues enjoined by Booker T. Washington on the heels of emancipation still represented the most viable strategy for the acceptance and advancement of America's Blacks. He argued that hard work, thrift, education, moral respectability, and self-respect would accomplish far more than antagonizing whites by nonviolent resistance, boycotts, and the like. For Dr. Jackson, the primary responsibility of the church was spiritual, not political, and "the role of the preacher was to bring the good news of the gospel to his flock, to save the members of his flock for Jesus, and to effect change by exemplary conduct."[5] Dr. Jackson was president of the largest black communion in Protestantism, and his views were shared by many elder statesmen of his generation. But despite his high office and his personal prestige, his was not the prevailing image of the appropriate role for the modern black clergyman. His strong personal opposition to the strategies of the increasingly turbulent civil rights movement had no significant effect on the involvement of the national Black Church, even among Baptists. But Baptist clergymen like Wyatt Walker, Fred Shuttlesworth, Ralph Abernathy, Leon Sullivan,* and others brought to the movement a vigorous, determined leadership which did much to dispel the Black Church's alleged proneness to passivity in the face of white Christian aggression and denigration. Yet, so formidable was Jackson's political control over the millions who came under his jurisdiction that he managed to retain the convention presidency until 1983, a total of thirty years, and long after the church-led civil rights threat had subsided.

Leon Sullivan and the OIC

The Reverend Leon Sullivan in Philadelphia provides another example of the Black Church at work in the struggle for human rights. Sullivan's own words suggest the psychological obstacles

---

* Respectively, executive director of SCLC, 1960–64; head of the SCLC affiliate in Alabama; close associate of Dr. King and his successor as president of SCLC; and founder of OIC (Opportunity Industrialization Centers) in Philadelphia and other cities. OIC provides training, skills, and placement for the "hard-core unemployed" of America's slums.

he, like all black clerical leaders, was faced with, but they also illustrate the power potential inherent in the Black Church:

> Although [the black preacher] has been criticized . . . for what has been called lack of leadership in the colored community, the fact is that without the influence he has exerted through his church, we black people would never have come as far as we have. . . . Every movement of significant proportions to survive in the black community has had its roots in the colored church. . . .[6]

Sullivan had been an active supporter of Martin Luther King in his various campaigns to integrate lunch counters in the South, but one day he awoke to the dismal realization that while the lunch counters of his own city, Philadelphia, were not generally segregated, all the people who worked *behind* those counters were white! What black people needed more than anything else was *jobs*. The dignity of an "integrated hamburger" without the means to acquire it seemed to him a specious dignity indeed. At Sullivan's initiative, four hundred black ministers of Philadelphia launched a selective patronage compaign against certain of the worst offenders among the industries that depended heavily on black patronage but refused to employ black workers except as menials. Their objective was to end job discrimination against Blacks by activating the latent power of the Black Church and bringing it to bear against the concerted power of big business. Despite its location outside the South, where rigid patterns of job discrimination were the norm, the City of Brotherly Love had a dismal record of brotherliness when it came to black employment.

> Up to 1958 in Philadelphia, although the black population comprised one-fourth of the city's population, less than one percent of the sensitive, clerical, and "public-contact" jobs were held by black people. The jobs blacks held fell mostly into the "service" field and into the most menial categories. As of 1958, in all the banks in the City of Philadelphia there were only a few colored tellers. There were absolutely no black salesman-drivers of trucks for such major soft-drink companies as Pepsi-Cola, Coca-Cola and 7-Up. There were no full-time colored salesman-drivers of major

baking companies, or any of the ice-cream companies . . . [or] of
oil trucks. . . . There were few black clerks in supermarkets, few
colored sales girls in department stores, and few black clerical
and stenographic workers in the large offices downtown. Everywhere you went where the jobs were good, you saw whites, and
everywhere you went where the jobs were poor you saw blacks.
And even those "black jobs" had white bosses. . . .[7]

The Philadelphia Four Hundred, in this case a determined
alliance of black ministers (rather than the patrician sodality
for which the city is better known), brought an end to the more
blatant forms of job discrimination by suggesting to their congregations that they avoid promoting discrimination by not doing
business with companies that practiced it. Selected companies
depending upon black consumers for a disproportionate share
of their revenues were visited by a committee of ministers and
invited to hire and upgrade black workers. When they refused,
on the following Sunday each of the four hundred black pastors
invoked selective patronage against those companies, declaring
that "we cannot in good moral conscience remain silent while
members of our congregations patronize companies that dis-
criminate against the employment of our people." For three years
the Black Church was locked in an unpublicized struggle against
a stone wall of discrimination that was as blatant as it was
merciless. The struggle was ignored by the Philadelphia newspapers, but the silence was finally broken on June 24, 1962, by
a feature story in *The New York Times*. After that, the Philadelphia movement became so effective that the selective patronage technique soon spread to Atlanta, Detroit, New York, and
other cities.

One preacher advised his small congregation gathered in a
storefront church in an area known for its high racial tensions:

Don't light no matches. . . . Don't set no fire. Don't break no
law. We're gonna burn [the merchants] with love! We're gonna
burn them with prayer! Yes Lord! We're gonna burn them with
unity. We're gonna put a big safety pin on our money pockets
and burn them with doing without 'til they come to their senses
and give us some of the jobs we been paying for so long!

The ministers in Philadelphia went a critical step further: they soon realized that, because the doors had never been open to them, few Blacks were trained for the jobs they were struggling to get. So they set up training facilities, called Opportunity Industrialization Centers (OIC). The first one was housed in an abandoned jail.

Leon Sullivan grew up in poverty in the back alleys of Charleston, West Virginia, and served his apprenticeship in the ministry in Adam Clayton Powell's Abyssinian Baptist Church in Harlem. For him, the success of the Philadelphia Movement is attributed to prayer, moral initiative, black unity, and the recognition that money is a prime determinant of human behavior. Prayer and moral circumspection are, of course, cardinal institutions in the Black Church. Indeed, critics of the Black Church have long contended that black people spend too much time praying and moralizing when survival in this world demands human initiative. While some critics are remarkably unsophisticated about the nature and complexity of religion, in our Christian society, where life for so many is so brutalized and unpromising, impatience with "religion" and "the church" is understandable. That is why the genius of Leon Sullivan and his school of black Christian activists must be seen through the same lens as Martin Luther King, Jr., and his nonviolent mission to bring about change through whatever legitimate powers the Black Church may have.

Leadership and the Divine Initiative

Both King and Sullivan owe the success of their movements to black togetherness. There is probably more unity in the Black Church than is commonly recognized. Ninety-five percent, possibly more, of all Blacks in America belong to but seven major communions in only three denominations,* an impressive statistic when compared with the extraordinary sectarianism

* In addition to the Baptists and Methodists, some three million Blacks belonged to the Church of God in Christ as of 1980. See also Charles V. Hamilton, *The Black Preacher in America* (New York: Morrow, 1972), pp. 70 ff., for a breakdown of membership in the lesser black communions.

that characterizes American religion in general. It is useful to make the point of denominational unity here, because obviously neither Dr. King nor Dr. Sullivan could have so much as dented America's tough racial carapace without the myth-shattering unity the Black Church displayed in Montgomery and Philadelphia and a hundred other cities where Blacks committed to peaceful change were confronted by a long history of violence. The fact that they not only survived but succeeded suggests that the power of the Black Church is limited only by the failure of black leadership to understand and fully appreciate the kind of entity the Black Church is.

For example, the Black Church's traditional reluctance to place itself in direct opposition to the white power structure grew partly out of the hard lessons learned from experience, both actual and vicarious. This experience was so confused with an overlay of myth and convention as to defy objective analysis in most cases; it resulted in a mystical invulnerability for all whites as a class, before which all Blacks stood exposed, helpless and contingent. Pushed to its logical conclusions, this meant that, ultimately, life itself depended upon the white man's goodwill, his charitableness, and his forbearance. This, of course, was precisely the psychological conditioning at which the ideology of slavery was directed: to inoculate the slave with the notion, nay, the *certainty*, that his welfare, his status, his *life* lay always in the hands of his master. Hence, the surest security was behavior which would evoke the master's active goodwill, and the greatest jeopardy was to rouse his annoyance or displeasure. This is the philosophy which produced Sambo, the grinning, shuffling nigger whom everybody thought well of and nobody wanted to see hurt.

Then there was the uncertainty about the reliability of black leadership. Since all Blacks were equal in their inequality, i.e., their lack of resources and power, there was a pervasive feeling that to trust any black leader was to invite disaster. The resulting guilt and self-hatred left little room for imagining any black man able to prevail in any contest with the white man. Black leaders had no access to training or preparation. They had little or no experience. Worst of all, since all Blacks were deprived and in constant need, black leaders could not be depended upon to resist the pressures to sell out for personal reward or security. Black leadership was considered a game which Blacks could never expect to win against the whites. The white man's ice was just colder, and always would be. Hence, the real goal of the black leaders must be a personal gain that would in effect permit them to win *against Blacks!* Such a game was at best a charade. At best, it could produce personal reward for the black leader, but only frustration and humiliation for all others. At worst, a foolish or unscrupulous leader could bring down the wrath of the white establishment, with great suffering and increased inconvenience for the whole black community.

Finally, there was a moral aspect to the matter which in various forms and guises has long haunted the Black Church. Essentially, it was the question of unfaithfulness to white friends who in times past were relied upon for such favors as they chose to deliver—charity, intercession, advice and protection, and other services which did not challenge but served to strengthen the white-over-black tradition. Tradition has it that black people never forget a favor and never remember a wrong. That is why, it has been argued, black slavery was so successful and why it lasted so long. Whatever the merits of this proposition, the concern for the sensibilities of "white friends" has undoubtedly been important in the structuring of strategy and the selection of leadership in the black community. Similarly, the church had to deal with the issue of the degree of the white man's culpability. The Black Muslims solved that problem by the simple expedient of declaring the white man to be totally demonic, totally depraved —a creation of Yakub, the very Prince of Devils. This religious fiat not only placed the white adversary outside the possibility of redemption, it also reduced the protocol of black-white relations to a very elemental level, a strategy long used by white Christians for similar purposes. But the Muslims' reversal of the white man's tactics is not at all representative of the traditional Black Church.

Cautioned and conditioned by history, the black Christians could scarcely be comfortable with a declaration that any people created in the image of God could be a race of demons beyond the scope of God's redemption, or beyond the proper concern of other Christians, even those who have been the targets of their abuse. Today, thanks to an emergent cadre of able and insightful black theologians, such issues are increasingly redefined in a way that permits them to be dealt with in the context of Christian theology. This bodes well for the faith and for its church, for a clearer understanding of the anxieties and concerns which define the chasm that divides black and white Christians is long overdue.

In summary, it can be said that the Black Church has often had to struggle with the problem of whether to struggle at all with the powers and principalities of this world, and whether such a struggle might not seem to question the righteousness and the sufficiency of God, who in His own way and in His own good time can always be counted on to set things right. The careful consideration of alleged white invincibility and the assessment of black vulnerability, the care and concern about the white man as another child of God, and the respect for the divine prerogative to change things add up to a mature and responsible religious posture that distinguishes the church from a mere instrument of group interests. This is a distinction less patient Blacks find difficult to understand or appreciate. And it is a distinction which some whites, long inured to the problem and the potential of the black estate, characteristically refuse to acknowledge when the Black Church does become aroused or involved in the continuing struggle for human rights.

Black Power

Although the Black Church has traditionally been the only real possibility of black power, gathered or ungathered, in the black community, the call for Black Power first appeared as a specter to plague the conscience of white America during the civil rights struggle of the sixties. It began as a slogan adopted by the young

Blacks of the Student Non-Violent Coordinating Committee (SNCC, or "Snick"), then led by Stokely Carmichael.* It was the summer of 1966, to be precise, when the mood of the black revolution had taken a very ominous turn. The ghetto disturbances accompanied by the destruction of white-owned property there, the receding white liberal support for civil rights, the uncompromising stand for freedom being taken by "unaccredited" black activist groups identified by the press as "militants," the amazing if tentative discovery that, stripped of his carefully guarded mystique, the white man was after all human, and being human he could be hurt, and the hardening resistance to proliferating black demands had all contributed to an escalation of racial anxiety that was approaching the point of explosion. Suddenly an anguished, defiant cry for Black Power! pierced the tension hovering over the Mississippi Delta and bounced off the cotton-choked landings of Memphis, and its startling reverberations were heard on Wall Street, Main Street, and Pennsylvania Avenue. It was a cry America was prepared neither to hear nor to entertain. Massachusetts's black senator Edward Brooke complained: "That slogan has struck fear in the heart of black America as well as in the heart of white America. . . . The Negro has to gain allies—not adversaries." President Lyndon B. Johnson declared: "We're not interested in black power and we're not interested in white power, but we are interested in democratic power with a small d." And Martin Luther King explained: "It is absolutely necessary for the Negro to gain power, but the term Black Power is unfortunate because it tends to give the impression of black nationalism. . . .[8] For five long hours," he confided, "I pleaded with a group to abandon the Black Power slogan."[9]

The Black Power cry, usually accompanied by a raised, clenched fist, originated in the SNCC faction of a coalition of civil rights groups marching through Mississippi in a show of

---

* The term seems to have originated with Adam Clayton Powell, who in an address at Howard University on May 29, 1966, declared: "Human rights are God given. . . . To demand these God-given rights is to seek black power, the power to build black institutions. . . ."

black solidarity. But solidarity was fading fast, and the cry for Black Power increased the threat to its virility. Dr. Nathan Wright observes:

> People who heard the cry when it was first raised reported feelings of both understanding and apprehension. Clearly the powerless black people . . . throughout the land needed power. Yet this was a new cry. It represented a new stance, which under the potentially explosive conditions of parts of the rural South and our urban slums, could herald a threatening imbalance in the power relationships through which progress had been previously charted.
>
> The continuation of the cry quickly made clear that the fears were justified, at least in part. Old mechanisms for the purpose of work for racial justice were being challenged and judged ineffective. Under the banner of Black Power, and in the manifest breakdown of patience, long-trusted and acknowledged Negro leaders were being by-passed, if not disclaimed. . . . There was a breach in the tired and time-worn mechanisms for communication.[10]

And Wright's analysis is echoed by Gayraud Wilmore:

> The reaction within the middle class, interracial coalition that was the civil rights movement was predictable. Dismay over the turn toward black nationalism spread a blanket of gloom over liberal whites in the National Council of Churches. . . . Black church leaders such as Dr. J. H. Jackson, President of the National Baptist Convention . . . deplored the nationalist trend. . . . Individual pastors who all along had stayed aloof from SCLC . . . were more than ever convinced that there were radical, anti-Christian elements with whom the Black Church was incompatible, working within the freedom movement. . . . The Black Christian radicalism which had made Martin Luther King, Jr., the high priest of the religion of civil rights . . . was giving way to a somewhat less sanctified, less precise and less American ideology of Black Power.[11]

It is ironic that the Black Church, which had always been the repository of whatever passed for power in the black community, should have been alarmed by the demand for real empowerment. But it is not inexplicable. The church wanted power on terms it conceived to be consistent with its posture of faith and moral responsibility, but the cry of America's impatient black youth was Black Power *by any means necessary!* The church wanted to share the white man's power in order to fulfill its own responsibilities to God and man. The new cry was for power because it was just; because it was politically and economically indispensable; and because neither to have it nor to be willing to struggle for it signified abject acceptance of an archaic arrangement that was patently no longer acceptable. For a moment the church faltered. King, who more than any other individual had led the Black Church to the tentative realization of its power potential, was caught off guard. He needed time to reassess his situation, for an increasingly somber mood pervaded the civil rights movement and new, unanticipated elements had been introduced into the struggle.

Some white liberals had quietly left the movement. Others were being asked by certain constituent organizations like SNCC and CORE* to give up their leadership roles so that Blacks could have a more determinative hand in making decisions about the black estate. The war in Vietnam had become a major competitor for the interest of white activists and for the conscience of the American people. And most disturbing of all, new groups of "militant" young Blacks for whom nonviolence was a synonym for Uncle Tomism were springing up around the country and gaining prominence in the press and in the streets. Some of them were probably left-wing or Marxist-oriented; most were not. But a common thread of black nationalism, the rejection of one-way integration as a solution to America's racial problems, and impatience with nonviolence and "Christian love" as effective techniques for social change ran through them all. To an alarming number of black youth the NAACP, the Urban League, and other traditional organizations were seen as ultimately under the control of the enemy—the white man. New Third World alliances were being talked about, as were new

* Congress of Racial Equality. Organized in 1942 for "non-violent direct action" in civil rights, it was the first group to use the sit-in as a direct-action technique.

kinds of revolutionary activity that did not rule out guerrilla tactics and other possible forms of violence.

The Black Muslims offered America's restive black youth a cryptic promise to "treat the white man the way he should be treated," and Malcolm X, their fiery polemicist, dominated black interest in the press and on television with his frequent public debates and lectures on the teachings of Elijah Muhammad. Muhammad's doctrine twitted the "so-called Negroes" about trying to love the white man, who, "by nature, cannot love you." He offered them instead the *lex talionis*, "an eye for an eye . . . a tooth for a tooth."

National Committee of Black Churchmen

After a brief moment of dismay, almost as if with conscious determination not to relinquish its leadership or lose the momentum it had generated over the preceding decade, the Black Church moved to deal with the issue of Black Power. Under the leadership of Dr. Benjamin Payton,* the National Committee of Black Churchmen was organized in New York City. NCBC was in some sense the Northern counterpart of SCLC, and its membership, particularly its leadership, tended to reflect a concentration of black Christians in white denominations—Presbyterians, Episcopalians, Congregationalists, and others outside the traditional black communions. This was to prove a serious handicap in the work and development of the organization as it sought to increase its relevance as an arm of the Black Church. As the church became more self-conscious about its blackness, its wariness toward those brethren with white denominational affiliations, particularly those holding important positions in the institutional structures of the White Church, would hardly be diminished by the formation of a New York-based organization. Indeed, the Black Church had never given SCLC its total blessing or formal recognition. Nevertheless, NCBC became a significant, de facto

---

* Then Secretary of the Commission on Religion and Race, the National Council of Churches.

expression of the Black Church and a timely spokesman for its interests. Initially, it was organized to

> discuss the almost hysterical reaction of the white clergy to Black Power, the way in which the slogan was being distorted by white churchmen and bandied about wildly and thoughtlessly by black spokesmen, and the obvious inability of the Southern Christian Leadership Conference to respond positively to the new situation and mobilize increasing numbers of radical black clergy in the North for leadership in the next stage of the struggle.[12]

The first public act of NCBC was to publish a statement in *The New York Times* entitled "Black Power" (July 31, 1966). Its goal seems to have been to put the issue into proper perspective —theologically, historically, and practically. The statement was addressed to "four groups of people in areas where clarification . . . is of the most urgent necessity": (1) the Leaders of America (Power and Freedom); (2) White Churchmen (Power and Love); (3) Negro Citizens (Power and Justice); and (4) the Mass Media (Power and Truth). The preamble of this extraordinary statement set the tone for the message to follow by labeling the white outcry over Black Power a "variety of rhetoric [which] is not anything new but the same old problem of power and race . . ." which has existed as long as the two races have been in America. "The power of white men and the conscience of black men have both been corrupted," the statement continued, the one because "it meets little meaningful resistance from Negroes to temper it and to keep white men from aping God"; the other because black men "having no power to implement the demands of conscience, the concern for justice is transmuted into a distorted form of love, which, in the absence of justice, becomes chaotic self-surrender." The churchmen were emphatic about the intention of the signatories to continue their concern for black improvement despite the popular sentiment that civil rights gains already made would be jeopardized. But they were also careful to disassociate themselves from the more radical and nationalistic elements by referring to America as "our beloved homeland." The document was signed by some of the country's most distinguished black clergy, including several bishops and other high officers of the church.

At first the White Church recoiled in disbelief, and many black churchmen were uncomfortable with such a forthright "political" statement. In the end, led by the National Council of Churches, white Christianity was moved to make its peace with the notion that the NCBC statement was a comparatively mild and reasonable statement of the new black determination to be totally and responsibly involved in the life of America. The next communication from the black community would be considerably more shocking and not nearly so easy to live with.

The National Committee of Black Churchmen established headquarters at the Convent Avenue Baptist Church in Harlem. Its formal organization was completed at a conference in Dallas in November 1967, and it soon became a factor in the development of black caucuses in every major white denomination. Beyond that, the organization was soon recognized as that representation of the Black Church with which non-church dissidents and radicals could communicate most effectively. It was through this agency in its role as a Black Church contact with America's more disaffected Blacks that James Forman made some very controversial history at Manhattan's Riverside Church.

Forman, once prominent in the leadership of SNCC but more recently eclipsed by the political flamboyance of Stokely Carmichael and H. Rap Brown, was able and experienced in civil rights strategy. After four years in the military he had interrupted his graduate studies at Boston University for more immediate involvement in the civil rights struggle. He helped organize the black farmers in Brownsville, Tennessee, who had been forced off the land in reprisal for their voting activity. Later he succeeded Bob Moses as director of SNCC's famous Mississippi Project. Although considered radical and Marxist, Forman enjoyed a close working relationship with the Black Church and had gained the respect of most of the black clergy involved in civil rights activity. He had participated in Martin Luther King, Jr.'s celebrated Selma, Alabama, campaign, and he was no stranger to the white power structure, its lawmen, and its jails.

For some time the black clergymen associated with NCBC had been concerned about black economic development as the next logical and necessary step in the freedom movement. The economic situation for a small segment of the black minority had improved, but for the black masses the economic gap between them and the rest of America was unconscionable by any standard, and getting worse. More than that, the progress of the few Blacks who could be pointed to was often linked to their willingness and ability to accept subservience to whites, who dictated the rules and the conditions from traditional bastions of power. This was progress in a vacuum. Nowhere were black people able to effect their own decisions, determine their own values, and still survive with a modicum of dignity. White power remained the sole arbiter of the style and the substance of black survival.

The Black Manifesto

In late April 1969, the Interreligious Foundation for Community Organization (IFCO) sponsored a Black Economic Development Conference at Wayne State University in Detroit. The official relationship between NCBC and IFCO is not always clear, but it is clear that they vibrated with a certain sympathy born of interlocking memberships and a common experience with the White Church establishment. In any case, Forman, who was not a member of either organization (but who was ultimately supported by both), appeared at the conference and read a startling Black Manifesto, which was approved by a majority of the delegates as the consensus of the conference.*

The preamble of the manifesto was written by Forman himself. Stridently Marxist in tone, it denounced American capitalism and imperialism and announced the intention of building a

---

* The person or persons who drafted the body of the statement were not identified. The preamble was James Forman's personal statement. There was disagreement as to whether the manifesto was properly introduced before the house, and many of the six hundred delegates abstained from voting. Rev. Lucius Walker, president of IFCO, announced that the vote for approval was 187 to 63. No action was taken to rescind the vote.

socialist society inside the United States. Such a society would be led by Blacks but would be "concerned about the total humanity of this world." Blacks who support capitalism were labeled "black power pimps and fraudulent leaders . . . contributing to the continuous exploitation of black people all around the world." Forman referred to the United States as "the most barbaric country in the world" and spoke of "revolution, which will be an armed confrontation and long years of guerrilla warfare in this country." Once Blacks are in power, whites would have to accept black leadership, "for that is the only protection that black people have . . . from [white] racism. . . ." Blacks were urged to "think in terms of total control of the United States. Prepare . . . to seize state power."

The text of the manifesto was considerably more restrained but no less startling. It referred to the centuries during which Blackamericans "have been forced to live as colonized people inside the United States" and demanded of "the white Christian churches and Jewish synagogues, which are part and parcel of the system of capitalism, that they begin to pay reparations to black people in this country." The manifesto demanded a total of $500 million from the white churches and synagogues, calculated at "fifteen dollars per nigger." It provided an elaborate schedule for expenditure of the money, which included a land bank for evicted black farmers in the South, publishing and printing industries, television networks, assistance to welfare recipients, a research center, training centers, a black university, and other benefits of a public nature for Blacks. It appealed to "all black people throughout the United States" for support and called for the "total disruption of selected [white] church-sponsored agencies operating anywhere in the United States and the world." Church properties seized were to be held in trusteeship until the demands of the manifesto were met.

The following Sunday morning Forman strode into Riverside Church, interrupted the worship service in progress, and read the Black Manifesto from the pulpit. For weeks, Western Christendom remained numbed by the shock waves. Although Riverside's pastor, the Reverend Ernest Campbell, and two-thirds of the worshippers left the sanctuary at Forman's intrusion, Dr. Campbell's statement of response proved him to be one of the few white church leaders able to see the issues that lay beyond Forman's political rhetoric and sacrilegious behavior. Said Dr. Campbell:

> Let's be done with rationalizing. Wherever you go in this country the white man rides higher than the black. He lives in better parts of town, sends his children to more desirable schools . . . holds down better paying jobs. In . . . Vietnam, more blacks are dying because the draft laws that prevail favor white youth. . . .
>
> And where has the Church been in all of this? By its silence it has blessed these arrangements and given them an extra aura of divine approval.

The Reverend Campbell then addressed himself directly to the issue of reparations, an issue most church leaders either ignored, evaded, or otherwise declined to come to grips with:

> Reparations, restitution, redress, call it what you will. We subscribe to the conviction that given the demeaning and heinous mistreatment that black people have suffered in this country at the hands of white people in the slave economy, and given the lingering handicaps of that system that still works to keep the black man at a disadvantage in our society, it is just and reasonable that amends be made by many institutions in society—including, and perhaps especially, the church. . . .[13]

The response of the White Church can be summed up as both varied and confused. Most official statements deplored racism and pointed to programs they already sponsored, or intended to sponsor, to reduce the effects of racism and alleviate poverty. They were prepared to expend funds through existing machinery within their own establishments, or through the Urban League, or through black caucuses within their own denominations, or even through NCBC. But they were not willing to concede the principle of reparations, or recognize James Forman, or hand any money over directly to the Black Economic Development Conference. The Jewish groups seemed particularly antagonized by the idea of reparations, and Jewish representation on the Board of IFCO was withdrawn.

The Black Manifesto is probably not one of the great documents of history, but as sociologist Charles V. Willie has put it: "The prophetic comes to us sometimes in preposterous wrappings." The Black Manifesto, said Professor Willie, "presented us with the uncomfortable task of sorting out the meaningful from the foolish." But the manifesto did more than that: it placed a mirror before the conscience of American Christianity and forced it to look at its own blemishes. What was seen was not complimentary to the faith.

The critical accomplishment of the Black Manifesto, though, was that its promulgation showed the world yet once again what more than thirty million Blackamericans must endure in white America, and it gave fair warnings of the dangers inherent in so anomalous a situation. The voice of prophecy is seldom welcome at the dinner table, and for black America it often seems that white America never gets up from the table—never has time to listen. This is possibly what Father Junius Carter, black rector of the Holy Cross Episcopal Church, was saying when he addressed the bishops of his church:

> Too long, bishops, you have sat on the sidelines and have not acted as our pastors! I urge you to . . . exercise the authority which has been given you by our Lord. . . . You've talked about black brotherhood, but forget it, Joe.
> You don't mean it. . . . It's nothing but a damn lie. You don't trust me, you don't trust black priests and you don't trust black people. You keep saying, "Be calm, be patient." I'm sick of you. . . . To hell with love![14]

The Black Church has not yet reached the regions of despair so agonizingly plumbed by Father Carter, but his may be a voice crying in a crowded wilderness. The church may be ordained of God, but it is also a creature of society. As such, the needs and aspirations of the people who comprise it may be read in much of what it does, or refuses to do.

The Crux of the Dilemma

The probabilities are that the determination of black people for responsible participation in the full spectrum of life in America will continue to be reflected in an aggressive Black Church. Participation means power. The presence of power is the absence of contingency, the sign of responsibility, of order and meaning in life. The Black Church has learned something of how power is acquired and how it may be expended to best effect, but whether the church in America has the power and the will to deal effectively with the American dilemma remains critical to its spiritual integrity no less than to its social relevance. Power without responsibility is tyranny. We have had enough of that. Responsibility without power is slavery. We have had enough of that, too. Slavery is the inevitable corollary of tyranny: you can't have one without the other; and the American dilemma is a cardinal expression of both. Hence, the ultimate challenge is not to the Black Church but to America.

But the Black Church can ill afford to wait any longer for the initiative of a more persuasive interest in the humane considerations of its excluded black contingent to manifest itself in the churches of the American mainstream. While the major white communions have an impressive variety of strategies, boards, commissions, and committees designed to deal with the embarrassments of racism at some level, none of them speaks effectively to the underlying causes which produce the embarrassments. In fact, while some are undoubtedly sincere and well-intentioned, most of the church commissions or agencies devoted to the issues of racism are embarrassments. Or they would be if we were not so effectively vaccinated against the possibility of an onset of Christian conscience. Incredible as it may seem, racism is primarily a problem to be dealt with overseas. But emphasis ranges from the most casual and incidental references, which merely recognize the problem, to in-house bureaucracies charged with doing something nice about it. In either case, such programs usually turn out to be ponderously innocuous.

Their chief accomplishment is the happy illusion that the problem is being addressed and that the Christians in *their* church can pursue their usual interests without undue concern about what they see in the streets or read in the press. Their dues have been paid. It *is* an illusion, and the great tragedy of our dilemma is the persistent notion that, having made our ritual ablutions, we are entitled to the peace of the blessed.

The Congress of National Black Churches

The vast majority of black Christians are not impressed by the quality of the efforts of the White Church to be truly relevant in the rollback of centuries of racially induced disability and exclusion. In their own churches Blacks have traditionally found a legitimation and assurance seldom evident in the churches of their white counterparts. In consequence, while there is an increased willingness to recognize and to anticipate a measure of moderation in the racist postures of the secular world, few Blacks are able to identify equivalent changes in the White Church, or to recognize significant "Christian influence" in the relaxation of secular proscriptions. The diminished expectations that the White Church will even address itself seriously to racism in America, and the increasing awareness of its own potential for self-help, have both agonized and energized the contemporary Black Church.

The Congress of National Black Churches (CNBC) is the most impressive recent evidence of the developing maturity and self-confidence toward which the Black Church is moving as it confronts the vagaries of existence in this world. The church has long been criticized for its alleged overcommitment to spiritual escapism at the expense of practical relief for Blacks in America. While such criticism has generally been insensitive to the larger calling to which the Black Church is addressed, it has not been insensitive to the need for Blackamericans to look to their own survival by whatever means their meager options afforded. The Black Church is the most obvious instrument of potential power accessible to black needs and interests, and from that perspective the rather generalized impatience with the black churches for their dearth of specific programs of racial uplift and relief is predictable, if not always credible. But, then, it is not easy to be credible, or even rational, when your gut growls and your feet hurt and the cold air calls you by your first name. In consequence, the church must always be permitted to be itself rather than a projection of the frustrations of its critics. But whether the Black Church can afford the luxury of its ideal calling is made moot by the preponderance of evidence to the contrary. The time will come when other institutions in the black community, the unions, the professional societies, and the endless number of other voluntary associations will realize that survival and racial uplift is everybody's business, and that the responsibility of the black clergy and the black churches to address this common interest is precisely the same as that of black doctors, teachers, bus drivers, professional athletes, and the organizations to which they belong. The black preacher is no longer the only rallying figure in the black community, nor should he be, and the Black Church is not necessarily the best talent around which to build a supermarket or a housing development or a pickle factory.

While the larger black community is still in the process of discovering its new potentials and its new responsibilities, and while it is unlearning its outdated perceptions of what the Black Church is and ought to be, the Black Church is obliged to continue to overextend itself because it has traditionally done so. While the black community is exploring its new possibilities, it is not yet comfortable or confident without the sheltering imprimatur of its church. Implicit is the faith that wherever the church leads, whatever may go wrong can somehow be retrieved because the church is ultimately affected with a divine interest which is self-redemptive. It is this faith and reliance that the Black Church finds it difficult to ignore.

The Congress of National Black Churches represents a more sophisticated approach to continuing church involvement in the whole spectrum of the black experience—spiritual, cultural, economic, and political—than has traditionally been true of the individual black churches or black denominational bodies or communions. It describes itself as "designed to provide the opportunity for the identification and implementation of program efforts which may be achieved more effectively than by any single organization."[15] Its strategies assume a common purpose needing only the solidarity of effort of the whole Black Church to replace the denominational individualism characteristic of black religion. The black churches have historically addressed themselves to an extraordinary spectrum of needs and responsibilities both within and beyond the purely spiritual concerns of their constituencies, but they have usually felt vulnerable to the persistent charges of being "too heaven-oriented," on the one hand, or "too political" or "too race-minded," on the other. The genius of CNBC is that it assumes the legitimacy of the practical-within-the-spiritual as a first principle of survival, thus avoiding the conventional contention over the church's "primary mission" in which the black churches have so often foundered. That issue has been a familiar ideological trap which has often compromised the effectiveness of individual churches and communions, and made bitter critics of the very people they sought to serve. A larger reality, as perceived by the congress, is that the peculiar needs of the black community are persistent and enduring, that the church is still looked to as a primary agent of relief, and that the line between relief that is spiritual and relief that is visceral becomes increasingly imperceptible. In consequence, the Congress of National Black Churches conceives itself to be, first of all, an ecumenical organization. Its collective means are addressed toward a more effective fulfillment of the extraordinary spectrum of spiritual and secular responsibilities traditionally accepted by the individual black churches. As a spiritual entity transcending the fractures of denominationalism, it is in pursuit of that ideal power which is greater than the powers of its constituents—a power which has characteristically eluded the black churches and the black community alike.

Organized in 1978, the Congress includes seven major black denominations: African Methodist Episcopal; African Methodist Episcopal Zion; Christian Methodist Episcopal; Church of God in Christ; National Baptist Convention of America; National

Baptist Convention USA, Inc.; and Progressive Baptist Convention, Inc. The first CNBC executive committee was chaired by AME Bishop John Hurst Adams, who initiated the interdenominational dialogue among the black churches from which the congress emerged. Other leaders from the other communions and a panel of lay and academic consultants worked closely with Adams in carefully developing the program and the strategy of the organization. From its inception, the congress steered clear of any activity or any ideological pursuits or pronouncements tending to challenge or compromise denominational autonomy in any way. Its interests are functional, not structural or jurisdictional.

The Congress of National Black Churches represents some twenty million black Christians in the 65,000 local churches of its seven charter denominations, and that constituency will be substantially increased when the smaller black denominations and the black churches in predominantly white denominations gain affiliation. National offices with a full-time staff were established in 1982 in Washington, D.C. The work of the congress is carried out primarily by task forces organized to deal with six priorities: theological education, employment, economic development, the media, evangelism, and human development and services. One of the most aggressive of these tasks forces, initiated by Dr. Lawrence Jones, dean of the Howard University Divinity School, and CME Bishop C. A. Kirkendoll, former president of Lane College in Jackson, Tennessee, is concerned with the recruitment of students to historically black seminaries. The objective is to increase the number of trained black clergy entering the ministry, and to provide strong continuing education programs in such fields as church management as a way of mitigating the handicaps of the large reservoir of black clergy that has not had the benefit of seminary training.

In economic development the congress pursues a number of innovative proposals to better utilize the vast resources of the Black Church. For example, black churchgoers annually contribute well in excess of a billion dollars to churches, and black church assets exceed another $10 billion. Hence, the formation of credit unions, insurance programs, and central purchasing plans are prominent among the plans of the congress, as are strategies benefiting the black community-at-large, such as collective banking with black banks, and collective buying from local black business enterprises or other entrepreneurs with demonstrated concern for improving the black estate. The concerns of other task forces include development of community-support mechanisms and networks better to assist the black family to survive. The possibilities are almost endless, and CNBC seems uniquely prepared to harness the vast potential of the Black Church and channel it into a program of self-help and self-reliance. Such empowerment can significantly improve the future of the entire black estate, and in the process go a long way toward helping America overcome its dilemma.

5

The Face of American Pluralism

The Spiritual Base of Civil Religion

A NY serious attempt to understand the religious situation in America must begin with at least two basic suppositions: that Catholics, Protestants, and Jews constitute the reigning religious triumvirate, and so perceive themselves; and that, while all three groups have black constituencies of varying degrees of importance, the collective significance of Blacks as Catholics, Protestants, and Jews is seldom considered a meaningful factor in assessing the religious mainstream in America. In consequence, the religious situation is structured in such a way that any investigation of religion in America has usually meant the religion of white Americans, unless "Negro," "folk," or "black" religion was specifically mentioned.

This conventional understanding of American religion suggests, of course, the spillover of prevailing secular values into the religious preserve. But then, American religion has always been self-conscious about its racial exclusiveness, and it has been very careful to disassociate itself from the religious proclivities of black believers even when willing to accept the physical presence of black worshippers. It is true that in recent times black religion has become increasingly self-conscious, but this is in part a defensive response to the long history of pariahism which has characterized the black believer's contact with white religion.

Our "white religion," or "American religion," has traditionally meant Christianity in general and Protestantism in particular. The Jewish presence in the developmental period of the American commonwealth was not significant in the establishment of religious norms. Being themselves under the cold and unsympathetic eye of religious and racial suspicion, the Jews understandably avoided attracting unnecessary attention to themselves, but with indifferent success. In the long run, the Jews paid the inevitable penalty for the preservation of their religious and cultural integrity, and their willingness to adopt the prevailing racial arrangements does not appear to have been a significant factor in improving their own acceptability.

Vestiges of anti-Semitism remain to this day, of course, but on the whole, Judaism and Americanism, for a complex variety of reasons—religious, cultural, political, and economic—have evolved a certain correspondence which has greatly reduced the more overt instances of American anti-Jewishness. Today the Jewish minority enjoys religious, economic, political, and cultural prestige considerably disproportionate to its numbers, and Judaism is a prominent feature in the American pluralistic establishment which is the shadow behind the substance of our official posture of the separation of church and state.

However, the religious pluralism which derives from the Catholic, Protestant, and Jewish rapprochement is scarcely reflective of their whole constituencies, for all have black memberships which tend to be discounted in the projection of the official image of the faith. In consequence, the restrictive character of black religion derives precisely from its involuntary disjunction with the religious mainstream in America. To find out how this came about, we must look more closely at what is involved in American pluralism.

In the absence of an official established religion, or where there are a variety of competing beliefs, religious pluralism may function to standardize the norms of acceptability. In America, pluralism has come to represent the spiritual base of civil religion, the secular base being derived from the peculiar complex of ideals and values borrowed from the Enlightenment and restated with such passion in the literature of the American Revolution. It was once commonly believed that civil religion could never be a factor of consequence in American life, for that possibility had been anticipated by the provisions of the First Amendment, which re-

quires that "Congress shall make no law respecting an establishment of religion, or preventing the free exercise thereof." True,
the most obvious intent of the First Amendment was to separate
church and state. The intent was to legally prohibit an official
church as was common among the nations of Europe. But the
effect of the law seemed even more profound: in refusing to
favor one church, the state put all churches and all faiths upon
common ground. Legally, their particularities of doctrine and
ritual gave none an advantage over any other. Against the power
of the state, they shared a common prerogative and a common
impotence. They could sow to a common parish—as broad as
the limits and the jurisdiction of the state—but no person could
be penalized for choosing one creed and rejecting another, or for
acknowledging no creed at all. At least, such was the theory
which underlay the notion of separation. But there soon evolved
in America an alternative *civil religion*, which retained many
of the salient features of the traditional establishment, and developed others compatible with our incipient political, economic, and
racial prespectives.

The point is that, while the sectarian impetus which figured
prominently in the founding of America implicitly encouraged a
proliferation of competing creeds,* the notion that a broad-gauge
sectarianism might someday threaten the integrity of the faith
and jeopardize the ideal of Christian unity was probably not
considered a formidable challenge at the time. Indeed, there
were those whose confidence was buoyed by the hope and the
expectation that the travail of sectarianism would ultimately
prove the salvation of the Church Universal. Their hope was that
out of the crucible of denominationalism might come a refinement of the faith so perfect and so pure as to transcend all
previous efforts to speak the faith effectively to man in all his
conditions of existence. Such a hope was current a hundred years
ago, and while most observers would agree that America has

---

* Sidney E. Mead reminds us that our mainline denominations were "the
direct descendants of the national churches of Europe . . . formed in the
old national church crucible," each concerned to preserve its sense of
identity.[1]

indeed developed a new religion, they may well disagree on the quality of its presuppositions, and whether it is more or less effective in its appeal to man in his universal condition.

If true religious pluralism achieved such a low priority in the thinking of those who founded and shaped the American commonwealth, then the possibility of a viable social pluralism received even less consideration. There was always a powerful faction of Americans dedicated to the prerogatives of social elitism, of course, but how to accomplish this without jeopardizing other values posed a problem which to this day has not been satisfactorily resolved. There were also those whose motives were less gross, to be sure, but neither the slave block nor the Statue of Liberty was ever representative of an unconditional commitment to democratic equality. Both presupposed that those who came to America would accept the niche already designed for them in the existing scheme of things by forces operating for the preservation of the existing order. Those who landed at Ellis Island in New York Harbor, like those who landed at Norfolk and Baltimore and Charleston all the centuries before, were faced with a *fait accompli*. The principal difference was that the descendants of those landed at New York, being white, could in time be Romanized if they were but willing to do in Rome what the Romans themselves were doing, while those whose forebears came by way of Charleston and Baltimore, being black and in chains, were scheduled to remain an underclass in perpetuity, no matter what they did.

The world is smaller now, and considerably more sophisticated. The old ideologies which for so long shaped the conditions of human survival are everywhere under challenge. The smug notions of religious or political manifest destiny for favored races and chosen people, while far from dead, are no longer fashionable, but they do continue to lurk like phantoms in the attics of the cult of the privileged. Our present ethos is said to be characterized by dialogue, by which is meant a commitment to discussion rather than to action. But those distressed by want and deprivation are no less hungry for food and dignity for all the talking that may be taking place. What happens if the dialogue turns out to be another exercise in *noblesse oblige*, and if after the dialogue is over, the initiative for change and the power to effect it remain where they always were?

Pluralism

What, then, is the dialogue all about? It is about the hopes and dreams of passionate men and women who long to see the society made whole; and it is about the anxieties and the fears we experience when we contemplate the specter of chaos we know to be dogging our pretensions with the tenacity of judgment. Americans make a brave showing of accepting the Rooseveltian dictum that all we have to fear is fear itself, but what we seem to fear most is each other. In a society where excess is considered sophistication and discipline is a dirty word; where all morals are individually determined and one man's behavior is as right as another's; and where the sanctity and relevance of the shared values once depended upon for identity and belonging have been so seriously eroded by the crusading zeal of ego-centered hedonism, the American social conscience has been battered into near-oblivion. We no longer feel much of anything unless it affects us directly as individuals, and even then we are no longer certain of what feelings, if any, are appropriate.

America is a society seriously at odds with itself, in which contending forces are momentarily and fortuitously stabilized. Such incidental pluralism is peculiarly vulnerable to both volatility and quietism. In the case of the former, the abrasiveness of the social flux, the mutual uncertainties and insecurities of constituencies jockeying for advantage, the absence of agreement or understanding defining the parameters of the critical particularities to be recognized by all, and by which all agree to live, all contribute to a condition in which the community's capacity to protect itself and to maintain order is sharply diminished. High levels of tension are characteristic, and people tend to adopt ad hoc attitudes about life and the circumstances of their existence. Concern for the future and the dimension of depth are not features of most social relationships. The feeling that "now is all you can count on" is not limited to an impatient generation of youth; it is experienced at all levels of the society. The result may be the illusion of a healthy, peaceful coexistence, when, in fact, all the elements of discord are present.

Social groupings presuppose a consciousness of identity, and identity seeks in turn to express itself in terms of its particularities. A pluralistic society, then, is one in which self-conscious social groupings are in significant contact with each other, sharing a common physical space. Each group is aware of its uniqueness but is expected to make an effort to live with the peculiarities of others, for pluralism recognizes that the freedom of one group to be itself and to celebrate its peculiarities depends upon the freedom of every other group to do the same. Wilbur Katz, of the University of Wisconsin Law School, puts it this way:

> A religiously pluralistic society . . . is one in which principal religious groups not only claim freedom for themselves, but affirm equal freedom for others, whatever their beliefs may be. Individuals are free to doubt or to believe. The model pluralism is also one in which there is a sensitizing to the differing needs of varying groups and a disposition to accommodate these needs.[2]

Effective pluralism, then, requires a conscious effort on the part of contending constituencies to protect each other's uniqueness in order that each may enjoy its own. It is toleration for the enjoyment of toleration. But more than that, it involves the active championing of the right to be different, a right which ipso facto must be extended to others in order to be realized by one's own group.

Pluralism is a practical way of ordering a society that is self-conscious about its diversity, but it does not address the hard questions which underlie the presumption of uniqueness, the parameters of authority, the unity of truth. Rather, pluralism deals pragmatically with these issues, but offers no final judgments. That is why it is often argued that pluralism is politics at its best —an informal acceptance of the presently possible rather than the fruitless pursuit of the philosophically ideal. Pluralism permits every constituency to indulge the fantasy of first among equals, and to so address itself to the world at large.

Living with Diversity

If mankind is truly one, and if the church aspires to be, there are consequences of unity which do not properly lend themselves to diversity. This is where the pragmatics of pluralism part company with those who worry about the true meaning of oneness, the deeper implications of unity. It is an old question. The notion of a common fold is at least as old as Christendom, and one fold implies one shepherd, one leadership, one rule, and one way. But Christianity is the fruit of an evolutionary process, which over some thousands of years succeeded in dissuading man of the possibility of his individual or tribal uniqueness in favor of the uniqueness of God and the uniqueness of mankind.

Certainly, man does not come naturally to the conclusion that he is one with all other men. In fact, most primitive societies learned to think of themselves as unique long before they accorded uniqueness to their gods. The function of the gods was to serve the people; indeed, to protect the uniqueness of the tribe, the clan, the race, the cult. Other peoples had other gods, but always the gods belonged to the people who worshipped them rather than the people to the gods. It was the people who were unique, and in practically every primitive culture we know about there were tribal names declaring their possessors to be *the* people. All others were counterfeits of the real, beyond the pale of humanity and the interests of the tribal gods.

The notion of God having a "chosen people" was a radical departure from the ancient tradition of the people having a chosen god, or gods. But even so, being chosen by God reinforced rather than weakened the notion of tribal, or racial, or cultic uniqueness. It simply meant that a reciprocal relation had been established. The chosen god in choosing the people had ratified what the people had always preferred to believe: that they were different from other people, and that their difference made a difference. The possibility that God might extend the category of his chosen to universal proportions would of course be resisted, because such a possibility posed an unacceptable threat to the notion of the uniqueness of those already elected. This resistance could be dissipated only if it could be shown that those subsequently chosen were, in all essentials, of the same tribal, racial, or cultic genre as those who first received the promise.

Learning to live with diversity is not one of man's most representative accomplishments. In fact, it is one of his more characteristic failures. The need to reduce all heterogeneity to a manageable uniformity (best illustrated in religion and politics by the medieval church and by classical Communism) is well documented. The question is why. Intellectually and philosophically, it probably has to do with man's understanding of truth—truth as consistency. Truth is the one and final expression of reality. Truth cannot be divided. It must be one. If A is true, and B is different from A, then B cannot be true. And by extension, if B is not true, then B is false and ought to be suppressed. Or at the very least, what is false (and not true) should not be permitted to enjoy the prerogatives of truth. Similarly, if truth is consistency, then truth is whole and cannot be divided against itself. Perfection is oneness. Wholeness. Uniformity. Whatever divides the oneness of an entity destroys the perfection that made it what it was and what it was meant to be. "A house divided against itself cannot stand" because a divided house has lost its integrity, its integrality—that quality of wholeness essential to its being itself rather than something different. To divide is not merely to weaken. To divide is to change the nature of a thing, to compromise its identity, to perjure its perfection: to make it something other than what it was or what it was intended to be.

When this kind of reasoning is applied to the church, the scandal of sectarianism, racial and denominational, is immediately apparent. Sectarianism balkanizes the church and leaves its truth open to pollution. If truth is one, to speak with many voices is not necessarily to confuse the message, but the risk is great. It is for this reason that all those who share an absolutistic interpretation of truth are unplacated by the relative effectiveness of pluralism, for if pluralism does not divide the truth, it grants respectability to what is not truth, and grants every claim equal accommodation in the marketplace of religious ideas.

Americanity

In contemporary America, any argument about religious absolutism is, of course, bound to be academic. There are those who do
weep for "the broken body of Christ," but for the most part they
sorrow in silence. Pluralism is taken for granted. It is its own
establishment. Predominant Protestantism no longer dominates
in any significant way, but with its own vast brood of religious
sub-entities it shares an easy understanding with those other
great religions from which it sprang. Religious pluralism in
America, then, means a mutually accommodative relationship
among Judaism, Christianity, and Americanity.

"Americanity" is a new expression of an old faith, or perhaps
it is more accurate to say that it is the vigorous offspring of a
marriage of faiths. It is the religion of the American culture,
"the religion of the Republic . . . , the 'national religious self-
understanding' that embodies and cherishes the ideals, aspirations
and hopes that have been traditionally associated with America."[3]
It is the natural child, it has been argued, of the Enlightenment
and evangelical Protestantism, from whose twin fountains flow
the clear, cold waters of our national heritage. That the waters
have long since been polluted is expressed in our national
dilemma. The Enlightenment in America, however, was snuffed
out by the issue of slavery before the flame was fairly set to the
wick. It never recovered, except as a ghostly chimera, a wasted
reminder of what America could have been if indeed we had
been less blind to the light of the Enlightenment, and if evangelical Protestantism could have been somewhat less evangelical and more humanitarian.

Americanity is the semi-secular, unofficial, but characteristic
religion to which most Americans appeal when an appeal to
religion is indicated. It is the religion most Americans *feel* when
they feel any religion at all. It transcends the classical sectarian
delineations and joins Protestant, Catholic, and Jew in a single
communion in a way no classical religion ever could. Those who
think well of America's culture religion see it as "a creative,

dynamic, and self-critical national religion that gives transcendent meaning and a high set of moral values to individual Americans, and produces just, humane goals for the nation."[4] Others see it as a "third force . . . a force that is capable of significantly altering a culture, or that is symptomatic of a significant new shift in the dynamics of a culture." The most important aspect of this third force is held to be its pluralistic quality. Indeed, it is suggested that this force is "the pietistic spirit of American culture itself," involving the American sense of mission and world leadership for the containment of Communism, our national sense of charity and stewardship, and "the sense of religious commitment and ideals that Americans ascribe to democracy and their way of life."[5]

Other observers of the contemporary religious scene are not quite so charitable in their assessment of Americanity, but there will be little challenge to its pluralistic implications insofar as its attractiveness to Protestants, Jews, and Roman Catholics is concerned, for, as Will Herberg has suggested, "to be a Protestant, a Catholic or a Jew are today the alternative ways of being an American."[6] That is precisely the point: the confusion of national goals and values with religious goals and values has produced in America a pseudo-religious modality with grotesque social and religious aberrations. How else can one explain our quite primitive racial and economic practices which, if they are not officially sanctioned by the church, are common expressions of our most respectable private citizens and national leaders without any consequences to their religious status or respectability?

This all-too-cozy bundling between what appears to be national policy and Western religion laughs at the alleged separation of church and state; and well it may, for it grants to civil power the support and respectability of religion without charging that power with a commensurate responsibility. It is little wonder that such antiquated notions as America's manifest destiny and "the white man's burden" persist and flourish in the contemporary code language which strives to retrieve respectability for notions no longer respectable, if indeed they ever were.

In the late 1950s, Henry Pitt Van Dusen wrote an article for

Life magazine[7] which was widely considered a warning to traditional religion to beware lest its influence in the world become increasingly overshadowed by the rapidly multiplying sects which make up the hinterland of standard Protestantism. While Roman Catholicism and mainline Protestantism were barely holding their own, Jehovah's Witnesses, the Church of Christ, the Seventh-Day Adventists, and similar sects were flourishing. Van Dusan saw these "fringe" groups as a third force. Any who were alarmed at his findings then would have no cause for comfort looking at today's statistics about church membership and religious influence. The national offices of the major liberal denominations are curtailing their operations and lamenting the wasting away of their congregations, while the fringe sects Van Dusen talked about have swollen memberships, new confidence, and an increasing sense of mission in the world. But for all their successes in keeping religion relevant while the standard denominations have been laboring to keep it respectable, the fringe sects are not really the third force. Not yet. Americanity, the religion of our national culture, is firmly fixed in that division. And it will probably remain so for a long time to come, for as the sects gain power and influence, a benign civil order will be waiting to accept *their* compromise, even as it has already compromised the religious mainstream.

Black Religion and a Distinct Identity

"Black religion" is hardly new to the American spectrum of faith, but it is new to the millions of American Christians who never venture from the familiar comforts of their mainstream congregations. Dr. Van Dusen would certainly have included black religion in his third-force collective had he been conscious of its existence and sensitive to its meaning. And while it is unlikely to find significant projection through the religious powers commonly relied upon to protect the conscience and define the morals of the nation, our racial patterns may well make black religion a *fourth* force in American religious pluralism. Excluded from the white churches in the past, demeaned and segregated where they were not excluded, black Christians, as we have seen, are hardly enthusiastic over efforts to include them in a united church. They listen to the arguments, but the arguments seem perfunctory and ceremonious because they do not seriously address the logical and moral aspects of our continuing racial dilemma.

Nevertheless, there will always be Blacks who opt for "Protestant," or "Catholic," or "Jewish" as their primary identity rather than "Black." And some will identify themselves merely as "Americans," to the exclusion of any racial or religious particularity. This is a prerogative inherent in the freedom of religion and the rights of citizenship which distinguishes a democratic society. In exercising it, Blacks are simply observing the options of self-perception and projection that millions of other Americans have used to specify identity. The problem is that self-perception and public reception are not always in agreement. No matter how Blackamericans may see or define themselves, to the mythmakers and census takers, the statisticians and the sociologists, and to white America generally, there are still white churches and "Negro sects"; and there is religion and "Negro religion," and the two are not generally considered to be the same.

As we have shown earlier, contemporary black religion is not particularly bothered by such rebuffs but takes in stride this strange American double vision as one more expression of our racial paranoia. Having rejected the "Negro" tag as one of the more insidious agents in the psychological arsenal of white racism, black religion is self-consciously black. Its claims to that identity are both legitimate and unique, and they rest securely upon the singularity of the black experience in America in the context of the theological reassurance that God does not just walk away from the oppressed. Theologian James Cone argues that:

> The task of black theology . . . is to analyze the nature of the gospel of Jesus Christ in the light of the oppressed black people so they will see the gospel as inseparable from their humiliated condition, bestowing on them the necessary power to break the chains of oppression. This means that it is a theology of and for the black community, seeking to interpret the religious dimensions of the forces of liberation in that community.[8]

Clearly, black theology has at last seized the initiative for a long-needed interpretation of the faith consistent with the black experience and with the way black Christians perceive themselves. The values at stake are in the category of the ultimate, for there hangs in the balance the question of whether Christianity in America can ever be totally inclusive, or whether its traditional perversions are so ingrained as to preclude altogether a truly common faith. The critical message of black theology is that black believers need never again be deceived by the white Christian's hot piety and cold love, for, says Cone, "black theology assumes that the possibilities of creative response among white people to black humiliation are virtually non-existent . . . [and] black people [must] seek to remove the structures of white power which hover over their being."[9]

In the West and of the West

Certainly there is no convenient place in the existing parameters of American pluralism into which this new independent spirit of black religion can be comfortably fitted. It is at odds with the traditional white American expressions of the faith, and it is not in the mood of stereotypical "Negro religion." Some black theologians and their disciples have, with varying degrees of caution, advanced the notion that the Black Church may be the saving remnant in Christendom; and not just in America, but wherever the uniqueness of Jesus Christ is acknowledged. The argument seems to be that Christianity as a Western religion, or more precisely as *the* religion of the West, has become entangled in the preservation and promotion of the cultural values of the West to such a degree that the universal values of the faith have been hopelessly compromised. From this perspective, Americanity is unique only with reference to its garishness, but it has substantial counterparts in every citadel of Western culture.

The uniqueness of the Black Church inheres not in its blackness per se, and not in any claim to being non-Western, but in the fortuitous experience of being in the West and of the West, yet being excluded by circumstances from voluntary participation in the moral decisions by which Western ascendancy was established and confirmed. In being left out, but forced to look on, the black people in the West cannot have their religious perspectives and spiritual experiences equated with those of their white counterparts who were the principal shapers of recent history. While the notion of a saving remnant sounds suspiciously like the assertion of a black manifest destiny, the possibility that their own degradation endowed black Christians with a more compassionate perspective on humanity, and a less febrile memory of the fundamental moral requirements of the faith, ought not to be dismissed summarily. There are substantial contributions to be made to the evolution of Western Christianity short of so consummate a benefaction as "saving remnant" implies.

Like every communion, the Black Church has its problems, but they are not primarily problems of the faith or of its interpretation. The most obvious question is whether the church is prepared (or preparing) to assume a role beyond its conventional parish, should such a role be thrust upon it. The notion of a "saving remnant" aside (for who can say if there will be a remnant worth saving?), it seems quite clear that if it hopes to survive, the Black Church must be prepared to assume an uncharacteristic leadership and a new relevance in the society. The increasingly formidable challenges of secularization will see to that, and when it happens, pluralism in America will be augmented, or supplemented or subdivided, by a *fourth force*, and the politics of God will be searching for a new rapprochement with the politics of the culture.

Despite the uniqueness of the black experience, and despite the wonted exclusiveness of the American religious establishment, the Black Church is not an island unto itself. It is still a part of the main, however tenuous and provisional its relationship. It is the spiritual embodiment of the black experience, but that experience is constituent to a larger social and cultural reality. This raises the question of whether the Black Church does in fact enjoy any significant immunity from the forces which corrupt the larger society, or whether its claim to uniqueness lacks the substance of reality. This argument implies that whatever is characteristic of white America will be replicated in the black community; and more specifically, that the lassitude and ambivalence which trouble the contemporary White Church will be found in counterpart in the contemporary Black Church.

Not necessarily. The argument falls apart when it is recognized that the conventions which have always conditioned social intercourse between the black subculture and the white overculture in America are still substantially intact. So while it is true that the Black Church to some degree is a part of the common religious heritage, it is also true that culturally and psychologically there is a significant spectrum of individuation and emphasis which ranges from what is the same or similar to what is quite different and distinct. While Blackamericans and white Americans share the same value structure informed by the same Judeo-Christian ethic, and while they share the same political ideals concerning the equality of persons and the sanctity of life and freedom, it is the interpretation brought to those common values in day-to-day human intercourse and the way they are translated into human experience which sets one group apart from the other.

All cultures borrow freely from each other, but American cultural borrowing is inordinately inhibited by the conventions of racial separation, and there is an inevitable disjunction between what white people are thinking and doing and what the black community is thinking and doing. Much of the borrowing that does go on is clandestine and not publicly admitted. We may safely conclude, then, that despite the inevitable overlappings of cultural experiences, neither the Black Church nor the black community is a replication of its white counterpart, but each pursues its own avowed distinctiveness. If this were not so, there would be no occasion to speak of a Black Church in the first place, for neither White Church nor Black Church would exist.

6

The View from the Narthex: Mormon, Muslim, and Jew

Outside the Mainstream

THE dominant religious influence on the black experience derives from contact with white Christianity, and most particularly white Protestant Christianity. The Atlantic experiment was initially an Anglo-Saxon Protestant undertaking, and the black experience was a development intricately intertwined with that event. In the history of our national development, the English were here first, and under the Anglo imprimatur the nation established its principal definitions, from which the culture took its unique development. The black estate is an aspect of that development, and the black estate is in part shaped and conditioned by the religious presuppositions and the religious behavior expressed in the Anglo-American Protestant tradition. However, American Protestantism, whether considered in isolation or as an aspect of the civil religion called Americanity, does not represent the limits of the black experience insofar as religion is concerned. The primary, even the preponderant, relationship between Blacks and Protestants is still intact, but as American history has been modified by other peoples and other faiths, so has the black experience in its turn.

There are three primary ways in which religion in America has affected the black estate:

- Some religions have been attractive to Blacks to the extent that Blacks have sought to identify with them, either as members or through vicarious association.

- Some religions have theological, or doctrinal, or conventional proscriptions which discourage, limit, or bar black participation.
- Some religions have tenets, conventions, or practices which are ultimately expressed in social, political, or economic policies inimical to the black estate.

None of these is necessarily mutually exclusive. Every religion aims first at the spiritual (and sometimes the practical) satisfaction of its own clientele, its own true believers. If it is successful, others outside its communion may be moved to seek or to accept admission. This is the primary way in which religions grow. But religions also grow by making themselves exclusive, by publicly rejecting specified publics in order to attract others considered more acceptable to the in-group. And finally, religions often seek to protect their own at the expense of others, particularly in the pursuit of scarce values, whether spiritual or mundane. Remarkably few religious practitioners, lay or professional, are able to recognize the inconsistencies, however bizarre, which often separate their commitments to righteousness from the pragmatics of secular advantage.

There are three religious communions outside the Christian mainstream with which Blacks have unusual relationships. While these relationships may vary in their impact on the black estate, they all reflect directly or indirectly aspects of the American dilemma. I refer to black relations with Mormons,* Muslims, and Jews. These religions all show at some point a common reference of belief, but they have little in common in their relations with Blackamericans. It is not a common theology or a common ritual, or even a common polity, which links them in their individual relationships with black people, but rather the peculiarities of the black experience itself, and perhaps the fact that each of them in its turn has felt the harsh jackboot of discrimination in

---

* "Mormons" is the popular name for the sect founded by Joseph Smith in 1830 whose official designation is Church of Jesus Christ of Latter-Day Saints (LDS).

America. But were they morally informed by this experience?
That is their dilemma.

THE MORMONS

The Coveted Priesthood

Until 1978 the Mormon Church had a very explicit theological
doctrine which effectively kept Blacks out of the church and
quite possibly out of Utah as well. Recent census figures show
that of that state's 1.5 million population, only nine thousand,
or less than two-thirds of one percent, are black, and only one
in thirty of these is a Mormon.° Since Utah is overwhelmingly
Mormon, and the government of the state is as near a theocracy
as exists in America, there is probably a high correlation between
the low estimate the church holds of Blacks and what Blacks
can expect in the way of civil and economic justice in a society
under Mormon control. The key to status in the Mormon Church
and to respectability in any Mormon community is the "priesthood." However, while a handful of Blacks were permitted to
become Mormon, the priesthood was closed to Blacks for more
than a century—in fact, for the whole history of Mormonism
save the first six years. Hence, the immediate effect of the denial
of the priesthood was to deny to Blacks any meaningful participation in the affairs of church and community expected of
all other Mormon males.

The priesthood is not only a matter of social importance; it is
critical to the Mormons' sense of spiritual adequacy and religious
fulfillment, and for that reason must be examined if the exclusion
of Blacks has any significance. In the first place, ordination to the
Mormon priesthood is not to be confused with ordination to become a pastor or a parish priest in Protestant and Catholic

---

° United States Census Bureau, 1980. There are fewer than one thousand
Blacks among the world's four million Mormons.[1]

churches. A Mormon priest is not a pastor in the conventional sense.

> The Mormons do not have a professional ministry; "divining for hire" was early regarded with some contempt. Instead, they make every man a minister. Every male, except those of black or African descent, is at 12 years of age ordained a deacon, the first of six orders in the priesthood; one rises, by faithful service in each rung, to the order of high priest. This authority to minister in the ordinances of the gospel is conferred on any male regardless of skin color—Indians, Polynesians, Melanesians, Orientals; only blacks are denied it.[2]

Only those who achieve the priesthood may even enter the Temple. Only they may have their wives and children "sealed to them forever" in a Temple ceremony. The integrity of the family has extraordinary religious and social value among Mormons, and it is through marriage to priests that women partake of the great benefits of the church. Only members of the priesthood may hold even the most minor offices in the church. In consequence, it is impossible for anyone who is not a priest ever to participate in church leadership or administration at any level. Black Mormons could not sing in the celebrated Tabernacle Choir, though they might have the voice of angels. Only members of the priesthood can qualify for a place in "Celestial Paradise." This means that, however moral and true to his faith a black Mormon might be, he could look forward to no improvement of his status, either here or in the next life. No one ineligible for the priesthood could assist with the sacrament (as twelve- to fifteen-year-old white Mormon males do) or bless or perform baptisms (as sixteen- to eighteen-year-old white males do).

Clearly, the priesthood represents the entry to the chief sacred and secular values of Mormonism. The church is ruled by males; and by making one's way up through the various levels of service, a man can attain great power and honor on earth and the assurance of a superior existence in the next dispensation. He can also baptize his departed relations, thus "blessing" them, and he can "seal" his family in the Temple, thereby opening the way for the women in his household to share with him the blessings they could not otherwise enjoy. But only if he is a priest.

Precept and Prejudice

The long-range effects of the Mormon exclusion of Blacks from the priesthood were far more insidious than mere spiritual inconvenience. Blacks of African descent alone are held by the Mormons to be cursed of God for various improbable reasons known only to the church. The fact that Blacks were cursed and to be avoided contributed to a generalized, guilt-induced teratology already deeply ingrained in the American culture. The millions of Mormons who accepted without question the denigration of Blacks in their church, and in the divine scheme as interpreted by their Apostles, were inevitably moved to accept the denigration of Blacks in the social order as normative. Indeed, so pernicious is the doctrine that not to do so would in effect place a conscientious believer in opposition to the will and wisdom of God. In an article published in *Look* magazine, an anguished white Mormon confessed:

> It is puzzling, unless one keeps in mind the attitude of overwhelming apathy that Mormons seem to have toward Negroes. Unfortunately, the very existence of the present Mormon Negro doctrine adds to this apathy. In fact, it gives Mormons a God-sanctioned reason for feeling superior to the Negro.
> This is where the Mormon question about the Negro merges into the larger question of racial prejudice. The best way to perpetuate racial prejudice is to provide as little real association between races as possible. Prejudice thrives on ignorance. The Mormons' Negro doctrine reinforces the ignorance of most Mormons about Negroes.[3]

The Mormons lay the responsibility of their doctrines on God, but the practical effects fall heavily upon people. Black people have for centuries been required to bear an inordinate share of misery deriving from other men's selected intimations of the divine. Wallace Turner, Pultizer Prize-winning former Nieman Fellow at Harvard University, in his celebrated study of the

Mormon Church found the Mormons to be "a fine people [whose] contribution to American life has been considerable." But he also found that

> Mormonism is a total way of life. A devout Mormon never really leaves his religious shell as he goes about his life in the secular world. So he never really leaves the feeling that black skin makes a man inferior. *This means that the LDS [Mormon]Church actually is one of the most influential organs of racial bigotry in the United States.* [Italics supplied.]

It is also Mr. Turner's opinion, and one shared by many others, that

> . . . the ultimate effect of this aspect of LDS doctrine is as racist as anything asserted by the Theodore Bilbos* and the Robert Sheltons† in the bigoted corners of the southern states. It separates the world into two groups: there are those who can become full-fledged Saints and thus God's chosen people; there are the African Negroes who are set apart from the rest of us to occupy a lesser station.[4]

Mr. Turner is right, except that the world has learned long since that all of the bigoted corners of America are not in the Southern states. Others are in Utah and Idaho and California where the Mormon Church has its primary strength. And some of them are in Washington, D.C., and New York City and dozens of other places far from Utah where that burgeoning communion has established stakes and built imposing edifices with the money drawn from faithful tithes and its vast commercial enterprises that range from newspapers to ranches to banks and blocks of real estate scattered across the country. The Associated Press reports the annual income of the Mormon Church to be in the billions, and its assets place it among the top fifty corporations in the country. Since the Mormons are the fastest-growing

---

* Former United States Senator from Mississippi, notorious for his anti-Black, pro-segregationist political philosophies.
† Ku Klux Klan leader.

denomination in America, such spiritual and economic leverage has obvious implications for the spread or the containment of strongly held social policies. So while the Mormons did not originate the corners of bigotry we find scattered through America, they are uniquely positioned to influence that bigotry for good or for ill by their great wealth and by the vigor of their crusading zeal. Known for its emphasis on self-reliance, achievement, sexual morality, and family integrity, the Mormon Church has some very impressive achievements to its credit, but its critics are practically unanimous in the opinion that "because of an antiquated racial position [it is] incapable of making any significant contribution to the solution of today's major moral and social problems."[5]

When in 1972 the Mormons decided to carry their message to New York City in the form of a $16 million, thirty-eight-story church to be built on the Upper West Side near the Juilliard School of Music, the proposal was considered a direct affront to the well-integrated international community on New York's Upper West Side. Nevertheless, the image of the Mormons as sober, law-abiding, industrious citizens brought forth cries of narrow-minded bigotry against those who thought the Mormons might be bigoted, and the issue was muted. Bigotry wears strange guises. In another twist of circumstances, in 1976 the Mormons' Washington Chapel, built in 1933, was put up for sale and its parish disbanded. The problem seems to have been that the neighborhood where the chapel stands had shifted from white to black. Perhaps to their credit, the Mormons made no pretense about servicing a changing community. When the racial balance shifted, they packed up and moved on to relocate among a more acceptable spiritual clientele.

The Mormon tradition is not to proselytize people of African descent. Blacks may (or may not) be admitted to membership if they insist on obtruding, but even if they are admitted, admission is likely a dead end. They have no meaningful part in the life and direction of the church. A black Mormon novice is a self-invited pariah in a church that with prior deliberation prefers to ignore his presence and discourage his participation. D. Stephen Holbrook, a Mormon missionary from Salt Lake City, reports:

> As a Mormon missionary, I served in Hong Kong and California, and found that it was the policy of the L.D.S. Church to allow equal rights for Oriental peoples, but we were instructed as representatives of the Church to bypass Negroes. The leaders of the Mormon Church instructed us to invite Negroes to the church of their choice, but not to the Mormon services, as we did every other person we came in contact with, going door to door. This practice made me feel very un-Christian.[6]

But Joseph Fielding Smith, grandnephew of Founder Joseph Smith and then-president of the Council of Twelve Apostles, and the church's most respected theologian, declared that the Mormons hold no particular animosity toward Blacks. In fact, he said, "darkies are wonderful people, and they have their place in our church."[7] However, even that "place" is not easy to come by. Dr. Glen W. Davidson, a professor in the Department of Philosophy and Religion at Colgate University, reports that in the Mormon missionary program, not even Smith's patronizing views are given currency:

> Mormon missionaries are directed not to proselytize Negroes and to keep out of "areas of transition." Not even Joseph Fielding Smith's invitation to "darkies" is tolerated in the mission program. The membership ranks are being filled with those whose religious commitment is to the maintenance of a racist society and who find Mormon theology a sanctimonious front for their convictions. President [Hugh B.] Brown° maintains that the Negro is barred from the priesthood today only because "he is not in sufficient numbers in the Church and [has] not advanced to the position where he could assume leadership." At the same time Brown admits that the increasing number of racists in the church will make development of Negro leadership even more difficult.[8]

° Hugh B. Brown was one of the two counselors serving Mormon President David O. McKay. In the Mormon administrative order, there are numerous "presidencies" of ascending order.

In his studies of the church, Davidson has found that it has indeed become attractive to many who wish to forestall association or identification with Blacks as long as possible. At the height of the civil rights struggles in the mid-1960s, the ranks of the Latter-Day Saints began to broaden as the racial confrontations increased. Davidson states in the September 1965 issue of *The Christian Century*:

> From interviews with recent converts in the south, and to a degree in the rest of the nation as well, I have found his fears well founded. A number of former Presbyterians, Methodists and Baptists confess to becoming Mormons because, as one woman put it, "I'm fed up with being told by some preacher that these niggers are equal to me." A number of missionaries working in the south this summer claim that there has never been more interest in Mormonism and that "our race doctrine is of the greatest interest."

The growth of the Mormon Church has continued apace since, and while it is not contended that the policies of the church are deliberately designed to attract racists, because we live in an era when *official* discrimination is no longer respectable, the very middle-class, progressive, and honor-bright Church of Latter-Day Saints must seem an attractive haven for thousands of frustrated Americans who may have less honorable motivations than the faith intends. Surely that is a problem the Mormons will have to face sooner or later, or they may one day find their church committed to a doctrine their founding fathers would feel compelled to repudiate.

The problem for Blackamericans is that every center of hardcore racial prejudice, whether "divinely inspired" or a manifestation of human perversity, is a threat to their welfare and perhaps to their very existence. It makes no difference whether the threat comes from people who are trying to save the country from the Communists or trying to save the country from the consequences of its sins; or people merely trying to salvage for themselves an ethnic security which has been battered by others in the inevitable vagaries of human intercourse. But black people are increasingly restive with being the convenient "it" for other people's enterprises or needs. Black people are tired of the familiar role of the religious culprit, the cultural nigger, the available ego dump for the racial paranoia that is the American sickness unto death.

The Mormon ostracism of Blacks derives from *nothing any black man ever did or was that raised a question of his moral fitness or his religious competence.* But, as has often been the case with others in need of a scapegoat, alleged black moral insufficiency was seized upon as a convenient way to respond to a crisis for which Blacks were in no way responsible. When Joseph Smith founded the Mormon religion in 1829, Blacks were as welcome as any others. As a matter of fact, *The Book of Mormon*, which the Latter-Day Saints believe to be divinely inspired, states emphatically:

[The Lord] . . . inviteth them all to come unto him and partake of his goodness; and he denieth none that come unto him, black and white, bond and free, male and female; and he remembereth the heathen; and all are alike unto God, both Jew and Gentile. [Nephi 27:33]

It is *The Book of Mormon*, believed by Mormons to be translated by Joseph Smith from secret gold plates shown him by an angel (Moroni), which is the basis and the beginning of the Mormon faith. Smith's translations were completed in 1829 at Palmyria, New York, the birthplace of the faith. Seven years later, in 1836, a black man, Elijah Abel, a mortician of Nauvoo, Illinois, was qualified and ordained as an elder. Abel, who is described as one of Smith's closest friends, was duly admitted to the priesthood and later ordained a "Seventy." He was probably the first—and certainly the last—black Mormon to be admitted to the priesthood until the new revelation of 1978.

What happened? Did this black pioneer in the Mormon Church somehow manage to desecrate the high office he attained? Did he fall from grace or lapse from his responsibilities, thereby putting himself and his race on record as unworthy? Incapable? Deficient?

He did not.

Abel was one of a handful of black Mormons who trekked on to Utah and the Great Salt Basin, and for nearly fifty years he served his church as a member of the priesthood in Salt Lake City. When he was seventy-five years old, he went on a church mission to Canada and came back to Utah to die, worn out and exhausted, in 1884.

The Missouri Compromise: The Mark on Cain

What did happen to the status of Blacks in the Mormon Church? In sum, here is the story from Professor O. Kendall White, Jr., writing in the *Journal of Religious Thought*:

> When the Mormons settled in Missouri during the 1830's the established residents quickly accused them of "tampering" with their slaves and identified them as abolitionists who were "endeavoring to sow dissensions and raise seditions amongst them." Perhaps even more importantly, the Mormons were accused of inviting free blacks to become Mormons and to migrate to Missouri to help build the kingdom of God in preparation for Jesus' second coming. This early pro-black posture generated considerable hostility among the established settlers who initiated a number of persecutions that eventually led to expulsion of the Mormon community. Attempting to reduce these pressures from antagonistic forces, the Mormons adopted a pro-slavery posture formulated in terms of the "curse of Canaan" motif of Southern Protestantism. Initially this was employed to explain the origin of black people and to justify slavery, but it later became the theological basis for the Mormon practice of denying the priesthood and prerogatives of the temple to black members. Theological explanations were subsequently extended to embody the Mormon belief in man's premortal existence by asserting that something black people did during their premortal existence determines their birth under the "curse of Canaan."[9]

So once again we recognize the cold pragmatics, the unfeeling opportunism of the American dilemma. What started out to be a significant and hopeful departure from conventional religious morality ended in accepting and promoting what was being resisted. Always it seems that for black people

> Between the idea
> And the reality
> Between the motion
> And the act
> Falls the Shadow[10]

The shadow. The ugly, wearisome, inevitable shadow. It is always there as a creature of "private truth" or "revelation." It is always insubstantial. Incorporeal. Try to deal with a shadow! How do you seize it? How do you pin it down for examination?

The Mormon objections to black people, which developed after their unfortunate confrontation and subsequent capitulation to the slavery interests in Missouri, are summarized by the Reverend Dr. Daniel Poling, religious editor of the National Education Association:

> The essential Mormon interpretation of the Old Testament asserts that the African race descended from Cain. For his crime against his brother, Abel, a "mark" was put upon Cain. Mormon theology teaches the idea that the "mark" was a black skin. Thus the skin color of blacks through all history is enough to condemn them on sight.
>
> Mormon doctrine lists another strike against the black community. According to their belief, the spiritual ancestors of black people failed to perform properly in their pre-existent state. In what Mormons call the "War of Heaven" (in which Lucifer and about one-third of the hosts of heaven were cast down) some groups took a neutral position during this celestial conflict. Mormons are taught that these despised neutrals are the spirits that have inherited black people now living on earth.[11]

So in biblical lore a mark was put on Cain for murdering his brother. But what has the mark on Cain to do with Blackamericans, who already have their hands full trying to cope with contemporary scars without having to take on Cain's problems of three thousand years ago? In a free society where people are judged on their personal merits, where a man can be President while all the members of his family, both lineal and sibling, remain quite ordinary people, the mark on Cain, even if it ever existed, would seem to be of no relevance to the American way we tout to ourselves and to the world. But more than that, nowhere does the Bible say what the mark on Cain was: an extra toe? red hair? a flat nose? yellow skin? blue eyes, perhaps? We do not know. And nowhere do the Scriptures state or even imply a divine intention to isolate Blacks from the dozens of races and ethnic groups by relating them and *them only* to Cain in the Genesis story. The absurdity is further confounded because, according to Genesis, God put the mark on Cain to *protect* him rather than to set him up as a target (Genesis 4:15).

The behavior of our "spiritual ancestors" in some alleged preexistent state is but another case in point. Most of us have not been privileged to know these ancestors, to say nothing of which ones were black and which ones were white or some other color. What we do know is that, whoever they were, we could hardly be held responsible for their behavior. It would be infinitely more logical to punish a parent for a crime yet to be committed by a child yet to be conceived in a world yet to be created.

The Revelation

It is not the Mormon priesthood that is important. There are probably other acceptable ways of realizing the blessings of heaven available to most men, including *black* men. What is important is that a major religious communion in the United States, however inadvertently, has long made a very powerful contribution to our racial problems by maintaining a climate conducive to the sanctification of racism. It is not enough to argue that religion is a private matter. It is. And it isn't. Certainly a man's personal relationship with his God is a private matter. But when personal relationships are influenced by a giant corporation with vast implications for the political, economic, and civil welfare of millions of people, a case for "privacy" is difficult to make. Mormons hold many high offices of public trust in the federal establishment. No matter what their political or professional competence may be, their attitude toward the black citizens they represent can never be a source of comfort until the implications of the promise of the priesthood are publicly and fully manifest. The revelation that couldn't come has come; but the revelation is but the shadow of the substance America longs to see.

On the ninth day of June 1978, the First Presidency of the Mormon Church issued a historic letter from church headquarters in Salt Lake City. The letter said, in part:

> [God] by revelation has confirmed that the long promised day has come when every faithful, worthy man in the Church may receive the holy priesthood . . . including the blessings of the temple. Accordingly, all worthy male members of the Church may be ordained to the priesthood without regard for race or color.[12]

The letter, signed by President Spencer Kimball, went out to Mormon churches all over the world. Many fair-minded Mormons breathed a sigh of relief, for they had found themselves and their church increasingly at odds over the church's official institutionalized racism. Indeed, so outraged were some younger Mormons over the church's refusal to admit black Mormons to the coveted priesthood that their increasingly vocalized criticisms seriously disturbed the very elderly ruling elite.* In 1976, Douglas A. Wallace, a white man and a high priest in the church, deliberately (and without authorization from his bishop) baptized black Mormon Larry Lester in a Portland, Oregon, swimming pool, and ordained Lester a priest. For his troubles, Wallace was excommunicated, and Lester's ordination was declared null and void. But the pressures on the church, internal and external, did not abate. The beleaguered hierarchy had long claimed that a change in its policy of withholding ordination from Blacks could come only by revelation from God, and since it was a divine option, that revelation could not be predicted or assured. Finally, however, the revelation did come; and in good time, as revela-

---

* The Mormon Church is a gerontocracy. It is ruled by a president and a self-perpetuating Council of the Twelve Apostles, in which age is the determining factor of promotion to power. Since the "First Presidency" is for life, it is not unusual for the governing power to be held by men in their eighties and nineties.

tions often do, for the Mormons were preparing for their biggest missionary drive in history—all over the world. At last, America's spiritual hands could bear examination.

Or could they?

The End of an Era? Or the Demise of a Symbol?

What were the less apparent subtleties involved? Why should the ordination to the priesthood in the Mormon Church be a matter of such moment to millions of Americans who had no immediate or personal interest in whether Blacks became Mormon priests or not? One prominent Mormon apologist undoubtedly touched some sensitive nerves with this challenge:

> How many non-LDS critics are truly Christian towards the Negroes? Is it barely possible that those Mormons and non-Mormons who accuse the Church of hypocrisy in this matter are themselves the hypocrites?[13]

It was not that many Americans cared one way or another about Blacks in the Mormon priesthood, but the fact that the Saints adamantly retained an official commitment to racism did muddy the waters of religious tranquillity at a time when most American communions were concerned to present an appearance of racial inclusiveness. Some of those most concerned were Mormons. One of them wrote:

> The doctrine of white-race superiority, so much the vogue in the early nineteenth century when Mormonism had its beginning, has been so thoroughly debunked as to catalogue its adherents today as either grossly uninformed or victims of traditional irrational prejudices, or both. Mormons as a group are not ignorant people; they rank high in formal schooling, with an extraordinarily high proportion of college graduates. Many of them naturally find it difficult to reconcile what they learn in college about racial differences and equalities with the stand taken by their church.[14]

One cannot escape the striking parallel between the devout, well-educated Mormons and the devout, well-educated Afrikaaners of South Africa whose attitudes about race and religion do not seem to reflect either spiritual or intellectual enlightenment. Is it possible that there is a correlation between such distinctive attainments and prejudice? Is this what the American dilemma is really about? In any case, Mormon intransigence was rapidly becoming a source of agitation and protest. Black athletes had rebelled against competing with teams fielded by Mormon universities, and some schools with black athletes had removed Mormon schools from their schedules. Suits had been filed by the NAACP against the Boy Scouts of America for alleged Mormon manipulation of Scout offices, and marches and disruptions had from time to time threatened Mormon-sponsored activities. The public, racially exclusive Mormon policy left some embarrassing blemishes on the surface of American racial reform, and Mormons running for national public office found themselves particularly vulnerable. More than that, ugly racial tensions were beginning to surface again. Black unemployment stood at an all-time high, and in a depressed economy whites who were increasingly anxious about hanging on to their economic prerogatives were impatient with arguments about honorific values which could not be translated into food and shelter. The Ku Klux Klan was boldly and stridently renascent, and racial violence was in the offing in Greensboro, Miami, Philadelphia, and Chattanooga, with no way of telling where the lines would be drawn.

What has been the effect of the change in racial policy enunciated in the Mormon revelation? For the typical American, it is no more than an embarrassing bother that is finally over. We are not unaccustomed to having our racial problems dismissed with solemn public pronouncements long before the hard evidence of that dismissal can be found. It takes time for new ways of thinking and behaving to cure, but in the case of Prophet Kimball's revelation, even the pronouncement fell short of the minimum assurance needed to lift the pall over the black members of the Mormon Church, and by extension over *all* black people. The Cain doctrine which Mormons believe to be crucial to the notion of black unworthiness was not repudiated, and the noisome theories about black neutrality during a mythological war in heaven were also left intact. The ban against inter-marriage with blacks ("lest the curse of Cain be extended to innocent blood") still stands.

When the battle is long and the foe is implacable, any con-cession is victory for the weary. One black college professor admitted:

> I'll praise [Kimball] to the skies. Why not? I don't want to be a Mormon priest. I don't want to be a Mormon. All I ever wanted was them off my back. And they're off . . . The last major organized public racism in this country dropped on Friday.

To him, and to many other Americans, the issue was the removal of the *symbol* of the act; the disavowal of the license to practice evil; the public repudiation of the last major *public* acknowledg-ment of racial chauvinism in a major American religious com-munion. That is not enough. The deficiency of pronouncement alone is symbolized by another black response, this time from a black Mormon in Utah:

> Don't expect me to thank Spencer Kimball. I'll thank Spencer Kimball when he announces that he has a revelation that Mormons will not practice racial hiring. Then I will be elated.[15]

Nevertheless, the revelation has come; the pronouncement has been made, and a black Mormon has been admitted to the priesthood. If the revelation is symbolic of a change in intention as well as in faith, the stage could be set—if much more were done—for a tremendous change in the impact of Mormonism in America and around the world, as America's most embarrassing religious appeal to racial bigotry has finally been officially abandoned.

THE MUSLIMS

The American Context

In the minds of those who believe in Western manifest destiny, the religions of the East, like the peoples of the East, have long since been consigned to the crumbling pages of an exotic past that is over and done with. The ascendancy of the West has always been read as the final devolution of the East. Eight hundred eighty-eight years separate the Battle of Tours from the arrival of the *Mayflower* at Plymouth Rock, and in that interim of nearly a millennium, Islam had long since been displaced in the important concerns of those who found in the New World a chance to fashion a more perfect civilization than that of the Old World from which they came. Although Islam had lingered on in the Spanish peninsula and is said to have been spread among the American Indians by Blacks serving in the Spanish expeditions to the Americas in the sixteenth century,[16] it had never been a serious aspect of the English experience, and the American commonwealth was from the beginning a transplant of the Anglo-Saxon culture and expectations. That original cultural impress has been modified by subsequent immigration, and by the development of an indigenous experience. But it has not been supplanted. Anglo-conformism remains the norm, if not the sine qua non, of American self-perception.

It is clear, then, that the religion of Islam is not in any substantial way a part of the most valued American experience. It has no purchase in America's antecedent European traditions, and it played no part in the principal development of the indigenous American culture. Black slavery and nationally selective immigration policies spoke eloquently of America's intention to reserve the country for Caucasians in general, and West Europeans in particular. In consequence, the development of our Western empire proceeded in what must now be recognized as a deliberate cultural vacuum, denying itself the wisdom and the culture of the East in what may prove to be a vain and shortsighted pursuit of a particular racial chimera that continues to bedevil our best efforts at Judeo-Christian democracy.

While our immigration policies excluded both Asians and Africans, our commercial interests did not. Among the millions of Blacks who came as involuntary immigrants, perhaps as many as twenty percent were Muslims. Exactly how many we shall never know, for the slavemasters had no interest in recording the religious and cultural achievements of their chattels. The slave trade required and maintained a determined myopia regarding the religious interests of its human commodities—first to avoid the queasiness of possibly selling an occasional African Christian, but more often in support of the convenient fiction that the very religious depravity of the Africans made them legitimate targets for spiritual rehabilitation through the tender mercies of chattel slavery. Under that charitable guise, even Africans who might be recognized as Muslims would fare no better than the rest, for Islam, when it was considered at all, was considered the supreme cabal of infidels. In spite of all this, the evidence of a substantial Muslim presence among the American slave population is slowly accumulating, but in South America and the Caribbean the Muslim presence was common enough to be taken for granted, and the cultural impact of Islam remains in high relief in those areas to this day.

In sharp contrast to the prevailing practices in Catholic Latin America, the Anglo-Saxon Protestant hegemony, which defined the culture and religion of our slaveholding South, considered it expedient to suppress *all* African religions of whatever kind. This practice effectively precluded the transmission of the cultic apparatus by means of which religions survive and propagate themselves. Still, accounts persist of Muslim slaves who committed the entire Koran to memory in an effort to keep the faith alive and to pass it on to others.* Ultimately, such heroic efforts were unavailing, of course, for the intransigence of the slave system, buttressed as it was by custom and convention, could not and did not accommodate itself to the recognition of slaves who were exceptional in any way not substantially related to the interests of the master. What the system did provide (after a hundred years of unconcern) was an alternative faith, for as slave generations succeeded each other, scarcely marked except by the momentary discontinuities of birth and death, into the vacuum left

* Such a man was Ayuba Suleiman Abrahima Diallo of Annapolis, Maryland. Diallo, also known as Job ben Solomon, eventually gained his freedom after 1731 through British interests impressed by his knowledge and his strict observance of the Koran.

by the proscribed native African religions, Christianity eventually made its way. It took the better part of a century for the decision to be made to begin; and the beginning was not auspicious.

Such is the backdrop against which black Islam has established a contemporary presence in America. Why "black" Islam? First, because it was the *black* Muslims, the "Moors" among the Spanish conquistadors, who first introduced Islam to the New World. Second, because in the English colonies the *only* Muslim presence was among the slaves imported from black Africa. Third, while there have been small enclaves of European Muslims in America for many decades, their presence has been characterized by clannishness and quietism, not by proselytism or public postures and involvement.

America's white Muslims were a very minor outpost of Islam. They were inundated, to all effects, by the ubiquity of Judeo-Christianity, the spirit and the symbol of Western ascendancy. Perhaps subconsciously they considered themselves logical targets for a Judeo-Christian jihad, unaware, or more likely unconvinced, of the protections afforded all religions by the American Constitution. In any case, they seemed content, or at least constrained, to keep Islam within their ethnic associations. Certainly, the white Muslims provided no more opportunity and even less incentive for black participation in the religion of Islam than the White Church provided for meaningful black involvement in Christianity. And while their respective statuses within the American social structure were hardly analogous, their responses to the black presence were not at all dissimilar.

The Memory of Islam: Behold! a Black Prophet

Fortunately, the image of Islam in America as well as that of Christianity has been gratuitously salvaged to some degree by the black converts' self-recognized spiritual needs, and by the ardent search for religious values which has characterized the black experience. In consequence, Blacks have seldom waited to be appropriated by religion. Instead, they have more often exercised the initiative and gone in search of those spiritual understandings they needed to give meaning and purpose to an otherwise uncertain existence. Their kindest critics have called them religious by nature; those less charitable have labeled them childish and superstitious. Both assessments may be right, for certainly man is born with the capacity for religion; and faith, which is the first condition of the religious life, is also the absence of that presumptiveness which distinguishes the innocence of the child from the cynicism of sophistication.

Perhaps another answer is that in the peculiar devolution of human history the African peoples have had longer than most, and more reasons than many, to ponder the inherent deficits of the human enterprise, and to accept in consequence the principle of contingency as a starting place for the ordering of human life. In any case, if the African, at home or abroad, has exhibited a decided proneness for religion, he has also demonstrated a remarkable capacity to make that religion, whatever its source, uniquely his own, and to make it work for him in terms of his particular needs. When Christianity was introduced to the African in America in the interest of his accommodation to bondage, overlooked was the fact that the African had known Christianity before, *at its source, and from its infancy.* Nor was it anticipated that he might accept the white man's begrudging proffer of the faith without necessarily accepting the white man's interpretation of what was being offered. Today the Black Church stands as a tangible symbol of the distinction between what was given and what was received.

Similarly, the Black Diaspora was no stranger to Islam. As with Christianity, there were disjunctions and separations as the African peoples had their turns and turnabouts in the flux of history. Although the effort was made by those who enslaved them to expunge every vestige of previous religious experience from mind and memory, there is a pervasive quality about religion that defies expunction, a fact well attested to by the African syncretisms which characterize Catholicism in much of South America and the Caribbean, and which gives Protestantism its distinctive flavor in the Black Church in America.

It is probable that the memory of Islam, however tenuous, was never completely lost to the slave experience. On the other hand, the major black Christian denominations were formed long before the Civil War, and though routinely denigrated by the White Church, they were at least a recognized part of the Christian community. If they were considered exotic, it was because they were black—not because they were alien—a problem Islam could not and did not escape.

There was no room and no requirement for a new religion for black people in post-Civil War America. The Black Church, divided between Methodist and Baptist denominations, offered the newly emancipated Blacks the chance for self-respect in the form of religious self-determination, the opportunity to *belong*— to be part of an existing, independent black spiritual confraternity. Drawn by so heady and so novel an opportunity, and pushed by the white churches in which they had previously held a debased and segregated membership, the new Blackamericans surged out of the White Church and became proud members of their own *black* churches: the African Methodist Episcopal Church; the Colored Methodist Episcopal Church; the National Baptist Convention, Inc.; and so on. Through all this, the memory of Islam persisted, but there was no occasion for its development. It was to be another half century before that memory would find vocal and physical expression among the hapless Blacks struggling for a negotiable identity and searching for their cultural roots.

In 1913, a black "prophet" from North Carolina established a Moorish Science Temple in Newark, New Jersey. Timothy Drew was not an educated man, but he had somehow learned enough about Islam to consider it the key to what would be called "black liberation" fifty years later. Islam was the religion of the Moors, the black conquerors from Africa who once overran part of Europe. How could anyone with such a heritage suffer the debasement which was the common lot of Blacks in America? Drew had no training in the social sciences, but he did have the perception to realize that there is a definite relationship between what you are called and how you are perceived, and between how you are perceived and how you are treated. "It is in the name," he concluded. The black man's problems began with his accepting a pejorative nomenclature. Drew, who was born in 1866 and given the Christian name Timothy, proceeded to give himself a name indicative of his "Moorish" heritage—Noble Drew Ali. His followers were no longer to be known as Negroes or Africans but as Moorish-Americans, thus preserving their recently won American citizenship but making explicit their Islamic heritage. Each "Moor" was issued an appropriate name and an identity card making clear his religious and political status in a society where "Negroes," however pronounced their Christian pretensions, were not generally held in high esteem.

Drew's movement spread to Pittsburgh, Detroit, Chicago, and a number of cities in the South. Although it made use of the Koran and what was known of the more exotic paraphernalia of Islam, such as the wearing of the fez and the adoption of Muslim names, Noble Drew Ali's movement was essentially a melange of black nationalism and Christian revivalism, with an awkward, confused patina of the teachings of the Prophet Muhammed. It was not Islam, but it signified a dim awareness of Islam. Ali died of mysterious causes in 1929, possibly of injuries received in a beating by the Chicago police. Thereafter, the movement languished, splintered, and was succeeded by a more vigorous and a more imaginative and demanding version of Islam led by Elijah Muhammed.

The Nation of Islam: Elijah Muhammad

Elijah Muhammad was born Elijah Poole in Sandersville, Georgia, on October 7, 1897. One of the thirteen children born to an itinerant Baptist preacher, Poole was destined to become one of the most controversial religious leaders of his time. But, controversy aside, he must be reckoned among the more remarkable religious leaders of the twentieth century. He made a considerable contribution to the dignity and self-esteem of the black undercaste. Beyond that, and more far-reaching in its implications, is the fact that it was Elijah Muhammad who must be credited with the serious reintroduction of Islam in America in modern times, giving it the mystique and thrust without which it could scarcely have penetrated the American bastion of Judeo-Christianity. After more than a hundred years, orthodox Islam in America had not reached the masses, white or black, and was scarcely known to exist before the Black Muslims, Elijah's Nation of Islam, proclaimed his Message to the Black Man in the name of Allah.

Elijah learned what he knew of Islam from the shadowy, mysterious evangelist who went by a variety of aliases, but who was most popularly known as Wali Farad, or Wallace Fard. Fard claimed to have come from the Holy City of Mecca on a mission of redemption and restoration of the Blacks in America. He taught that members of the black African Diaspora were all of Muslim heritage, "lost-found members of the tribe of Shabazz." The essence of his message was that black debasement had occurred over the centuries because Blacks were separated from the knowledge of Allah and the knowledge of self. They were estranged from the one true God to whom they owed allegiance, and ignorant of their own history and their previous high status in the hierarchy of human achievement. The problem was to restore the truth to the Lost-Found Nation, the only truth that could make Blacks free. This was the formidable task assumed by Elijah Muhammad when, after three years of preaching, Fard ostensibly returned to Mecca after designating Elijah "Messenger of Allah."

In his own words, Elijah set out to "cut the cloak to fit the cloth." Previously, there had been no spiritual options, because there had been no available religious traditions or models except Judeo-Christianity. Elijah undertook to redress these deficits. His methods were sometimes ad hoc, and usually controversial, but they were always addressed to the reality that the Blacks in America were the pawns of other *people*, not the playthings of the gods; and that the same kinds of cultural mythologies which were used to keep them debased could also be used to free them and give them dignity and power. Against him was a formidable array of forces, not the least of which were three hundred and fifty years of solid Christian tradition in an avowedly self-conscious Christian society which routinely appealed to the faith as a justification of black oppression.

Elijah's initial parish was the slums, the black ghettos of the industrial cities; and his potential converts were the slum-created outcasts of a developing technocratic society. His targets were those who were most battered by racism and stifled by powerlessness, and whose experience of the white man's "invincibility" made the acceptance of black inferiority seem as reasonable as it was pervasive. The black intellectuals would scorn Elijah, and white-appointed black leaders would denounce him; the Christian church would oppose him, and the local enclaves of orthodox "white" Islam would repudiate him. But Elijah Muhammad was not only charismatic; he showed none of the fear and caution characteristic of more prudent black leaders. When harassed by federal agents, local police, and others determined to silence him, he declared:

> I am the Messenger. . . . I am guided by God. I am in communication with God. . . . If God is not with me . . . protecting me, how can I come and say things no other man has said?[17]

Muhammad drew freely on the Bible, on religious and secular mythology, and on the lore of his own experience. He met his converts where they were, ministering as far as he could to a spectrum of needs which transcended the spiritual to find their cruelest expression in more immediate psychological, economic, social, and political needs. His official book was the Koran. His law was the *lex talionis:*

> Never be the aggressor; never look for trouble; but if any man comes to take advantage of you lay down your life, and the whole planet Earth will respect you.[18]

His God was the same one he knew as a Baptist preacher, a fighting God bent on vengeance and the liberation of his people. Elijah proclaimed him to be "a *black* God whose right and proper name is 'Allah'!"

Elijah Muhammad did not achieve orthodoxy for his Nation of Islam, but orthodoxy was not his goal. What he did achieve for the first time in our history was a pronounced public awareness of a religion called Islam. Temples or mosques sprang up in a hundred cities where none had existed before. Suddenly there was a visible, exotic religious presence in the form of a hundred thousand Black Muslims—conspicuous in their frequent rallies and turnouts, and in their grocery stores and restaurants and bakeries and other small businesses. The clean-shaven young Muslims hawking their newspapers on the streets, celebrating their rituals in the prisons, debating their beliefs in the media gave to the religion of Islam a projection and a prominence undreamed of in Christian North America. Suddenly the prison warden and the social workers and the people who depended on black labor were saying that the Nation of Islam had done a better job of rehabilitating the black underclass than all the official agencies addressed to that task. And it was frequently argued in the black community that the Black Muslims had done more to exemplify black pride and dignity, and to foster group unity, than some of the more reputable middle-class organizations.

By the time Elijah died in 1975, the Nation of Islam was no longer exclusively a community of the poor and the fallen. With Malcolm X as its chief public representative, the Nation had attracted a substantial number of college students and a small element of black intellectuals and numerous former Christian ministers. A large number of celebrities of the world of sports and entertainment, clearly influenced by the Nation, became Muslims, even though they tended to affiliate with the more orthodox branches of Islam. A notable exception was Cassius Clay, who, following his recruitment by Malcolm X, became world champion of heavyweight boxing and was given the Muslim name Muhammad Ali by Elijah Muhammad.

Under Elijah Muhammad, the Nation of Islam became the prevailing Islamic presence in America. It was not orthodox Islam, but it was by all reasonable judgments *proto-Islam;* and therein lies a religious significance that may well change the direction of history in the West. After shaping and guiding the Nation of

Islam for more than forty years, Elijah Muhammad passed the mantle of leadership to Wallace Deen Muhammad, his fifth son. But Wallace Muhammad was destined to walk in his own way rather than in the path of his father.

Toward Orthodoxy: The First Imam

Immediately following his election as Chief Minister of the Nation of Islam, Wallace Muhammad began the decultification of the following he had inherited from Elijah. In the cult phenomenon, few successors are able to hold intact the disparate forces controlled by a charismatic founder, and Wallace was no exception. The transition of power was neither complete nor fully successful, and while the movement did not shatter upon his succession, as was widely predicted, there was dissatisfaction, disillusionment, and an inevitable erosion of membership. An undetermined segment of the Nation either drifted free from involvement or elected to follow the independent movement of Minister Louis Farrakhan. Farrakhan, who succeeded Malcolm X as Elijah's chief spokesman, became the most prominent exponent of the original teachings of Elijah Muhammad. Whatever the fortunes of Islamic orthodoxy, Farrakhan's movement (which retained the name Nation of Islam) will scarcely be affected, because for the millions of Blacks whose lot has not been measurably improved by the cosmetics of racial change, the vision of Elijah Muhammad's Nation of Islam still represents a self-determined identity and a tangible effort at reversal. And it remains a visible expression of the rage and hostility that still pervades significant segments of the black undercaste. To the Nation of Islam it is quite clear that the denied and the disinherited are still black; the deniers and the disinheritors are still white; and Armageddon* remains an inevitable necessity if things are to change.

---

* Elijah Muhammad taught that the "Armageddon," a final clash between the forces of good (i.e., Blacks) and the forces of evil (i.e., Whites), must take place "in the wilderness of North America" before the Black Nation could be fully restored.

Confirmed in his leadership role as successor to Elijah Muhammad, Wallace himself is recognized as orthodox, and as First Imam of what is now called the American Muslim Mission. The Imam has made it clear that his first priority is to eradicate completely the black nationalist image so carefully nurtured by Elijah and to establish complete orthodoxy for the cult Elijah fathered and made internationally famous as the Nation of Islam. If Wallace, fluent in Arabic and well known and respected in the Muslim capitals of Asia and Africa, can bring the erstwhile Nation of Islam into fully recognized communion with international Islam, he will have accomplished a master objective for the rapid expansion of Islam on the North American continent. A prominently visible, orthodox Muslim community in the United States would have political, social, and economic implications which in time might well be expected to reverberate far beyond the ghetto which gave it birth, a possibility for which the traditional American religious community has done little, if anything, to prepare.

Perhaps the most imponderable obstacle between orthodoxy and the Nation of Islam is not the opposition of the purist keepers-of-the-gate inside Islam but the far more elusive and impalpable body of tradition that defines black religion in general. Black religion derives, in the first instance, from that aspect of the black experience which found it difficult to resolve the apparent incongruities between Christianity and black slavery. It was not only a repudiation of the concept that slavery was acceptable to God, but black religion has always been a critical medium through which the black community has institutionalized its efforts at black liberation. Inevitably, this has meant a certain estrangement of the Black Church from *Christian* orthodoxy as understood and practiced by the White Church, for the salient tradition of black religion has always been the sufficiency of its own insight.

Since practically all members of the Nation of Islam (and its successor organizations) trace their religious origins to the Black Church, there is little reason to believe that the notion of orthodoxy is of overwhelming significance for most of them.

Further, since orthodox Islam is no stranger to the enslavement of Blacks, even in contemporary times, in the minds of those who came to the faith through the Nation of Islam, Islamic orthodoxy may well be viewed as the Islamic counterpart of white Christianity—a possibility certainly not overlooked in the careful strategies of Elijah Muhammad. Since the black experience has provided more than sufficient reason to question orthodox interpretations of the faith, *feeling*—the *direct* experience of the Divine rather than the official formulas and prescriptions of the experts—is the hallmark of black religion.

There is impressive evidence that Wallace Deen Muhammad has given such problems painstaking scrutiny as he determines his strategy for making Islam the major religion in America after Christianity.* The catalogue of changes he has accomplished to date includes radical modifications of doctrine, structure, and administration; changes of name, style, role, and office. Moreover, official attitudes about race, political involvement, and military service have all been revised to reflect a strictly normative American stance. The Fruit of Islam was disbanded. Key elements underpinning Elijah Muhammad's mythological doctrines have been allegorized, reinterpreted, or quietly abandoned. And the "blue-eyed arch-enemy," the "white devils," are now welcomed into the mosques as brothers. The American flag is displayed in every Muslim school, and the Pledge of Allegiance is made before morning prayers.

Ministers of Islam are now imams; temples of Islam are called mosques, or masajid, and Wallace himself is now Warith Deen Muhammad. The fast of Ramadan is rescheduled to coincide with the lunar calendar used by other Muslims throughout the world. The roles of women are upgraded, military service is no longer forbidden, and believers are urged to take an active part in the civil process. The name American Muslim Mission, the

---

* Such a projection assumes that since Judaism has only about six million adherents in the U.S., it could be numerically eclipsed in relatively short order by a crusading Islam. But such a projection must also be encouraged by a significantly increased Muslim immigration brought on by recent changes in our national political and economic policies.

Imam explains, which "speaks more to our aspirations and thrust," became official in 1980. "My greatest desire," the Imam has said, "is to one day hear that a Muslim, a real Muslim, a genuine Muslim from our Community has become a governor, or senator, or head of some big corporation."[19]

Imam Warith Deen Muhammad's "desire" and Reverend Martin Luther King's "dream" are in essence quite similar. They both want for their people the participation in the American Dream that other American citizens take for granted. How strange it is, and how sad, that the route to participation is so circuitous, and still remains uncertain. The Black Muslims originated in protest against the exclusion of black people from the American Dream, and as an attempt to find an alternative route to participation. Elijah Muhammad was canny enough to tap the only source of proto-power there was in the black community—*black religion*. He looked at the paralyzing effects of the white man's mythology and created a countermythology of his own. He deposed the traditional white God and dared to install a black God in his place. He denied the white man's reading of history and substituted a black history filled with the glories of black achievement. He made the white man a "blue-eyed devil" in place of all of the black devils the West had conjured up for centuries. And he announced the coming destruction of the whole devil-race at Armageddon, as a Righteous God metes out justice to those who oppressed his people. Then Elijah stood forth in the midst of the icons he had toppled and announced:

> I am the man. . . .
> I am not trembling.[20]

It worked.

The black ghetto was electrified. Blacks recovered a measure of dignity; whites found new respect for them, and when it became clear that every Muslim response called for an eye for an eye, public harassment declined dramatically. Suddenly it was beautiful to be black; and suddenly in those cities where the Nation of Islam could fill the streets with hordes of clean-shaven, well-disciplined Muslims, the power establishment from the governor's mansion to the petty politicians and moguls of industry paid their respect to Elijah Muhammad and courted his favor. But, for all that, few doors of consequence were opened. Elijah's greatest achievement was to expose to black people the true nature of their bondage, to help them regain their dignity, to show them that in solidarity there is strength, that in strength there is *power*, and that there is nothing oppression respects more.

Warith Deen Muhammad's search for the Dream transcends the parochial approaches of Noble Drew Ali and Elijah Muhammad. For the older men, the goal was to create an oasis of independence in a desert of contingency—to develop, if possible, a kind of immunity for themselves and for their followers by repudiating one identity and claiming another. This could work within limits (as it did with the Nation of Islam), not because the enemy believed in the identity claimed, but because the *faithful* believed in it. Having shucked off the image of guilt and worthlessness consigned by a slavery-oriented Christianity, Elijah's black followers were free to become what they perceived themselves to be. But the process of becoming can be both long and hazardous. And in the meantime there was no outside agency of reference or corroboration to bolster the transition should it be challenged or meet with difficulties. Hence, the Nation of Islam, whatever its successes, would always be contained.

Warith Deen Muhammad's struggle for orthodoxy is, first of all, a struggle to break through the double isolation involved in being black in white America and Muslim in the citadel of Western Christianity. Both Warith and his predecessor were aware from the beginning that there is a world beyond the West, but while Elijah's claims to affiliation and affinity with the world of Islam were both tentative and pro forma, Warith Muhammad fully intends to enlist that world by enlisting in it. If he is successful, the isolation of black Muslims qua Muslims will of course be transcended in the international fellowship of the Islamic faith. Today, as a result of the modification of our immigration policies, our economic and military interests in the Middle East, the influx of Muslim students, and the continued growth of indigenous black Islam, it is reliably estimated that there are between two and three million Muslims in the United States. At the present rate of growth, the Muslims will soon be our third largest religious presence following the Protestants and Catholics. How this will affect a religious climate which has always considered Blacks a class apart awaits the determination of history, but there is a convention that every new religious option makes the neglected soul more dear. In that case, Islam may well play a vital part, direct and indirect, in the reconstruction of our traditional attitudes about race and religion.

THE JEWS

Among the more pernicious effects of the continuing dilemma is the tragic shift in the relations between Blacks and Jews that is popularly known as the Black–Jewish encounter. The word "encounter" is both inaccurate and provocative: inaccurate because it conveys the subtle notion that Blacks and Jews are (finally!) engaged in an ethnic vendetta which, if it proceeds, will produce the effective destruction of at least one of them; provocative because to repeatedly suggest an encounter is to create one.

There is no Black–Jewish *encounter*. There is a Black–Jewish *discovery* which could lead to a mutually disastrous encounter if Black and Jewish leadership proves too dull, too shortsighted, and too certain of what has never before proven to be a sure thing. That discovery is that, while Blacks and Jews compete for the same values, they are differently equipped for contention. What remains for Black–Jewish leadership to make clear to their respective camps is that their contention is not necessarily with each other, or for any one indivisible prize. In America, there is enough for all. (Isn't that why we are all here in the first place?) The problem is that Jews and Blacks have never really gotten to know each other beyond the stereotypes on which our national dilemma feeds and fattens. In the critical days ahead, Jews and Blacks will have to look beyond convention and rethink the new roles and attitudes they must adopt to be in consonance with the very changes they labored together to bring about.

> Look back if you would plot the course ahead
> For past and future in life's grand design
> Are tethered by one solitary line
> And what will be is anchored in what was
> For nothing is except it finds its cause
> In what has gone before.[21]

The way in which Jews and Blacks have experienced each other in their common pilgrimage from exclusion toward increased participation in the full range of options and values considered normative to the assimilated society is the history of cooperation and conflict between two subcultures with superficially similar but fundamentally disparate experiences. In the context of history, they have met before, but under circumstances not precisely replicated in their American experience. Jews and Blacks are not strangers to each other. Their Western experience is in some sense but a resumption of a relationship that is rooted in antiquity, and documented in biblical and secular lore.

Into the Melting Pot

In the undisciplined idealism of the men and women who launched the American experiment in the seventeenth century, this new outpost of Western development was destined to become a supercivilization of European cultural eclecticism under the controlling imprimatur of the Anglo-Saxon experience. Two hundred years later, the rhetoric of politics and the premature conclusions of insufficiently tested social theory proclaimed America to be a vast melting pot from which countless millions of immigrants—Germans, Italians, Poles, Czechs, Irish, Scandinavians, and others—would emerge, after proper seasoning, a new entity: *American.* Was it not Emma Lazarus, a Spanish Jew, who wrote the official welcome a confident America inscribed on the Statue of Liberty, the nation's symbol of its perceived destiny to mold and give to the world a new civilization and a new people? Here is the challenge to the Old Country:

> Give me your tired, your poor,
> your teeming millions
> yearning to breathe free . . .

And so they came by the millions in search of the promise of being American in America. All that was required was to be white, European, and possessed of the urge to merge, that is, to have a certain eagerness to be melted, as it were, into conformity with the developing American archetype.

It is evident by hindsight, of course, that there were some immigrants for whom the urge to merge held no attraction. These were the dissidents who left the Old Country less with the intent of being molded into New Americans than with the hope of finding the freedom to be left in peace to be what they were. The notion of being shorn of their treasured cultural or ethnic identity and melted into an anonymous general population was particularly abhorrent to some of the European expatriates. Inevitably, they paid the price for their recalcitrance; and, indeed, some continue to pay to this day. Still others found the melting process to be effective mainly in the imaginations of the True Believers. There were barriers to assimilation, some of them formidable. Perhaps the new way could be for their children, or for their children's children. But not for themselves. For themselves, it was perhaps better to give priority to more immediate needs, keep to their own communities, and look after their own in the traditional ways they knew best. These, too, paid a price—for their defeatism and their doubt.

But for the Old Settlers and those who wanted to be mistaken for such, assimilation via careful Anglo-conformism was the narrow gate to the *real* America and to being *real* Americans. It was the surest path to the American Dream. If the assimilation process was slow and uncertain, it could be catalyzed by certain strategies calculated to more speedily close the gap between the dream and reality. For example, if one were both enterprising and determined, he could swallow his accent, adopt a new religion, and Americanize his name by dropping the last syllable or two. More than that, if the new dream was worth more than an old identity, he could even forswear the comforts of endogamy and take an "American" wife.

The point is that people, or more accurately, *certain people*, could indeed be melted and assimilated, but like so many other theories of human behavior, the melting-pot theory was notable for its exceptions. It did not take into account what could (and did) happen to millions of European immigrants; and excluded from its purview altogether, of course, was the black experience in America. The melting-pot theory was politically and morally misleading, and it provided the grounds for a multitude of false assumptions which still condition our thinking about why some have made it in America and some have not.

At the height of the European immigration to America in the late nineteenth century, Blacks already constituted a sizable population. But it goes without repeating that their peculiar disabilities barred them from assimilation into the general population. To call them American was to observe a political courtesy scarcely grounded in reality. It did not seem to matter that, unlike the immigrants from Europe, Blacks spoke the language, having learned it over three centuries of intimacy with the oldest of the Old Settlers. They had no unpleasant accents, only the approved regional inflections of the indigenous Old Stock. While it is said that Episcopalianism was a very potent religious catalyst for the more impatient Europeans who were willing to convert, the Blacks, who had long since become Methodists and Baptists, saw little need to reconvert. Nor did they have to worry about changing their names, for their given names were principally from the Bible or from the familiar legends of Greece and Rome, and their surnames were the proprietary symbols of the families who founded and ruled the country. And as for exogamy as a strategy of assimilation, it was hardly an available option in any case.

In spite of all this, it was inevitable that some Blacks would want to test some of the options available to others, law and convention notwithstanding. While Europeans often changed their names and not infrequently their religion, assimilation-minded Blacks simply changed their race. Unlike national or ethnic identity, *race* in the United States is primarily a matter of complexion. *Nobody sees the genes!* Continuous racial miscegenation from the earliest times created and sustained a substantial pool of fair-skinned men and women who, once outside their immediate environments, could, Janus-like, look either way for a racial identity. Under the pressures of expedience, thousands passed back and forth across the color line at will. Many still do, although new feelings of ethnic pride, and the amelioration of some of the most offensive and inconvenient forms of segregation, have lessened the urgency to escape the onus of blackness by passing. Nevertheless, it is not unreasonable to suggest that over the generations of our common experience in America, through the simple act of passing, enough black people have become white people to seriously qualify the meaning of being white. If, as the laws and conventions dealing with the matter commonly declared it to be, a person having "any Negro blood whatever is, with all his descendants, a member of the Negro race," then race in America is not a state of being; it is a matter of speculation about American sexual history. Certainly it would be inexpedient for many Americans to search too closely for their roots should our technology ever perfect a reliable racial spectroscope. The anxieties our racial purists would suffer under the most casual probings might prove unbearable, and the whole society might well stand in need of immediate reclassification.

Passing for white was the most effective option available to some Blacks intent on escaping the disabilities of race. And, by tradition, it was and is the best-kept racial secret, and a prized source of in-group ridicule and humor regarding the pretensions of whites who are not as lily-white as they would prefer to believe. Another option suggested by the Jews' apparent ability to escape harassment on religious grounds (although certainly less apparent to the Jews) was sufficiently impressive to a very small minority of Blacks to suggest that their own condition might be relieved with a public change of faith. What they were after, of course, was a *cultural* identity which they confused with religion, which appeared to be its most salient characterization. Hence, Blacks who were physically incapable of changing their race were not altogether lost. Perhaps changing their religion, if not the best option, might at least improve the chances for escape from the white man's imposition of Negroness. To be a Jew, or to be a Moor, or a Muslim, was certain to provide a more effective insulation from abuse than being merely black.

Black Jews

In 1969 *Time* magazine reported that there were about 350,000 black Jews in the United States.* While this figure is almost certainly inflated, the report that there are *any* black Jews in America probably came as a shock to many within and without the Jewish communion. But Blacks have had a long association with Judaism. The Falashes of Ethiopia date back to the sixth century B.C., tracing their origins to Solomon and the Queen of Sheba. In America there is a scattering of Black Jews in the congregations of a few white synagogues, but the major concentrations are found in three principal all-black sects known as the Black Jews, the Black Hebrews, and the Black Israelites. These groups vary in their interpretation of Orthodox Judaism, but all believe that they are "true" Jews who have been trapped in the interstices of history and alienated from their heritage and their destiny.

Most black Jews look forward to an eventual return to their "homeland"—Israel—and since 1969 at least a thousand Black Israelites have migrated, or attempted to migrate, to Israel. The Israeli Law of Return makes it mandatory to accept anyone born of a Jewish mother, or Jewish converts who are not members of any other religion and who seriously pursue the practice of Judaism. The first few hundred Blacks were admitted to the country and given the privileges of immigrants while their claims were reviewed. However, it is reported that the Black Israelites

---

* *The Negro Almanac* (1971) puts the figure at 44,000.

managed to become their own worst enemies. They soon let it be known that they, not the white Israelites, were the only true Jews, and that they were but the vanguard of millions like themselves who would eventually arrive to claim their ancient homeland. After that, the Israelis' reception turned from tentative to decidedly hostile. No more Black Israelites were admitted under any circumstances, and privileges, including jobs, housing, and education, were withdrawn from those already there. By the middle 1970s, only a handful of Black Israelites remained in Israel, and these faced deportation if they did not leave voluntarily. They adamantly refused to "convert" to Judaism—claiming that they could not become what they already were.

The Starting Lines and the Color of Privilege

The Blackamericans who opted for assimilation by changing their race or their religion are an intriguing facet of the American dilemma, but they are not our present focus of interest. Nor are those Jews who compromised *their* identity and forfeited their history by changing their names and becoming Protestants or Catholics. It is the Blacks and the Jews who have remained Blacks and Jews who are the principals now involved in the Black–Jewish collision of interests. They are both avidly in pursuit of the American Dream, but the pursuit has been on different terms and under disparate circumstances, for they have arrived at their present state of relationships via different routes and through a vastly different set of experiences. Historically, the Blackamerican has simply wanted to be *American*. Period. But American racism has always clouded that possibility, requiring the Blacks to rethink the whole question of identity and its meaning in America. Historically, the Jew, too, has wanted to be American, but what he really wanted to be was an American *Jew*. There is a difference. For most Jews, the options for entering the American mainstream at the sacrifice of religious and cultural identity were not attractive, although there is recent evidence that "Jewishness" is not a high priority for many contemporary youths from Jewish families. But to black people it has often seemed that the Jew has been able to have it both ways. He could be "Jewish" when he pleased. Or he could just be "white." Whatever disabilities he suffered seemed to Blacks to be relative.

While such a view is undoubtedly simplistic, it is nonetheless true that anti-Semitism in America has always been mild in comparison to the hatred and disablement of Blacks. In the first place, the American dislike for the Jew was essentially a second-hand experience. Folk anti-Semitism, it was called. Oppression of Jews was something that occurred elsewhere; i.e., in the ghettos of Europe, or the Soviet Union. It was something Americans read about, or learned about from non-Jewish immigrants, or from the Jews themselves; but there was little evidence that the American religious ethos was compromised to any significant degree by European-style anti-Semitism. J. R. Marcus, a noted Jewish historian, reveals that "there was probably not a single law in the land in the eighteenth century that had been enacted for the purpose of imposing a disability on Jews alone,"[22] and that Jews were often socially preferable to Roman Catholics. Nor were they particularly singled out for physical assault, if our sordid record of extra-legal violence means anything, although they experienced heckling and taunts from the nativists, as did other ethnics. But of the recorded 3,200 lynchings in America between 1889 and 1919, 2,522 of the victims were black. Only one was a Jew.°

It is undoubtedly true that the facility with which the Jew has been able to appropriate his host culture, improve it, and make himself comfortable in it, while retaining his own peculiar identity, has for centuries been a continuing irritant wherever he has gone. But in the United States, where a newly developing civilization was at stake, the Jew's creative industriousness was

---

° R. G. Weisbord and Arthur Stein, in *Bittersweet Encounter,* point out n a footnote that one other Jew (Leo Frank) was lynched along with a Black in Tennessee in 1868, twenty-one years prior to the beginning of the NAACP compilations. Two other Jews, Andrew Goodman and Michael Schwerner, along with black James Chaney, were lynched in Mississippi in 1964.

too important to be forfeited, and his religious and cultural aberrations could be tolerated so long as his numbers were small and his contributions were great. Rabbi Louis Finkelstein, retired president of New York's Jewish Theological Seminary, once recalled: "Each pilgrim who crossed the Atlantic received sanctuary. Yet, he did not come empty handed. For bearing his gifts, his skills, his talents, his genius, he freely and gladly offered them to the land of his adoption. . . . the land that is their beloved home."[23]

In short, "given the conventional measure of success in America, the Jew has succeeded. . . . He has 'made it,' " at least in his own estimation, as Jewish scholars Robert G. Weisbord and Arthur Stein attest. "This is not to say that millions of Americans do not harbor hostility toward Jews," Weisbord and Stein would caution us. "They do. . . . But who can deny that Jews are privileged, not deprived? In the main they are comfortably ensconced as members of America's bourgeoisie. . . . If Jews live in ghettos today, they are golden ghettos for the most part, and Jews live there by choice."[24]

Blacks came to America under considerably different circumstances. They, too, had gifts, skills, talents, and genius which benefited America three hundred years. And for free. And they, too, adopted America and tried to make it *their* beloved home. But America was having none of that. If the Jews were welcomed, the Blacks were not, and their total rejection was rooted deeply in guilt and economic interest. The white man enslaved the African, and has sought ever since to justify that behavior. Black labor, while absolutely indispensable to the early survival of the American commonwealth, was eventually locked in an inverse relationship to European immigration and developing technology. As the need for black labor declined, the black presence and all it signified became more and more onerous, and less and less tolerable. In consequence, guilt, fear, and the need for justification all contributed to the severity of the oppression directed toward Blacks. The new Americans from Europe, anxious to prove worthy of the new lease on life America meant for them, sometimes outdid themselves in being more American than their hosts in keeping the Blacks in their place. Some Jews were inevitably a part of this performance, although the whole Jewish scenario is exceedingly complex and subject to oversimplification. The Jews, more than any other group, came to America with a profound appreciation of their own history and a peculiar body of religious and cultural preconceptions derived from it. Perhaps "the Jew . . . unaware of the great expectations his history aroused, unconscious of the fact that his only ritually remembered thralldom made him seem a brother to the Negro, simply viewed the black man as other white men did. The result was that when the two did meet, their very different images of each other and their contradictory concepts of their relationship bewildered the Jews and infuriated the Negroes."[25]

The confusion marked by this Jewish "bewilderment" and black "fury" escalated sharply after World War II. As the two minorities have pursued their respective destinies, their perceptions of themselves and of each other have been inevitably affected by the disparate circumstances which have conditioned that pursuit. Their separate priorities of needs and interests and their respective strategies for realizing them have underscored their differences, and their pool of recognized common interests has progressively diminished. There seems to be a growing belief among Jews that Blacks have become anti-Semitic. On the other hand, many Blacks see this alleged black anti-Semitism as nothing more than a product of Jewish guilt over the Jews' progressive abandonment of the civil rights cause. To many Blacks it seems that the Jews have often secured their new status by making common cause with white racism against the Blacks who remain in the struggle. This is the critical point of misunderstanding between Blacks and Jews. Many Jews appear to feel that their open (and sometimes lonely) support of black causes in the past should in effect provide them with some immunity from black rage when Jews themselves assume the role of oppressor. But Blacks are likely to view *any* Jewish oppression as being doubly damnable because it is two-faced. In most instances, there is probably no bad faith on either side, but merely a collision of interests exacerbated by the racial prism through which all our relations are refracted. In such cases, Blacks are no more reacting to Jews as "Semitic" than Jews are reacting to Blacks as "Christians." The issues are much more likely to be economic and visceral than they are to be cultural or religious.

In their carefully researched volume on Black–Jewish relations, Weisbord and Stein have found that historically

> Jews were certainly not in the front ranks of the oppressors of the Negro. Neither were they in the vanguard of his defenders. . . . Finding themselves in a precarious situation, Southern Jews for the most part tried to be as inconspicuous and as inoffensive as possible. Despite the tragic European past of their own people, they must have found it extremely difficult to identify with their degraded, dark-skinned neighbors. If they were able to empathize at all, practical circumstances prevented Southern Jews from demonstrating their concern.[26]

But Norman Podhoretz, a Jewish intellectual who once edited the very influential *Commentary* magazine in New York City, is quite candid about the repugnance he feels about black people, even though he is far removed in time and circumstance from those Jews who lived in the slaveholding South two or three centuries ago. Says Podhoretz, who grew up in Brooklyn "fearing and hating Negroes":

> The hatred I still feel for Negroes is the hardest of all the old feelings to face or admit, and it is the most hidden and the most overloaded. . . . It no longer has . . . any cause or justification. . . . I know it from the insane rage that can stir me at the thought of Negro anti-Semitism, I know it from the disgusting prurience that can stir in me at the sight of a mixed couple.[27]

While it is doubtful that Podhoretz's fear and hatred of Blacks can be rationalized, or that it is systemic within the Jewish community, it does illustrate another important difference between Blacks and Jews which ramifies in a disparity of contemporary perspectives, including Podhoretz's problem with mixed couples. The black man is a readily recognizable target, and if the con-

ventional opinion held by Blacks that the Jew can change identity
at his convenience is somewhat overdrawn, it at least has some
basis in fact. White is the color of privilege in America. *Anybody*
who is white is automatically presumed to warrant certain
prerogatives, privileges, and protections. Anyone who is black is
not. The Jew does not have to take advantage of his color. It is
an advantage thrust upon him. "Only in America," writes Jewish
historian Lenora Berson, "was the Jew a white man."*

This assertion notwithstanding, prevailing Jewish sentiment
takes being "white" for granted and goes to some pains to make it
clear that, being white, individual Jews have behaved more or
less like other whites, and that they have been neither better nor
worse than other whites with whom they are associated. Unfortunately, this may not be the most viable basis on which to rest
the Black–Jewish relationship, for it seems to imply that being
white creates a license for the abuse of black people, or that it
makes that abuse less offensive.

The problem is probably exacerbated even more by the distinction that Blacks have always made, informally, but quite
definitely, between "Jews" and "white people." However the
Jews see themselves, most Blacks seldom think of them in terms
other than their Jewishness, as Blacks perceive it. Jews are
almost never seen simply as "white," and the conventional
understanding of white oppression does not usually include the
Jew except where Jewish identity is blurred by circumstances.
To the typical black man-in-the-street, Black–Jewish relations are
of a distinctive order, usually more benign, and without the
threat to black existence that always underlies black-white
relations.

---

* Weisbord and Stein declare: "Even if white Gentile America had desired
to set the Jew completely apart enforcement would have been difficult for
an obvious reason—the Jew is white." Black tradition ordinarily places the
Jew somewhere between white and black on a racial spectrum. The belief
that Jews are "covert Negroes" is very strong in black folklore and traditional black humor. In contemporary times there is still a residual ambivalence about Jewish racial identity which inevitably affects black perceptions
about Jewish behavior.

The Perils of Success

In recent times, however, the traditional view of Jews held by most Blacks has been severely strained by the fact that not only do Jews increasingly appear to stress their "white" identity but Jews have at the same time become increasingly visible in the white power structure. This could mean simply that the Jewish strategy for infiltration is working, a strategy against a common problem which might well be applauded if it also means that Jews will still remember their traditional alliance with Blacks, and now intend to work from the inside in the common interest. But what if the Jew, feeling himself fully accepted as white, now decides to *be* white, to act out his new identity? What happens to the traditional Black–Jewish understanding? Blacks are apprehensive about how the Jew is going to deal with the success of acceptance, and they are often resentful of what they anticipate.

Will success spoil Joe Goldberg? That is the question Blacks are nervous about. Some already perceive a new Jewish hard line toward Blacks, and they attribute it to the supposition that since the Jews have finally arrived, and Blacks are no longer needed as levers for their advancement, then Blacks are expendable. In consequence, the argument goes, the sooner Blacks learn to go it alone, or to look elsewhere for allies, the better off they will be.

What appears to Blacks as a sudden determination of Jews to be white, and to be so perceived, is almost certainly in part a manifestation of increased Jewish secularization, in which the values of religious and cultural identity are eclipsed by other satisfactions. White is a state of mind. An ideological construct. But only those who look the part can play it with conviction, and this poses no substantial risk for most Jews (and, irony of ironies, for some Blacks!). So it is not the Jews' skin color that makes the difference. It is a question of what values and behavior are considered more appropriate to what pigmentation or lack of it. Hence, the increased secularization cued by the new confidence

Jews have come to know as more barriers have fallen between them and their full and rightful participation in American life may have little to do with concerns about being white. The barriers have not fallen because mainstream America suddenly recognized Jews as white; that question was never seriously at issue. It was Jewish religion and Jewish culture which placed them outside the mainstream and beyond the pale. But America never pursued objections to these values more than halfheartedly. Prejudice against Roman Catholics, which was often quite virulent, was probably more intense for most of our history than antipathy to Jews. But it was hard to tell who was a Catholic six days a week, while the Jew maintained a persistent, even defiant, cultural visibility which even his whiteness could not wholly excuse. In consequence, his recent arrival at respectability has been accomplished both because he has been willing to moderate his Jewishness and in spite of it.

The Jewish arrival derives to a significant degree from the determined black push from beneath. When the pot boils, the first visible action is at the top. Jewish philanthropy and the long, ardent, direct Jewish participation in the civil rights movement were critically important factors contributing to the degree of success the civil rights movement enjoyed. But if the Jews had done nothing at all to help the cause, as a designated American minority they would still have reaped some major benefits from the black struggle. American acceptability presupposes an order of priority—a racial-cultural pecking order. In order for the Blacks to move up at all, all those aspiring minorities which rest on the bedrock of Blackamerica must first be moved up to make new space for the black advance. But in relation to all the others the Blacks are still at the bottom no matter what their progress may have been. The Jews are not responsible for this scenario, nor are they the only group to benefit significantly from it. But the Blacks are determined to change it.

The problem now is that Blacks are tired of playing by the old rules because the rules are all contrived and the deck is stacked, and, to mix a metaphor, black people's feet are tired? Earl Raab saw selected aspects of the problem quite clearly a full decade ago:

> In order to join the American parade, the Negro community has to find its own identity, and shake itself loose from the degradation and self-degradation of the past. This is Black positiveness, power, pride, dignity as a preface to economic integration. In addition, an obvious piece of political realism has come to the fore: the black community was not going to be able to take a serious part in American pluralism until it established its own political strength and instruments. It had to shake loose from the coalitions long enough to do that.[28]

But Mr. Raab didn't report the whole story. From the black perspective, the increased abrasiveness characterizing contemporary Black–Jewish relations also reflects the Jew's apparent determination to be a part of the System, and the Blackamerican's belated but determined repudiation of the conventional arrangements which make him the perpetual nigger to the System. For the Jew, the American Dream has, in the last three decades or so, taken on substantial form and substance. For him, overt acts of bigotry have disappeared, or have been directed to new targets. There are considerably fewer barriers to his success, and life for him is sweeter in America than anywhere else in the world. The American Dream is beginning to look like the stuff of the Promised Land, the search for which has been an awesome odyssey for thousands of years. That is as it should be. But for the Blackamerican, the Dream is still a will-o'-the-wisp. To him it seems that every time he lays his hand on a piece of the Dream, there is some other hand under his. So he is increasingly impatient with the System which seems always to operate to defer the American Dream for him, in favor of somebody else.

The Jew qua Jew is not the adversary. That must be clearly understood by Blacks and Jews alike if they are to avoid some foolish, futile confrontation that may well turn out to be of extraordinary and protracted disadvantage to all concerned. The adversary to the legitimate black estate has not changed at all. The adversary is still whoever subscribes to the cold, calculated racist ideology which perpetuates Blacks as America's *niggers*, in order to deprive them of their fair share of the common values of this society. The adversary is whoever takes unfair advantage of black disability, and whoever stands in the way of black rehabilitation and recovery. That is the enemy.

The travail of Blacks and Jews is the tragic saga of two minorities trying to gain full participation in a society which, despite the political and moral rhetoric to the contrary, is basically intolerant of racial and cultural diversity. Blacks and Jews are not the only groups involved in the struggle, although they are, at this time, the most prominent, and possibly the most competitive. They have pursued a common goal with differing degrees of success, a matter largely determined by factors familiar to, but not within the control of, either of them. Their struggles have been conditioned by their separate histories, and rewarded or negated by the attitudes and intentions of the larger society from which they have both been excluded in varying degrees. Had their travail remained a common struggle rather than become an occasion for counterstruggle, the history of America might well have been different. It is not too late to build again on the foundations we now seem ready to abandon as unworkable.

As Jews qua Jews have never represented a focus of anti-Black feeling, it is also true that classical anti-Semitism has never curdled the emotions or perverted the social behavior of black people. As a matter of fact, the Blackamerican has, for most of his history, been so preoccupied in his struggle to establish his own humanity and his right to belong that there has been little energy left for denigrating or for hating anybody except himself. The determination of conventional American opinion that black people were "different," and should be treated differently from anybody else, took an inevitable toll of self-appreciation and self-esteem. The American discrimination against Blacks has been so common, so overt, and so unremitting that much of the time ordinary black people did not even know they were being discriminated against, and could not identify the discriminator if they did. A black woman who lived all her life in Selma, Alabama, admitted that she had no sense of discrimination or oppression until Martin Luther King went there. Differential treatment was so normal as to be unrecognized. Who, then, could single out the Jew as a special target for black anti-Semitism if he were behaving the way white people normally behave?

The truth is that the black man's animus was for the most part uncertain and unfocused. He was vaguely aware that "Polacks" and "Jews" and "Italians" and "Irishmen" and "poor whites" were somehow against him. But then, weren't *all* whites? And if the "Honky" or the "Polack" took his job, or the Irish cop busted his skull, or the "poor whites" lynched him while the "good whites" looked the other way; if the Jew cheated him and the "Dago" sold him bad meat, who was he going to single out to hate? He hated himself. He hated himself for being the object of so much hatred. And so long as he hated himself he lacked the self-confidence necessary to say to any particular group, "You are oppressing me and I intend to fight you!"

Again, when the pot boils, the first action is at the top. Today the Jews, among others, stand to benefit substantially from the Black Revolution, no matter how abrasive Black–Jewish relations may become. But it is also true that a hard boil stirs up the sediment at the bottom, and soon the whole pot begins to throb. It is reasonable to expect that, as the black struggle for parity intensifies, the conventional order of things will be challenged again and again. There will be alignments and realignments dictated by perceived group interests, new sources of immigration, and increased voter registration and political sophistication. There will be short-term advantages now for the one, now the other group. These need not create adversary relationships. In the long run, coalition is better than confrontation, and working in full mutual respect and confidence is better than selling, or being sold, down the river.

Some Jews, like some Blacks, have been able to get through the emotional shock of feeling betrayed every time some divergence of their respective interests produces behavior that is more ethnic than collaborative. Those who have not will have to learn all over again that Blacks are not Jews, Jews are not Blacks, and the best of coalitions may come unraveled under pressure of some more compelling expediency. After all, coalitions are political alliances, and politics is the art of the profitable. To any people whose history is measured in terms of the quality of oppression they have experienced, every new rung up the ladder from the pit must seem worth the bitter struggle. The fact that some rungs are less sound than others, or that rungs that go up also go down, is seldom considered except by hindsight—after the fact, and after the fall. In any case, coalitions are the free expressions of cooperation between independent entities sharing some interest for some indefinite period of time. *They last as long as the promotion of a mutual interest is possible.* And, barring the cat-scrapping that marks the parting of the immature and the unsophisticated, every coalition that has served its purpose well lays the groundwork for another. It would be helpful if Jews and Blacks could trust each other enough to be open about their conflicting interests and to solve them between themselves. The sense of betrayal is hard to avoid when one group feels compelled deliberately to ally itself with forces known to be antagonistic to the other in order to resolve issues that are in-house or parenthetical. Such ad hoc alliances are inevitably read as spiteful. They are not easily forgiven, and they may well prove embarrassing down the road.

Rabbi Albert Vorspan makes the case realistically and with sensitivity when he declares: "I submit: no segment of the white community of America has had more empathy with the plight of the black man or has given more support to racial decency [than Jews]." And Rabbi Vorspan will find even more support for the observation that

> . . . the black man, by himself, [cannot] bring about the needed social revolution in America. He will need allies in the white community, including Jews, because the ultimate arena is political. But no longer will Blacks be dependents, supplicants, mere symbols of injustice, or objects of our efforts. . . . The more understanding among us will recognize that this is a new day, a new

ball game. We must shift gears. We must learn to play a supporting role, must learn to forgo control and domination in the
interest of true cooperation.[29]

Truer words have not been spoken, and added to them must
be the reminder that the social revolution that is needed in
America is not solely the responsibility of Blacks, although they
are presently the most inconvenienced. We all need allies with
as wide a spectrum of leverage as can be managed. And the
black leverage will be significantly different tomorrow from what
it was yesterday.

It is bad enough for Jews and Blacks to continue growling at
each other over spoils they don't yet have, or that they hold so
tentatively. Even more demeaning is the fact that the spoils they
are allegedly trying either to wrest or to protect from each other
are not the spoils of any consummate victory but retrievals from
a mere series of skirmishes. Perhaps that is why they take on such
emotional significance—the pervasive fear that the next skirmish
may see them disappear again into the oblivion of a more pervasive prejudice well known to both. The ultimate enemy is
racism, and racism is the silent presence at every so-called
Black–Jewish "confrontation," and it is to racism that the fears
of Jews and Blacks alike are ultimately addressed. Jews do
understand the traumas of exclusion and privation. Their private
nightmare, according to Robert Klein, Jewish manager of radio
station WDAS in Philadelphia, "is that the white Christian elite
will set the Negroes and the Jews upon each other, and then sit
back and enjoy the fireworks. . . . Suppose this country takes a
decided turn to the right and white support is withdrawn from
the Jews. Jews would then be classed along with Negroes as
outsiders."

Whatever the validity of Mr. Klein's assessment, Blacks have
their own scenario. They have no fear of Jews as such. The Jew
has money and influence and in the past he has used it in the
interest of their common advancement. But Blacks have finally
learned the value of political mobilization. Their potential as
voters is several times that of our relatively small Jewish popula-

tion, and other allies will find coalition attractive. Things will even out eventually, and the Jew will get back his investment in the black struggle with interest, if he proves consistent. But if the Jew who makes it into the system reverses his sentiments and his tactics to make common cause with the black man's age-old oppressors, the black struggle for a more reasonable and responsible participation in America will be inconvenienced, but it will not be turned back. Similarly, there are still those who resent the increased visibility and presence of the Jew in traditional racial sanctuaries where once there were no Jews, and who long for the status quo ante. There will be increased pressures on both groups to abandon an allegiance that has worked to common advantage for promises that appeal to emotion rather than to substantive interest. They must be resisted by Jews and Blacks alike.

The anxieties of Blacks and Jews illustrate the classic example of how the American dilemma reaches into the most interstitial aspects of American life and is often the most crucial, if unrecognized, factor in the ordering of relationships which seem far from its interests or influence. The American dilemma has far from run its course; the forces which hold Blacks and Jews alike to be anathema may be less discernible for the moment, but they have never really quit the scene. Blacks will need Jews; Jews may again need Blacks. The millennium is not yet. Not for Jews. Not for Blacks. Not for America. Tomorrow has yet to be encountered. It is foolish to burn bridges on the strength of today, a commonplace that the politics of religion of whatever race or color might well give a more prayerful consideration.

7

The Legal Route to Remediation: From Desegregation to Affirmative Action

THE American dilemma persists, but there have been some earnest efforts to undo it. Some churches, for example, have gone beyond mere tokenism by doing away with the legal structures which effectively denied Blacks meaningful participation and responsibility. The United Methodist Church, the leading example, since 1964 has been routinely electing Blacks as bishops and assigning them with little regard to the racial composition of their jurisdictions. No other denomination has gone so far in depth and determination as the Methodists, but a few others have taken steps which would be encouraging were it not for their obvious symbolic intent. A serious problem for the American church is that to endorse carefully selected Blacks for unusual appointments, or even to elect a few Blacks to high national office, is one thing; it is quite another thing to bring about inclusiveness at the level of the local church. Here, even the Methodists are no exception. It is the American dilemma all over again: high ideals with low-grade implementation. Form without substance. Paralyzed motion.

Since the Second World War the most important efforts to dismantle the structure upon which our troublesome dilemma rests have been made in the courts, and in most such efforts the Black Church has been an important direct or indirect participant.

Money, manpower, mobilization, a lot of prayer, and a lot of preaching made the Black Church the home base of the civil rights movement from the beginning, and it is still in the Black Church that the principal energies of the black will to freedom continue to ferment.

The legal attack on the structure of racism has had the most telling success in two cases which finally came before the Supreme Court of the United States. The first to dramatically break the long pattern of civil inertia was the celebrated case of *Brown vs. Topeka Board of Education*, which struck down legal segregation of the races; a quarter of a century later, *Bakke vs. Regents of the University of California* sought to remedy some of the cultural devastation caused by three centuries of slavery and segregation by official recognition that a class of people deliberately and systematically crippled by the state and by society for so long could not realistically be expected suddenly to compete without help against the favored majority. These cases are of great significance in our recent social and political history for their impact on the American dilemma.

Brown vs. Board of Education

Brown vs. Board of Education, decided by the United States Supreme Court in 1954, was a momentous ruling in the history of American jurisprudence. In that decision the Court destroyed the legal basis of racial segregation and put the country back on the road toward the completion of the emancipation process begun at such tragic cost a hundred years before. The *Brown* case changed forever the social and political topography of America. It signaled the beginning of a process which has changed and will change significantly the character and the fortunes of the black estate. *Brown* is significant because, in changing the rules for public exclusion, it changed the rights of the Blackamerican from the simple right to be free to the right to be free from segregation. Left intact was the problem of being free to *become*. That assurance was needed to give full meaning to being free, but America seems still unconvinced that freedom has to be facilitated, or being "free" is so much sound and fury signifying no value of substance. We have learned by hindsight, but in 1954 *Brown*, as the cumulative fruit of a long history of litigation, was heralded as the logical fulfillment of the promise inherent in the Constitution of the United States.

Decisive action was indeed overdue. We were foundering in the aftermath of a long war which was all the more frightening for the problems it left unresolved and for the implications it raised for the future. As we looked for familiar structures and conventional landmarks in our efforts at personal and social and political reconstruction, it was clear that the world had changed. And we had changed with it. We would never again be the way we were. Too many new truths had been discovered; too many old myths had been decoded; too many sacred taboos had been violated. Too many icons had been defaced; too many hole-cards had been exposed; too many brass idols had been toppled. And alas! when the dust had settled, they all had feet of clay! *Pedes terra cotta!*

A Vegetative Undercaste?

There is no romance and there is no glory in modern war, for wars are no longer contests of valor fought in isolation from the people. Whatever the business of war uncovers, the people share it and react to it. This century has been characterized by a succession of wars of liberation of doubtful consequence if the welfare of the designated "captives" is considered, but war sometimes inadvertently produces effects not considered in its motivation or strategy. Whatever the fortunes of the liberative intent on the battlefield, liberation from the constraints of political and social tyranny sometimes occurs at home when conventional enforcement is strained by the exigencies of the larger struggle. For example, nothing did more to destroy the white racial mystique which had been so assiduously cultivated in this country for three and a half centuries than the exposure of the autistic savagery of the ulta-civilized Germans, unless it was the official American refutation of the Nazi theories of a master race. It stood to reason that if the allegations of a master race in Germany were spurious, why not in America? And if the Jews deserved liberation, why not the Asians? Why not the Africans? Indeed, why not the black people of America, right here at home?

But it was more than a war and its implications for new ways of seeing things that marked the timeliness of *Brown vs. Board of Education.* Nobody seemed to realize that the black community had changed, and that that change would inevitably seek its logical expression in some modification of American social relations. The social patterns which defined the society, most particularly in the South, were given definition when the South recovered its regional hegemony hard on the heels of Reconstruction. But the South had its own notions about the nature and character of the African Diaspora it once legally enslaved, and these notions reflected not so much on the African character and personality as they did upon the psychological needs of the alleged master class—now burdened by the twin failures of arms and ideology. The views that became the foundation of Southern "reconstruction" were obviously not consonant with any objective learnings derived from three centuries of contact with black people. Instead, the South chose to reconstruct a private reality not substantially different from the fantasies of the old regime which had just been toppled. The erstwhile masters, however presently reduced in circumstances, were still not prepared to accept the suggestion that the Blacks among them were quite as human as themselves, and that black people had all of the potentials for glory or for disgrace with which the human species is everywhere endowed. Indeed, had America been sober enough or clairvoyant enough during its reconstruction to have made this notion a principle of its regeneration, we would have been spared the agonies, the tragedies, and the tremendous waste in human energy and human lives we had to experience before *Brown vs. Board of Education* could bring us some relief.

However, it seems that, for some, history, once it has been wound and set, has to run its course before the people are willing to recognize the destructive forces they have set in motion.

It turned out that when the War between the States was ended and the national order had been restored, the Blacks were called free, but there was no room made for their freedom. The apparent expectation was that they would simply disappear, or that they would vegetate in a kind of cultural oblivion while the rest of America got on with the business of its temporarily derailed manifest destiny. In the light of the Southern experience this would seem to be a curious reading of history, for it was precisely in the South that, for generations, black ingenuity in agriculture, construction, the mechanical arts, animal husbandry, and the like had been translated into white economic advantage. And it was in the South that black initiative was legendary in the countless instances where, for years on end, black slaves met the harsh requirements of the slave workday, and then worked on in the determined effort to purchase themselves and their families. If the desire for freedom was such a powerful incentive for initiative, why should not the realization of freedom fan the fires of initiative even more? Further, the expectation that the new black citizens would constitute a perpetual, culturally stagnant undercaste apparently gave no consideration to the systems of legal and conventional proscription which had fixed the limits of black performance when Blacks were slaves, and which were retained as completely as possible to continue that arrangement now that they were free. Why, one wonders, was such an elaborate system of constraint necessary to control a people who were "naturally" indolent, vegetative, unaspiring, and satisfied with their lot?

Whatever the expectations may have been, in the nine short decades between emancipation from absolute slavery and the removal of some of the more crippling of the residual civil restraints by the Supreme Court decision of 1954, Blackamericans managed some remarkable accomplishments for an allegedly primitive people. They sharecropped for subsistence; but they also bought land and farmed for themselves. They continued to work as servants and menials; but they also opened their own small businesses—often providing employment for their families and others. They homesteaded and gained local reputations for honesty and industry, but they also traveled the country and learned new ideas and ways of doing things and relating to people. In most instances they were effectively excluded from meaningful political participation in the larger society, but they learned and practiced the political arts in their religious, fraternal, and social organizations. They developed major institutions such as the Black Church, the black press, the black college. They founded banks, insurance companies, and a network of voluntary social organizations for the expression of their cultural interests. They produced great scientists and men of letters; actors, artists, humanists, musicians, politicians, educators, notables in sports and entertainment. They went to war for their country whenever their country went to war, and they won their fair share of recognition for exceeding the requirements of duty. They saw the world and its peoples and learned from them; but, above all, they struggled to be educated, for from the beginning they were committed to the notion (however arguable it may be) that, in America, education is the key to adequacy, to acceptance, to access. From almost total illiteracy to near total literacy in ninety years—and with signal achievements far beyond—that is the record. Of all of the liberated peoples in history, few have come so far so fast. And yet the black odyssey has always been a struggle with a liberation that was imperfect from the start—a travesty of justice in this citadel of human justice we call America. *Brown vs. Board of Education* was a belated acknowledgment of that fact.

Time to Change

But *Brown vs. Board of Education* was also the official recognition that the black estate had changed and that more change was indicated. In 1954 there were more Blackamericans in college than there were students in a majority of the nations of the world. The Blacks in the armed forces of the United States numbered more than the men under arms in many sovereign states. Blackamericans earned and spent more money than was represented by the gross national product of half the countries we were courting politically in order to dispose of our excess production. Clearly the black undercaste, while still severely restricted by the racial policies of the United States, had been something more than vegetative and indolent. It was time for a change which gave proper recognition to the realities of the black contribution to the material, the moral, and the cultural substance of America.

Change finally came, and the rest is history. But it is history in the making, not an act which has been accomplished. We need not document here the extraordinary social frustration and disruption occasioned by the decision of *Brown vs. Board of Education.* What we shall do instead is to examine some of the consequences in terms of what appears to have been the basic intent of that ruling: to extend more fully the blessings of liberty, responsibility, and participation in the common ventures of the American commonwealth to the black estate and to its posterity.

Education

Perhaps the place to look for the critical effects of the *Brown* case on the black community is in education, for that was the fundamental issue of the suit. The consequent question is whether the education of black children has been significantly improved by classroom desegregation. But that issue is far more complex than the question admits, and it cannot effectively be resolved in a simple statement of personal impression. In the first place, the intent of the decision has undoubtedly been frustrated to an important degree by the politics of delay and erosion; by the necessity of new logistical arrangements to achieve racial balance; by the elimination of large numbers of black teachers and administrators from their jobs and from positions critical to the need of black role models for black children; by the hostility and indifference of some teachers to black students; by the crisis atmosphere pervasive in some schools; and by the racial clannishness which characterizes the academic enterprise at all levels.

As a result, expert opinion on the basis of the accumulated research is predictably divided, and the measurement of benefits to black children in integrated classrooms is inconclusive.

Considerably more concrete is the fact that the per capita amount spent to educate the black child is for the first time in history at, or near, that spent to educate his white counterpart, and that professional preparation of black teachers must now approximate that of white teachers. Inadequate physical plants for black children suddenly improve or disappear under threat of integration, and the differential school year of six or seven months is no longer a feature of Southern education. On the other hand, while the integration of classrooms is desirable as a de facto evidence of racial parity, and as an important learning experience in social relations for both races, these are not the principal concerns of the black estate.

To put it another way, the presence of Blacks and whites in the same classroom is, or ought to be, considered the normative mode for the educational process in a society seriously committed to the democratic ideal. In such situations peer relationships and understandings find their own common denominators, and the influence of external, stereotyped determinations are minimized. However, the private notion that racial proximity functions or is expected to function in the osmotic transfer of intelligence from one race to another is universally rejected as a particularly subtle form of racial chauvinism.

Beyond the Secondary Level

Three decades after *Brown*, well over a million black youth, or at least twenty-five percent of the eighteen to twenty-one age group, were pursuing some form of higher education. About sixty percent of these were in two-year community colleges, or in trade or technical schools, but fully twenty percent were enrolled in the 144 traditional black colleges whose critical usefulness to the black estate has not been diminished by integration. The significant conclusions to be drawn from these informal statistics must include the following. First, there has been a sharply improved perception of the value and the need of higher education among Blacks. When the high dropout rate at the high school level, the concomitant low level of encouragement or preparation for college most black students experience in integrated high school settings, the high cost of college matriculation, and the dwindling base of support opportunities for black college youth are considered, then a black college population of twenty-five or twenty-six percent would seem to compare reasonably well with the thirty-four percent of white youth who are in college.

Second, access to technical and para-professional training has helped to modify the traditional patterns of black employment. Except during national emergencies such as World War II, black employment has always been heavily concentrated in unskilled, menial occupations relieved only by a relatively small number of professionals—doctors, teachers, clergymen, and the like—whose services were almost exclusive to the black community trapped behind the walls of segregation. There was no substantial tradition for skilled, technical, or para-professional training, because neither the training nor the positions it implied were generally available to black people. The accessibility of such training increased substantially after *Brown*, and more than a half million Blacks—many of them previous dropouts or working adults—were attending these middle-ground institutions in the early 1980s. If they can find jobs, they will be a significant factor in improving the traditions and the configurations of black employment.

Third, the traditional black colleges remain the critical components in black higher education. In terms of aggregate enrollments, more Blacks now attend white colleges than black, but while seventy percent of black students attending black colleges complete their degrees, seventy percent of black students in white institutions drop out. Furthermore, the distorted readings of the *Bakke* case notwithstanding, the impact of black enrollment on the white college campuses of America is minuscule—a mere five percent of the total, distributed in more than a thousand white institutions. But even that small presence suggests a very painful paradox. American education has always assumed that a relevant education is one which reflects the interests, the values, and the potentials of the white middle class. And since Blacks and their interests are generally excluded from serious recognition in the conventional American universe of significant values, American education must be considered a vital factor in the way our society is organized and maintained. In consequence, the low self-estimate of Blackamericans, dictated by their prescribed place in the body politic, is continuously reinforced and encouraged by our systems of education.

Only the black college has seriously addressed itself to the rebuttal of racial dogma enshrined as education, for the black college considers its very existence to be a de facto refutation of innate black inferiority. Born in the poverty and hostility of Southern "reconstruction," none of the black colleges in the relatively short span of their existence has been able to amass endowments or to develop the graduate and research facilities of the long-established white institutions. Yet these black colleges have produced a more than creditable number of scholars, scientists, statesmen, and clergymen, whose contributions to America and the world are eloquent argument for their respectability.

Of greatest significance has been the success of the black college in providing realistic, available role models for black youth in confounding the incredible racial myths and taboos designed to stifle black genius before it is born, and to fix and fortify the parameters of development and achievement before they are even tested. More than any other institution, the black college has provided a solid affirmation for black identity, freeing the battered black ego from the nagging doubts which are the inevitable corollaries of a total life experience washed in denigration and constraint.

In consequence of these and other factors, it is probably in higher education that the blessings of *Brown* are most mixed. The saw cuts two ways, and even as the decision opened up a whole new world of opportunity for technical, graduate, and professional training, it also threatened the survival of one of the institutions most crucial to the black estate. Since *Brown,* the black college has become an endangered institution, for desegregation has brought a number of problems in its train. Some are cruelly paradoxical. Others illustrate the depth of America's naïveté about racial matters. For example, a most persistent and exasperating issue stems from the curious notion that integration ought to mean the abandonment of black colleges because black students may now attend white institutions! Those who hold this view give only the most impatient consideration to the individual merit of black colleges, or to the enormous cultural investment they represent, or to the fact that they are still the first choices of some two hundred thousand black students. Nevertheless, in the early years of the implementation of the *Brown* decision, the black colleges lost most of their best students and faculty to prestigious white institutions, and their support from private philanthropy was seriously eroded by the notion that they were suddenly superfluous. The problem was compounded by pressures from the federal government to desegregate the black colleges by requiring a sudden white presence in the faculty and student body. It is ironic that the black colleges had never received more than five percent of the federal budget for higher education, and that private black colleges had never required segregation in the first place! Segregation in education was ordained by the several states, and state-supported black colleges were created precisely for the purpose of legally avoiding "race-mixing" in academe! To add insult to injury, when, following *Brown*, it became clear that the continued maintenance of state-supported black colleges would no longer protect white state-supported institutions from the admission of black students, some Southern states quickly developed strategies for submerging their black colleges in white universities, or else phasing them out altogether.

Few white institutions make any serious provisions for their small communities of black students who expect to find in the college experience increased opportunities for the understanding and appreciation of black culture as well as its white counterpart, and who, like white students, are in search of the usual intellectual and social stimulants of self-affirmation. Even worse is the

substantial threat to identity some state-supported black colleges have experienced with reverse integration of increasing
white enrollment and the concomitant arrival of increasing
numbers of white faculty, who further reduce the small reservoir
of black role models, and diminish the only secure job market
black graduates ever had if they expected to enter the academic
profession.

Employment

It is difficult if not impossible to separate education from employment as the most important factor determining the quality
of life in America. The *Brown* impact on black employment has
been far-reaching, but its ultimate influence is still a matter of
conjecture. In theory, *Brown* and its successors did away with
conventional understandings which openly or tacitly defined
"Negro work," or which reserved certain categories of employment for whites. Traditionally, Blacks were expected to perform
whatever labor was hot, heavy, dirty, menial, low-paid, and
devoid of any satisfaction deriving from a sense of creativity, or
from the possibility of advancement. Over the decades since
1954, the employment base of the black community has been
broadened and diversified, and Blacks who are well prepared
are less frequently rejected by racial selection when they apply
for the jobs for which they have been trained.

Nevertheless, discrimination remains a formidable factor in
employment. Blacks still have only token representation at the
policymaking levels in most unions, and there is still a very large
number of skilled jobs and professional positions in industry,
communications, management, etc., which are considered racially
sacrosanct. In the wake of *Bakke* and its attendant cases, Blacks
still hope that these preserves will eventually be breached under
pressure of affirmative action, the pragmatics of economic interest, and the performance of black workers in collateral fields.

More troubling is the growing conviction that, while *Brown*
and its progeny have brought increased expectations, these expectations are being frustrated by a future that appears increasingly

bleak. For example, advanced technology has all but eliminated the need for the kind of labor the unlettered and the unskilled are equipped to do, thus threatening these unfortunate people with obsolescence as workers *and as persons* at precisely the time that Blacks have developed a sense of self-esteem. But machines are cheaper and often more efficient than people. Machines require no fringe benefits; they can be amortized for tax credits; they have practically no absenteeism, and they require no humanitarian consideration. Hence, the numbing fear is growing that substantial numbers of the vast reservoir of unemployed black workers may never again have sustained employment. Even more depressing is the specter shadowing unskilled black youth, many of whom will never in their lifetimes have the experience of a regular job. The available alternatives point to a national junkyard of human potential: all black; all poor; and all around us.

Political Involvement

Except for the brief interlude of the Reconstruction, the black involvement in the American political process was, until quite recently, essentially ceremonial. In the South, Blacks were effectively disenfranchised by the poll tax and other strategies. In the North, the patterns of residential segregation, combined with the cavalier attitudes of both major parties, served to neutralize the black vote in most cases. Hence, the sense of powerlessness was pervasive in the black community and deeply etched on the black psyche. There were no black senators, or governors, or mayors, or state representatives, or commissioners, or heads of school boards. The tedium of exclusion was relieved only occasionally by the rare election of a black congressman, such as Oscar DePriest or Adam Clayton Powell, who was made to function as the symbolic representative for the whole black community.

But the typical black citizen, whether in Birmingham or Buffalo, Memphis or Minneapolis, arose to face each day with the comfortless knowledge that in the world beyond his front door he was a nonentity, and that whatever transpired in the day-to-day order of human events would not reflect his existence one way or the other, except insofar as he was an object to be manipulated. For a hundred years, he had been a citizen bearing all the burdens that citizens bear, but for that hundred years he had shared none of the responsibilities that citizens share in a democratic society. He was a nonperson and he resented it. When at last his cup of anguish would hold no more and he screamed out for a share of power, America was alarmed, aggrieved, annoyed, and unforgiving.

But times change with the votes. The successful registration of over a million additional Blacks through new voting-rights legislation in the wake of *Brown* opened the door for meaningful black participation in the political process. With the help of federal registrars, and despite the most determined opposition, by the early seventies voter-registration campaigns had broken the back of black disenfranchisement in the South. The breakthrough was timely, for in the North (which had become the new battleground for civil rights) the ardor of protest confrontation was considerably dampened by the defection of the more visible white liberals. There were also other problems, including the internal dissension in the protest organizations, the increased ferity of the opposition, the uncertain interests and intentions of the Federal Bureau of Investigation, and the mounting competition of mushrooming liberation groups spawned in the furrows of the civil rights movement.

In the South, none of the gains imposed by such "outside agencies" as the Supreme Court or the various civil rights organizations could be considered final until they had received local ratification. In consequence, a breakthrough in registration and voting was in the long run the indispensable corollary to the implementation of *Brown*, for, in the absence of the diligent exercise of the black franchise at the state and local levels, experience has shown that there is no effective way to protect the interests of the black estate, no matter how well intentioned the federal establishment, or how carefully drawn its decrees.

As black voters, South and North, began to recognize the

potency of a unified black electorate, some remarkable things began to happen. Suddenly there were black mayors in the big cities of the North and West, and in the cities and small towns of the South as well—Chicago, Philadelphia, Los Angeles, Detroit, New Orleans, Atlanta, and Birmingham, to name the principal ones. Blacks appeared in substantial numbers in the state legislatures, and by 1983 there were more than twenty black United States congressmen. There were black faces in the state highway patrol, in the sheriff's uniform, and on the judge's bench. In the 1976 Presidential election, ninety percent of the Blacks who voted cast their ballots for Jimmy Carter, thereby insuring his election as President of the United States—the nearest Blacks had ever come to being decisive at such a high level in the political process. In 1984, Reverend Jesse Jackson ran as a serious candidate for President, and forced a new era in American politics. His successful negotiations with Syrians and Cubans for the release of American and Cuban prisoners, and his "rainbow coalition" policies focusing on the rights of women, ethnics, and other neglected constituencies, caused many Americans for the first time in history to give serious attention to a black Presidential candidate.

All this adds up to power. But how much? It depends on how you look at it. There is not a formidable amount of power inherent in having a black mayor of a city like Gary, Indiana, or Newark, New Jersey, or even Detroit or Chicago, as we have seen, for while such an office is certainly not ceremonial, the economic and political realities are such as to rule out an extravagant exercise of personal whim or racial prerogative. This was a lesson brought home to Chicago's black mayor, Harold Washington, soon after his election in 1983. Before he could be properly installed in office, the well-organized opposition within his own party made it quite clear that the policies of his administration would be under the closest scrutiny, and subject to the sufferance and the ratification of a white power structure which did not welcome his intrusion. Nor are there any black state legislators sufficiently independent of white support to accomplish any programs unilaterally. Politics, as we have said, is the art of compromise, and if he wishes to stay in office, it is an art the black politician must learn early and perform well.

The number of black elected officials is still minuscule—barely more than one percent of the total. Moreover, the black vote was considerably less decisive in the 1980 Presidential elections, thus signifying that black voting power may be of crucial significance only when the rest of the country is unable to resolve its ambivalences. Despite the size of the black population, black political influence does not at present begin to approximate that of an ethnic group like the Jews, for example, who have perhaps one-fifth the potential numerical voting strength of the black community but who seem to manage an intensely disproportionate impact on domestic and foreign policy. The difference is a matter of political diligence, daring, and determination supported by the cultural unity and self-confidence by which the Jews have survived as minorities for thousands of years in practically every nation in the civilized world.

How much power? Not much if power means the control over critical decisions which affect the integrity and interests of the black estate. Few would argue that Blacks have attained the feared "black power" visualized by a hysterical white establishment in the late 1960s when *all* the power was in white hands. Black power, as such, does not exist, but there are significant gains in the power potential of black people. First of all, the legal disabilities regarding the franchise have been substantially removed, and black citizens everywhere have an increased opportunity to participate in the political process. This is the crucial first step. There are still pockets of intimidation, and there are still islands of apathy; but the official barriers are down and the option is generally available to those who care enough to pursue it. Second, some black office-seekers *are* being elected, as are whites who are sensitive to the interests of the black estate; so the black citizen is no longer a total cipher. If his vote counts, *he* counts, and the recognition that he is a force to be reckoned with is an important indication of the power participation that could be developed.

Despite the practical limitations on the power of black mayors and others who hold high elective offices, it is significant that for the first time in history increasing numbers of Blackamericans all over the country represent the elected leadership for local constituencies of all races. They are elected by Blacks *and* whites, and sometimes others as well. They are highly visible; and considering the fact that they are often reelected, their performance must at least be on a par with that of the white officeholders who preceded them. To be voluntarily governed by Blacks is something new for Americans, and the fact that black political aspirants continue to win some elections may be a signal that America has finally matured enough, and that white Americans finally feel secure enough, to share some of the power at least some of the time. That is an auspicious omen for the country and for the black estate. We have come a long way, and we have a long way to go down the same road together. Sharing the power and sharing the responsibility is the best way to get there with expedition and with grace.

Regents vs. Bakke: Redress in the Form of Opportunity

Opportunity is a close correlative of power, and inordinate power corrupts the human equation to the end that those who were created equal soon become unequal in their access to the common values to which all are equally entitled. Whether by arrogance or artifice, when the power of opportunity is arrogated to a particular race, and this arrogation is facilitated by the machinery or the agents of the state, then the state is a party to the abuse and the suppression of the most fundamental rights citizenship is designed to bestow.

If equality means equal rights to the common values of society, then justice requires equality of access to those rights. When the evidence shows clearly that such access is consistently denied to some, whether by intention or by inadvertence, or by caprice, it is in the interest of justice and it is the responsibility of the state to relieve that situation. To this maxim every democratic society should be particularly sensitive, for no free people in a free country can be compelled indefinitely to accept arbitrary constraints which compromise and nullify the very freedom that being free implies.

In the present instance, the Blackamericans' access to education, employment, promotion, and advancement has been severely impaired by centuries of institutionalized racism in which the state itself has been a prime agent of facilitation and a principal barrier to change. But in the process of history, change, however imperceptible, is also ineluctable, and change has come to America. Elemental justice requires that the anomalous, arbitrary compromise of the rights of black citizens be redressed. That redress is not accomplished by meretriciously equating the circumstances of those whose impairments derive from our pernicious racial syndrome with others in the society whose claims derive from a set of causes that are clearly less invidious and less determinative. No other minority or ethnic group in America has ever felt the concerted effort of the whole society and all of its principal institutions directed at its suppression and degradation. Hence, the black citizens' impairment is as unique as it is conclusive, and millions of those now considered to be their peers and partners in disadvantage have been, however innocently, the longtime beneficiaries of their distress.

That is the tragic flaw in the Supreme Court's ruling in the *Bakke* case.[1] When the medical school of the University of California at Davis set aside sixteen seats for "minority" applicants (some of whom could well have been white), Allan Bakke, who had been twice rejected by the school, sued on the grounds that he had been discriminated against because of his race. Bakke argued that since some of the sixteen minority applicants scored lower on the admission test than he did, they were admitted only because they were black, or Mexican-American, or Asian-American, and he was white. Overlooked was the fact that at least seventy-nine whites with scores comparable to his, or better, were also rejected on the two occasions he tried for admission, *and* some of the minority applicants scored higher than he. In 1978 the case was heard by the Supreme Court, which said in a somewhat ambiguous ruling that race might be one factor taken into consideration in college admissions practices, but that no "quota" for disadvantaged persons could be countenanced in attempts to provide special opportunities for disadvantaged Americans. Bakke was admitted to Davis and the affirmative-action programs across the country were left under a pall.

Whatever else may be gleaned from the *Bakke* case, the fact that we still harbor a pervasive fear (and perhaps a resultant antipathy) of black people is quite evident, both in the nature of the suits and in the implications of the decisions. And whatever his own feelings may have been, Allan Bakke's moral support came from an unsilent majority who interpreted any remediation of the black estate to be a de facto encroachment upon established white prerogatives, and a threat to other established norms which are even more sacrosanct. The justice of such remediation, the propriety, the humane imperative was dismissed as immaterial, or of no consequence. Hence, *Bakke* is symbolic of much more than one man's desire to go to medical school. None of the disadvantaged applicants competing for the sixteen seats set aside for them at Davis Medical School had any interest in barring Mr. Bakke from Davis, or in taking from him a place to which he was entitled. They did have an interest in participating in a modest effort at redressing somewhat the enormous imbalance that exists between whites and nonwhites in the medical profession (and all other professions) in California and the United States at large. Bakke's suit was directed at the *concept* of affirmative action. It was the repudiation of a remedial effort believed to be innocent of any violation of any just claims he or others may have had against the university in its limited attempts to redress a history of injustice. It served notice on such programs everywhere that there is no clear and certain mandate for the remediation of impairments occasioned by racial deprivation.

The Regents of the University of California vs. Bakke illustrates the extraordinary difficulty the people (and the courts) have in coming to terms with the facts and the consequences of our peculiar national development and underscores our earlier suggestion that neither racial nor ethnic pluralism was a goal (or a serious possibility) anticipated by those who laid the political foundations of the American commonwealth. All Blacks were relegated to a caste apart, and all others were expected to rinse away the telltale blotches of ethnic imperfection in the pure, crystal waters of Anglo-conformity. Great care was taken to exclude the unassimilable from the melting pot, and in those cases where this was occasionally impracticable (as with the Indians, the Chinese, and the Filipinos), the effort was made to create racial or ethnic enclaves which could be drawn upon for labor, when needed, but which like the black caste would have no official standing in the body politic.

Our present problems as symbolized by *Bakke* demonstrate the obsolescence of race and racial conformity as instruments of socialization or criteria of human worth. While the vision of social fusion in some mystical melting pot fired by Anglo-Saxon traditions and producing in a generation or two the proper American still persists, the notion that Blacks are infusible at any temperature supplied by any cultural fire, however long sustained, also persists. Nor have we abandoned the idea that America is (and always will be) a white, Christian nation, and that all those not initially favored with the prerequisite credentials can only hope to subsist by the sufferance of those who are.

Bakke vs. Regents is rife with subtleties, with critical implications for the future of affirmative action as an instrument of justice. One particular subtlety, so obvious to some but either overlooked or considered inconsequential to very many others, is that the reserved seats at Davis were not reserved for Blacks but were set aside under a special admissions program for those students who, according to Dr. Sarah Gray, chairperson of the Special Admissions Committee, showed "evidence of a serious desire to eventually return to a disadvantaged area similar to that from which they came (mainly inner city ghetto, rural area, or Indian reservation) to provide health care. . . ." This would seem to mean that the program was minority-oriented rather than racially oriented and that, presumably, even whites could apply if they met the requirements which pledged future service in a disadvantaged area. However, the Special

Admissions chairperson conceded that "with these criteria, it is not surprising that most of the students who have entered the program have come from racial minorities, since they are the ones who predominantly inhabit California's disadvantaged areas. . . ."[2]

Now, the critical issue is not whether Allan Bakke was deprived of his rights because, being "a characteristic Caucasian male . . . tall and strong and Teutonic in appearance,"[3] he is not a member of a racial minority. Rather, the critical issue is whether Blackamericans are members of such a minority as that term has been traditionally applied and understood, and whether the deprivations and impairments of black people occurred under that particular imprimatur. Obviously, they did not, and the judgment rendered in *Bakke vs. Regents* should in no way affect the right and the duty of the federal government to continue its remedial efforts on behalf of Blacks. It is not here intended to denigrate or to waive the just claims of the traditional minorities, whether they be racial or whether they be minorities of the white majority. What is intended is to call attention to a device, a social fiction, if you will, which if unchallenged will once again consign the tenuous interests of black people to the familiar limbo of double jeopardy.

Most Americans find security in the convention that our founding document—the Constitution—is sufficiently clairvoyant to anticipate all possible issues of political and social relations, and that our system of jurisprudence is invested with a clairvoyant wisdom and sophistication by means of which the basic law will always be interpreted in the interest of justice, barring judicial error or incompetence. This is a very useful convention, one that is commonly considered fundamental to the effective governance of this democracy whose mandate, we are reminded, derives from the consent of the governed. The principle of justice at stake in the *Bakke* decision depends first of all upon certain issues which have to do with the rationale that ordained the Constitution in the first place. The Preamble lists the following six objectives: to form a more perfect Union, establish Justice, insure Domestic Tranquillity, provide for the common Defense, promote the general Welfare, and secure the blessings of Liberty to ourselves and our posterity.

It seems clear that the Founding Fathers had considerably more than mere national autonomy or political aggrandizement in mind—they opted for political autonomy as the surest means to the security and enhancement of individual human existence. The reason for the state they sought to fashion was to insure justice, peace, security, opportunity, freedom, and its derivative blessings for all those individuals who were to hold membership in the political corporation.

The problem is that, despite the nobility of rhetoric and the magnificence of intention, the earnestness of passion and the reality of sacrifice, the commonwealth they struggled so hard to perfect in embryo was nonetheless born with a taint. That taint, as we have seen, has dogged our destiny and compromised our peace, qualified our liberty, and mocked our justice from the moment this nation was conceived. The taint, of course, is the formal institutionalization of a racial differential in the basic law of the land—the ultimate political creed to which we must all refer for an understanding of who we are in the political context, and to which we must all appeal in the uncertain search for justice. It is the taint of the color line.

It is one of those little ironies that haunt the record of human performance that, had not the statesmen who drafted the initial version of the Declaration of Independence yielded to bigotry in the interest of political trade-off, the issue would have been dealt with summarily and American history may well have taken a different course. As it turned out, of the extensive catalogue of sins for which the British king was indicted, the one charging him with violating "the most sacred rights of life and liberty" of black people was quietly deleted—an ominous clue to the temperament and the intentions of some whose efforts were critical in the formative stages of the country. What was implied in the revision of the Declaration of Independence was made explicit in the Constitution itself, which still bears the reminder that the federal establishment was born with the conviction that the value of black individuals was three-fifths that of whites.[4]

Bakke and its train are the fruit of the American dilemma, the contradiction implicit in the virtue of American ideals and the shortfall of American behavior. The issue is neither the deprivation of whites nor the preferability of Blacks, but whether a reasonable belated effort to make less consummate the institutionalized privileges and prerogatives of whites will at last be attempted. The implications of the *Bakke* decision transcend altogether the dubious issue of "reverse discrimination," a policy patently incapable of realization so long as discrimination requires the power of enforcement. The true issue is the refortification of the prevailing system of racial hegemony brought under siege by *Brown vs. Board of Education* more than a quarter of a century ago.

Legal experts have argued that certain inherent weaknesses in the *Bakke* case rendered its outcome doubtful and possibly hazardous for affirmative action from the beginning because there was no history of discrimination against minorities at Davis Medical School, since it had been only recently established. A more pervasive weakness in that case and in most such cases argued in recent years is that, since *Brown vs. Board of Education,* we have progressively experienced transposition of the national commitment to the rehabilitation of Blackamericans— whose plight derives in large part from long-term specific national policy—to a more generalized concern for the interests of "minorities." This sinister policy which lumps together Blackamericans and other "minorities," particularly those minorities who together constitute the white majority, ignores the most conspicuous features of American history and gives currency to a pernicious fiction which confuses the issues and creates for the struggling Blacks a whole new class of competitors. It is a strategy which, if successful, can only accomplish for black people a reversion to the *status quo ante.*

In the long generations which fixed the disabilities Blackamericans are now struggling to have reduced, Blacks were *never* considered a mere minority or an ethnic group—either in slavery or out. "Ethnic" implies, at a minimum, historical continuity and a legitimate, recognized culture. No "Negroes" or

Africans were considered capable of such, and this convention is everywhere memorialized in American religion, letters, politics, myth, legend, social behavior, and law. Similarly, "minority" implies an order of relationships with a majority in which the will of the majority may prevail but the rights of the minority are respected. *But at no time in the history of America have the circumstances of the black estate issued from a majority-minority relationship.* In the course of our history, Blacks have outnumbered whites in countless political units or jurisdictions, but their numbers did not determine their rights one way or the other.

Harvard University's Oscar Handlin has argued that in the American understanding of "minority" the term "was not given a quantitative meaning. . . . Rather, it reflected an awareness on the part of some groups in the United States that they were underprivileged in access to the opportunities of American life." This argument is rendered moot by the fact that, in America, *race* has always been the *supreme* measure of human worth, with all other sortings and evaluations intended to be subsidiary to, but in careful recognition of, that primary understanding. But then, Professor Handlin recognizes this when he finds:

> Of the groups marked off by color, the Negroes were the most important, by virtue of their numbers, of their long history in the country, and of the tragic injustices to which they had already long been subject. . . . Emancipation . . . had stricken from them the shackles of legal bondage, but it had not succeeded in endowing them with rights equal to those of other citizens. . . . No other group suffered the total burden of discrimination the Negro bore.[5]

This is the *true* issue here: the disabilities of Blacks in America are of a different *genre*, a different *origin*. They derive from the peculiar implications *race* has for white America, *and* from the peculiar ways in which those implications have found their expression in the social and psychological life of the society, no less than in its political and economic life. We live with the evidence that Chief Justice Roger B. Taney's infamous dictum, "Negroes have no rights that a white man is bound to respect,"[6] expressed the conscience, and reflected the behavior, not only of his generation but of the generations that followed. Taney's conclusions were based on the theory that "the class of persons described in the plea [i.e., Negroes] whose ancestors were imported into this country and sold as slaves" were not "constituent members of [American] sovereignty" and that "they were not included, and were not intended to be included, under the word 'citizen' in the Constitution. . . ." *This language has never been applied to any other American "minority,"* and while it is true that amendments to the Constitution *created* citizenship for Blacks and gave them the franchise, those amendments did nothing to rectify the accumulated damage of two hundred years of human bondage.

On the other hand, the pejorative stereotypes invented to justify and to effectuate Black subjection have persisted, and in the conventional American mind, *all* Blacks are still a people apart, a peculiar excrescence in the body politic toward which a peculiar and distinctive class of differential behavior has always been considered appropriate. We know by bitter experience that, in the absence of compassion, whoever is differently perceived will be differently received; and, in the absence of morality, one man's travail is merely another man's convenience. Arnold Toynbee provided some revealing insights concerning the prospects of the victims of these stereotypes for normal participation in the social order. Says Professor Toynbee of "the white-skinned western Protestant of modern times [as] regards his black-skinned convert":

> The convert may have found spiritual salvation in the white man's faith; he may have acquired the white man's culture and learnt to speak the language with the tongue of an angel; he may have become an adept in the white man's economic technique, and yet it profits him nothing if he has not changed his skin.[7]

Professor Toynbee could well have added that, here in America, neither citizenship nor franchise nor valor in war nor industriousness in peace nor cultural contribution nor moral suasion nor scientific understanding have individually or in combination been of sufficient moment to overcome the stigma of being black. That is why the sudden recognition of Blacks as just one more minority among *competing* minorities, or one more ethnic group among a nation of ethnics, is both transparent and profane.

Blackamericans are indeed a minority. This is an obvious fact, and beyond question. It must be equally obvious that Black-americans are ethnics. Their good fortune is a synthesis of the legacies of many African, Indian, and European civilizations woven into the common fabric of the black experience in America and expressed in a distinctive subculture of which they may well be proud. But to make this fact determinative so late in the game, when there are such compelling antecedent considerations to be dealt with, is to regress from the avowed effort to bring about the racial parity required by *Brown vs. Board of Education*, and to impair seriously the promise implicit in the implementation of affirmative action. It is a patent effort at confusion of the issues and circumvention of justice.

This is a pluralistic society. No one would be so unsophisticated as to argue that the Poles, the Serbs, the Italians, the Jews, the Spanish-surnamed, even the Anglo-Americans may not have legitimate minority claims against our common government. Nor can it be supported that Blacks have prior rights to any of the common values this nation holds in trust for its citizens. However, if, as the Founding Fathers declared, a fundamental concern of the nation is *justice* for all its constituencies and for all its individuals, then justice demands a reappraisal of what we have done and what we are doing, and *why*. If justice is rendering to every man his due, then justice must be neither blind nor deaf. Justice must be informed, and it must always consider the circumstances out of which what is due arises. It may be just to honor one man and hang his brother if that is in fact what is *due* them respectively. In a society where all men are created equal, and so recognized and proclaimed by the state, justice must also redress the inequality of opportunity which precludes for some a reasonable participation in the scramble for scarce values which the pursuit of happiness requires in our kind of society. Inevitably, we are compelled to return to the wisdom of Justice Blackmun in *Bakke vs. Regents*, who, except for Justice Marshall, came closer than any of his colleagues to seeing the case in proper perspective: "In order to get beyond racism we must take account of race. There is no other way. And in order to treat some persons equally, we must treat them differently."[8]

The promotion of Blacks to "minority" status not only redefines the arena of struggle; it sets up a potentially endless succession of arbitrary adversaries from the majority minorities whose own interests are suddenly discovered to be threatened. Ironically, this perceived threat is not recognized as originating in the white majority in which they hold birthright membership, but is viewed as coming from the conventional knave, the persistent intruder who has the temerity to want help from the very society which conspires in his exclusion. Observes *Time* essayist Charles Krauthammer: "Because civil rights is justly considered among the most sacred of political values, appropriating it for partisan advantage can be very useful. The fiercest battle in the fight over affirmative action, for example, is over which side has rightful claim to the mantle of civil rights."[9] Thus emerges a cryptic and sinister protocol for the maintenance of the *status quo ante* through the spurious proposition that being black in America is merely an inconvenience of the same order as being Jewish, female, or Appalachian.

After three centuries of selective myopia, the grim realities of a different world emerging from World War II forced us to take a furtive look at what we are rather than what we had always proclaimed ourselves to be. What we saw was frightening. And well it may have been, for the American dilemma is not a game of chess. It is a prime purveyor of suffering, hostility, and death. Every step forward seems to demand a counterstep of reassurance that concerns for social justice are essentially cosmetic and academic, and that when the sound and the fury of public debate have subsided, and when the strategies of implementation have been refined to innocuousness, the way things will be will not be different from the way things always were.

The *Bakke* case was considered the first real test of the affirmative-action concept. Looking at the record Justice Thurgood Marshall gave so much of his life to put together, one can imagine the anguish, the outrage, and the shame he must have felt when he realized that his colleagues on the High Court were quite impervious to the hauntings of the past. Certainly Justice Marshall's grim catalogue of helplessness and horror, of struggle and sacrifice, of justice perverted, justice postponed, and justice denied, did not register with the urgency of firsthand experience on the rest of the Court. To Justice Marshall, the tragic legacy of what America did and what America failed to do is everywhere apparent, but most white Americans, however sagacious and however well-intentioned, find it difficult to recognize any moral relationship between that legacy and themselves. As a result, the national mood regarding the peculiar plight of Blackamericans may on occasion be one of sympathy, but seldom one of empathy. Hence, *noblesse oblige* rather than justice has been the relief most often considered appropriate for our racial ills. But *noblesse oblige* merely reconfirms the presuppositions from which the problem derives in the first place, and postpones the final reckoning when the problem must be settled on its merits. It offers no strategy for permanent relief.

The Court was not haunted by the apparitions which tortured Marshall because the other members of the Court were born protected from the experience so common to Justice Marshall and all other Blackamericans. They were born white, and that is precisely the point: the black experience *is* different *from the beginning until the end*, and Marshall was hard put to understand why anything so obvious could elude the venerable Court. He complained that

> . . . it is more than a little ironic that after several hundred years of class-based discrimination against Negroes, the Court is now unwilling to hold that a class-based remedy for that discrimination is permissible.
>
> In the light of the sorry history of discrimination and its devastating effect on the lives of Negroes, bringing the Negro into the mainstream of American life should be a state interest of the

highest order. To fail to do so is to ensure that America will forever remain a divided society.[10]

Justice Marshall's warning is as clear as his logic, but the *Bakke* decision seems to turn on other, less compelling concerns. There is a muddling of the issues which seems likely to insure protracted confusion and litigation, for the Blacks who have so lately and so conveniently been merged with the majority minorities and other nonwhite ethnics arrived at the merger with a substantial schedule of preexisting disabilities accumulated under a more maleficent arrangement. This in itself would seem to deny the probabilities of a common solution, for the problems they share are not in every case common problems. It seems clear that any viable approach to affirmative action in the future must take into consideration the following reminders, which summarize what we have contended thus far:

- Historically, the basic issue of American social relations was race, and the unique condition of the black minority derives from the absolutism of a racial caste system.
- The impairments of caste and color are of a different order from those which derive from any other minority status or ethnic difference.
- The cumulative effect of the color-caste syndrome on the Blackamerican has been to condition his understanding of reality in a way that stifled his ambition, crippled his development, compromised his access to the common values of the society, and lowered his expectations for achievement, reception, and participation.
- The cumulative effect of the color-caste syndrome on white America is such that the presumption of "natural" prerogatives and superior "rights" has hardly been abated despite the changes which have occurred since *Brown vs. Board of Education.* Most of those changes were made under duress, and the convenient convention that Blacks are "undeserving" and "interlopers" persists with the force of religious conviction.
- The perception of Blacks is still conditioned by the same

"forgotten" arguments and rationalizations which consigned them to a separate order in the first place, and the American mind-set is still such that, however styled at the moment, Blacks remain involuntarily distinguished from all other ethnics or minorities.

• Justice implies restoration, which in the present instance requires a serious effort on the part of the state to do whatever is necessary to restore to the black estate the dignity and the proficiency necessary to compete realistically with those who have not experienced the extreme level of black disablement under the imprimatur of the state, the connivance of its principal institutions, and the racial consensus which prescribes and enforces the parameters of life experience in America.

• Affirmative action is an instrument of justice employed by the state in the interest of ameliorating the impact of past injustices through the removal of some present impairments which derive from those injustices.

• Because of the long history of white racial prerogatives in America, the resultant impairments of black people are more insidious, more pervasive, more enduring, and more decisive than those of any other group; and because of their distinctive nature, they may at times require distinctive remediation.

For purely pragmatic considerations, the invention of the Negro may well have been the most ingenious economic contrivance in the history of Wetern ascendancy. However, "the Negro" as conceived by his inventors is as obsolete as the occasion for his invention. But, as so many of America's adventures in pragmatism seem to illustrate, fate reserves the right of serendipity, often blessing our less notable enterprises with some unanticipated good. Black people now constitute about twelve percent of the American population. Their contributions to the culture are both impressive and distinctive, but their *potential* as contributing Americans remains seriously underdeveloped. Between "what is" and "what is possible," between contribution and potential contribution, falls the shadow of impairment. It is in the national interest to remove that impairment as speedily as possible.

It is a national obligation for the state to heal itself, but that obligation can never be met in full, for the most precious losses are beyond restoration. What can be restored is a measure of dignity. It is conceded that dignity, like responsibility, can never be directly bestowed on anyone, but both dignity and responsibility are the natural fruits of meaningful participation in the common ventures of human intercourse, and if the tools which open the door to that participation can be distrained, they can also be restored. Restoration is a moral imperative to dignity, and dignity is the prime condition of human development and social health. Surely the state has, or ought to have, an unavoidable, inextinguishable interest in the restitution of opportunity to every citizen bereft of it, and this by every possible legal expediency.

We know by experience that some Blacks, like some whites, are going to prove out against the odds, whatever the odds may be. Every generation has its contingent of irrepressible men and women who were born to fly, however pedestrian their circumstances. These are the few. It is not necessary to argue whether the masses will ever take wing; it is sufficient to be reminded that they deserve the opportunity, that so long as they are citizens of the United States they have a vested right to try, and America has a vested interest and an inescapable obligation to provide that opportunity.

If the focus on the uniqueness of the black estate has been protracted, it is compelled by the conviction that no resolution of the American dilemma can be final until that most obvious and most enduring claim has effectively been met. The whole thrust for civil rights and human rights in America has moved principally on the impulse of the black struggle for justice. Deprivation is a relative condition, and countless American minorities, both real and euphemistic, first discovered their "deprivations" and their rights to relief through the dogged determination of the black struggle rather than by the suffering of direct experience. But however desperate a tardy discovery proved their lot to be, there was some consolation to be had in the recognition that the black condition was, and always had been, infinitely worse. The entire history of the black struggle for human rights, and the legal, political, and social effervescence created by it, has invariably clarified the rights, enlarged the opportunities, and otherwise benefited unnumbered groups and individuals beyond the black protagonists who have borne the brunt of continuous encounter. As previously suggested, when change does occur, all those classes and individuals which rest by accident or design on the black caste are pushed up *in order* through no necessary effort of their own. It is gratuitous mobility. Much of the resistance to affirmative action, and most of the anxieties about "reverse discrimination," derive from the fear that somehow the *order of progression* will be changed.

It is reasonable to expect that a serious strategy of affirmative action must begin where the problem is most real and most pervasive. The American Dream is for all the people, but the luster and attractiveness of that Dream can be compromised beyond retrieval by making the efforts to attain it a political and economic rat race instead of an orderly process of social adjustment. Nothing in our history, early or recent, gives substance to the fears of an inversion of the racial pecking order, but the evidence to the contrary is overwhelming. The new rights won by Blacks have inevitably, and quite properly, been interpreted in the interests of all Americans—sometimes to the momentary inconvenience of the very Blacks suing for relief.* Once again, equity is the remedy indicated. Equity makes the distinctions without which justice is a mockery. Having reaped the monstrous windfall of three centuries of the most insensate racial proscriptions, it is difficult to accept at face value the arguments of those so conveniently benefited by the past who now insist that justice suddenly become color-blind.

The *Bakke* case avoided the full implications of the racial issue, but left it as a possible consideration, *inter alia,* for *some*

---

* The *Bakke* decision is a case in point. Justice Powell cited the disregard of provisions of the Fourteenth Amendment as "the fatal flaw" in the Davis admissions program.

affirmative-action programs. But the judicial language of *Bakke* is vague and apocryphal, perhaps by design, and the varied and tentative opinions of the justices need to gel into a more mature and comprehensive consensus. One thing remains clear, however: no matter how unique the needs, or how just and compelling the claims of America's black citizens may be, the accumulated inequities of American racism will not be significantly lessened by affirmative action until the principle of specified relief for specified distress is recognized and established.

Beyond Bakke

After *Bakke*, it was widely anticipated that the then impending case of *United Steelworkers vs. Weber* would make the intent of the Court somewhat clearer. It did not. In the *Weber* case the Court gave a highly qualified approval to a race-conscious affirmative-action program initiated by a private employer, but did not entertain the fundamental issue of the rights and responsibilities of federal or state agencies to effect the relief of a specified class of citizens whose distress was in large part occasioned by the open and continuing collusion of the state (or its agencies) with another specified class of citizens. *Fullilove vs. Klutznick*, next in the affirmative-action cases to come before the Supreme Court, may finally turn out to be the landmark case *Bakke* should have been. In *Fullilove*, the two opinions constituting the majority decision seem to make it clear that Congress, an agency of the state, may officially recognize the peculiar implications of race in America in its allocation of interests controlled by the state. Writing for the majority, Chief Justice Warren Burger finally made the declaration the nation had long avoided and justice had so long required: "We reject the contention that in the remedial context the Congress must act in a wholly color-blind fashion. It is fundamental that in no organ of government, state or federal, does there repose a more comprehensive remedial power than in Congress."[11]

It is still not clear to what extent Blacks qua Blacks have improved their standing at the bar, but the official recognition of race as a factor the state may be called on to consider in its remedial efforts is encouraging. Certainly, it has the potential for a dramatic dismantling of the formidable political and economic machinery which kept the privileges of American apartheid intact for three centuries. It must be noted, however, that the *Fullilove* ruling *does not* distinguish among the races of the minority— thus again avoiding the fundamental issue of the implications of slavery and its aftermath. Blacks, the Spanish-speaking, Aleuts, Asians, and Eskimos are for the purposes of this ruling lumped together as a class. To be sure, the "minority" ground is narrowed to some degree, and none within the class are minorities of the majority. This ruling is perhaps indicative of future possibilities, but until the implications of *Fullilove* are tested, its meaning for the American dilemma remains unclear.

One reading of the *Fullilove* decision is that the Court conferred upon Congress the power to use racial quotas to remedy past racial discrimination. But once again *the essence of affirmative action is not in the recognition of quotas but in the recognition of classes*. Quotas made up of a confusion of disparate classes do not necessarily meet the needs of equity, and may in fact exacerbate the problem. The agencies of the federal establishment have for a long time been dealing with Indian claims, for example, but when the Indians sue for the restoration of some fraction of their land, justice would hardly be served by lumping the Indians with other minorities like Jews and Puerto Ricans and then dealing with them as a class on the question of tribal lands. Such an act would be farcical because the Indians' claim has a unique and distinctive point of reference rooted in our common history, and well known to us. It would be no less Jesuitic to defend inaction on the grounds that a remedy which required the present landholders to *share* the land with the Indians would be an inconvenience to "innocent" successors (who in their "succession" have grown quite rich on its produce). The relevant issue, of course, is not that Jews or Puerto Ricans or Filipinos may be landless minorities, but how the *Indian* who is landless *got that way*, and what the state and society can do now to remedy the situation. That is the only real meaning affirmative action can have, but for Blacks, a judicial reading to that effect has been most elusive.

In consequence, *Fullilove* must be accepted with caution. Whether or not the "minorities" recognized in the case constitute an arbitrary class, or whether they are presumed to have a distinctive community of interests which may be protected or enhanced by the blurring of history, is of critical importance. It happens that *Fullilove* had to do with a ten percent "set-aside" of federal construction grants aimed at insuring the availability of participation for specified minorities. Since construction is widespread and is carried on in all kinds of ethnic and racial settings, the reasonableness of the unusual class of minorities in this case is not at issue. But in any other context a classification that brackets Blacks, Eskimos, and Asians together would certainly appear contrived in America as we know it, and might well be suspect. If the pragmatic lesson to be distilled from the various affirmative-action cases is that the courts need not be blind to color, then the moral lesson still to be learned is that neither must they be deaf to history. Somewhere beyond *Bakke*, *Weber*, and *Fullilove*, when the pragmatic and the moral find their proper legal conciliance, affirmative action can proceed to do its job in the common interest of all Americans.

The Strain on Black Ethnicity

In the meantime, it is fair to say that the quality of life for selected segments of the black community has been changed dramatically since the *Brown* case was argued in 1954. There are young adult Blacks in Mississippi and Alabama and North Carolina who have never seen the back of the bus from the inside, and who have never had to go to the alley entrance of a restaurant to buy a sandwich. There is a generation of black youth who do not find it strange or awkward to compete with whites in sports, or in the classroom or in the job market, or to have white friends. They have no special animosities, no epithets or strategies reserved for the whites with whom they are in contact day by day. If through their survival mechanisms they know intuitively that they themselves are still perceived as "different," and that to most white people their difference makes a difference, that is dismissed as the white man's problem. Only he can solve it. These black youth have no identity problems, no strong racially based anxieties. Although they are aware that America is still a racist society, most of them have had no direct, personal racial confrontation of any consequence.

Who is this generation of Blackamericans? They are the sons and daughters of the newly emergent black middle class. Their fathers and mothers are black professionals who struggled against the odds of segregation and discrimination to educate themselves for what was then, at best, an uncertain future. The odds paid off far better than expected. The implementation of *Brown* first required thousands of instant Blacks in highly visible positions in industry and government and academe. This was followed by affirmative-action programs intended to give an element of solidity to what was initially superficial compliance. In the meantime, as the older Blacks, who were mostly educated in the black colleges of the South, dug in to preserve and maximize their new opportunities, their children, with greatly increased expectations, prepared themselves for a considerably broadened spectrum of opportunities. They are the self-confident young men and women who are today finding their way into job categories not even known to their parents when *Brown* was in its infancy. Sometimes they find doors open even beyond the job. Perhaps they have finally cornered, though they have not yet captured, that elusive will-o'-the-wisp the French call *fraternité,* which means *mutual acceptance* in America.

There are signs that the bonds of caste have been broken. To the degree that this is so, a reconstruction of the model on which American society has heretofore depended must also be underway. The two groups most likely to participate in new levels of interaction are the Liberated Black Elite (LBE), that fraction of a fraction of the black middle class, and their counterparts among upper-class whites. The white middle class is considerably less receptive because of its insecurities about its proximity to the class beneath, and because upwardly mobile middle-class Blacks are often overqualified for normative middle-class stature except for race. For example, the entry level of many jobs attractive to well-prepared Blacks is relatively high, and the jobs available are relatively few in number. This translates into a situation in which middle-class black professionals and managers are often more likely to have peer relationships with high-status whites than with middle or lower-middle-class whites. This would seem a continuation along more structured lines of the traditional dentification of the Old Line white liberals with the interests of the achieving/aspiring black middle class.

There is another aspect of this development which deserves attention. The options of the black masses appear to be in steady decline even as the black elite search for their niche in the American Dream. The gulf widens; the old bonds are raveling under the tension of new opportunities, new privileges, new interests, and new horizons—*for a few.* But there is nothing new for the black masses except the permanence of their exclusion and the threat of total abandonment. In the old days, all Blacks were members of the same black undercaste, and the black undercaste was absolute. In an absolute caste everybody is equally disprivileged, and mutual concern is the price of survival. There may be pretensions of differential status, but the ceiling on upward mobility is an absolute instrument of equalization for all to whom it is addressed. Before it, the pretensions of class-in-caste evaporate in the acid of reality. Hence, the class structure within the black caste never amounted to much: the black bourgeoisie and the black bootblack were alike subject to the embarrassments of external evaluation which recognized no distinctions between them. Now the integrity of the black estate is at stake because the rules have been changed. The lines have been laid between the very few and the very many, and the challenge to the few is to prove themselves worthy to be a people apart from their roots. In short, there are strong signals that America is prepared to write off the black masses in exchange for accepting the Liberated Black Elite, and that the ambivalence of the LBE is slowly but progressively diminishing after the initial agony and guilt have been faced.

It is a sad tale; a pernicious proposition. To divide the black community is to destroy the black estate. The black elite is the flower, the creative exponent of the black masses, and there has always been a certain security for the black estate in the tacit understanding that Blacks who somehow surmounted the barriers of caste and color almost always returned to their origins for spiritual nurture, bringing with them the benefits of extra-caste achievement and the valuable leadership of a less parochial experience. By the same token, it was inconceivable that the distinctiveness of the black subculture could ever be lost, for the exigencies of personal survival have always made living beyond the ghetto an adventure in loneliness and frustration.

There have been some changes. While the pattern of close social and cultural ties with the black community is still the prevailing mode for Blacks who now live in traditionally white enclaves, the sense of marginality is considerably less compelling. Personal and social needs that once could be met only "at home" can often be managed satisfactorily in their new environments. More than that, the LBEs who live and work among whites seem resigned, if not altogether eager, to make the personal adjustments required to reduce any exotic or alien impact their presence may entail for their newfound associates. Such adjustments are usually dismissed as just another aspect of the price of the job. In consequence, more Blacks find themselves accepted as exceptions, and as such, they turn up with increasing frequency at social functions in their new white neighborhoods, and (considerably less often) even at white churches on Sunday morning. In short, the conventional wisdom about black marginality, while still reliable, is no longer conclusive. And while it is still undoubtedly true that the distinctiveness of the black subculture cannot and will not be maintained by its expatriates, it is also true that the inconveniences of expatriation are a declining factor in maintaining the integrity of the black community.

Where does that leave the black estate? If the white establishment has written off the black masses as unproductive, unsalvageable, and undesirable, and if the Liberated Black Elite in full pursuit of the normative American rewards for individual diligence, education, and effort accept the long-overdue fruits of their exertion, what is the future of the black subculture? The accumulating evidence is not yet decisive, but the prognosis seems ominous: the black estate is in grave danger of having its potential leadership and its most creative genius siphoned off, just at the point when the promise of *Brown vs. Board of Education* should reach its logical maturity.

It will be a long time before we know in what segment of society the principal benefits of *Brown* will ultimately be found. We can hope that America as a whole has benefited, that participation in the American Dream has been broadened, and that the American dilemma will someday be rendered obsolete by a new and more positive reality. The Black Church will rejoice, and the vast energies it has had to expend to counter the pain and the agony, the misfeasance and the nonfeasance, the cruelty and the malevolence engendered by the notion of race may finally be redirected in the common interests of humanity.

8

Principles, Problems, and Prospects

Moral Resources for Resolution

Every culture defines for itself the critical values by which it will be judged and motivated, and every culture develops the standards which determine the degree of variation permitted from the accepted norm. From time to time the values that undergird and presuppose normative social behavior change. This transformation is usually gradual, for it is characteristically related to changing social experience, which may gradually erode established values. When values are in flux, there is an uncertain wavering of standards—a pendulum effect—as social opinion swings back and forth between what is remembered and revered and what is "new" and "progressive."

Here in the United States, the process of erosion and growth, the transformation of values, and the accompanying agony of reappraisal and redefinition were greatly accelerated by two world wars in a single generation. War is the supreme distortion of social relations, a phenomenon always marked by the suspension of many cardinal values, conventions, and obligations. Such distortion creates a climate in which "alien" values and ideologies may flourish, and it accelerates the proliferation of unconventional experiences, which in turn encourage new ways of looking at old institutions. In the aftermath of war, whether for good or for ill, some conventional notions and behavior may never recover completely the obligatory status they enjoyed previously. This is the inevitable risk of war (and perhaps it is one of the subliminal factors contributing to its occasion).

We are still struggling in the backwash of the most destructive war experience in history, and the normal evolutionary changes characteristic of human society are racked and distorted by the dislocations of that war and its implications for the future. The chief legacy of World War II is a prevision of World War III as the Final War—the sudden, cataclysmic, self-determined conclusion to all human experience. This is a unique consideration for human society, and it carries with it an excessive burden of human anxiety. True, man has contemplated the ultimate before, and religion itself is in part a response to the expectation that there will be a termination of terrestrial human experience, *but not by human initiative.* The difference is critical. As long as the end of the world—however imminent—was in the hands of forces beyond man's control, which is to say in the hands of God, there was hope for something beyond terrestrial experience, and this hope could be strengthened by an adequate moral response. In consequence, whenever human society has been faced with impending calamity, the characteristic human response has been a rededication to the old ways, i.e., to conventional standards of moral behavior. Implicit in such a response is a religious factor that recognizes not only the moral requirements of God but his faithfulness and consistency as well.

With *man* at the console of human destiny, all this is changed. There is a sense of futility which robs morality of its reason and of its promise. Indeed, morality becomes meaningless because if man has usurped the divine prerogative to destroy the world, since man is merely a destroyer and not a creator, what hope can there be beyond man's destruction? What is the payoff of morality? The values to be realized in the future run the very grave risk of not being realized at all, for we may well run out of time. Traditional Christian morality with all its sanctions is in a death struggle against hedonism, that ancient enemy which is now beguiling the "Now" generation, which finds itself trapped in the haircloth of social responsibility. The courage to endure and to win is no longer a salient aspect of who we once believed ourselves to be, for the call of hedonism is the call to structure reality around those values capable of immediate realization, without concern for either truth or consequence.

And what is the function of religion in all this? Religion begins where self-sufficiency ends. Or, to be more precise, religion begins with the *awareness* that self-sufficiency is an illusion, and one that can seriously compromise the struggle on earth and the availability of heaven. The function of religion is to make the human individual acceptable to God (who created him) in the hope that God will save him from himself. Religion anticipates change, just as conversion is itself change. *Change for what is better.* Hence, the catalogue of *changes* addressed by religion is as inexhaustible as the catalogue of human weakness and perversity, but among the more generic expectations is the belief that true religion turns darkness into light, foolishness into wisdom, deficiency into wholeness, strife into peace, hate into love, and bondage into freedom. Black religion begins with the unshakable faith that *all things are possible with God;* and in the confusing context out of which the Black Church developed, there was good reason to believe that *only* God could change the fate that had been designed for them by their "masters" on earth.

Private and Public Religion

Like other expressions of the uniquely human experience we call religion, the Black Sacred Cosmos—the peculiar spiritual mantle which identifies and distinguishes African-American culture—is not monolithic. It lives and operates in two realms of reality—the "spiritual" and the "public," or the "private" and the "communal." Professor Martin Marty, one of the most reliable interpreters of the practice and meaning of religion in America, identifies these opposing realms as "private" and "public" religion.[1] This spiritual polarity recognizes the most vital personal interests of the individual without abandoning or avoiding the interests of the community to which the individual is attached by bonds that include religion, but may also transcend it. While this concept does not exhaust the catalogue of possible interpretations of the private/public duality of religion, it does offer valuable insights for understanding black religion as a response to a bastion of grace recognized and shared by millions of Americans whose underlying cultural roots are as varied as those of the first convocation at Pentecost.[2]

The critical significance of the Black Sacred Cosmos will not be apparent wherever people believe that the Black Church is merely a kind of folk rendition of white mainstream religion.[3] Given the peculiar social and religious history of America, this very common belief may be understandable because it is consistent with other conventions which structure social and religious understanding in our society. The fact is, however, that every authentic religion is a precipitate of peculiar cultural experiences, experiences which shape identity in relation to some Ultimate Presence beyond the self and other selves cast from the same clay but fired in a different furnace. The Black Sacred Cosmos is addressed to the urgencies of the black experience which seem to lie beyond effective human resolution. The cultural mind-set that produced "mainline American religion" is not only of a different order, but of a different origin. It remains an unremitting backdrop against which the travail and triumph of the Black Church must accomplish its mission.

From the beginning, African Americans were involuntary adhesions to a host society in which their creative participation was severely limited by law, by tradition, and by caprice. Accordingly, the concerns of the host society were inimical to the most compelling concerns of the black bondsmen, and vice versa. In consequence, black religion takes its origins not from established religion in America, but from *the black experience in America,* which was and is a singular illustration of the complexities of the human predicament, and of the spiritual resources available to the Black Church's mission to overcome.

The Mission of the Black Church

From its inception, the mission of the Black Church was to do for its peculiar constituency of black slaves and freed men what no one else was willing to do for them, or to have them do for themselves. There was no consistent effort to bring Christianity to the slaves in America until the (Anglican) Society for the Propagation of the Gospel in Foreign Parts[4] established a spiritual presence of sorts on the plantations of the South in 1701—almost a hundred years after the first Africans arrived at Jamestown in 1619. The price the planters exacted from the SPG for permission to exhort the Blacks to convert was the written assurance of the reigning Bishop of London that in no case would "conversion work manumission." This understanding constituted an effective nullification of any dreams the slaves may have had of burning their bonds in the fires of the faith by confessing Christ, as was the tradition in England—but never in America. Nevertheless, it was not until the sense of the Bishop's spiritual ruling was codified as the law of the land that the slaveholders were willing to risk their property to the hands of the Christian missionaries. But the SPG was persistent, and by the middle of the eighteenth century, selected retainers from the Big House often held "auxiliary" membership in some of the white churches.

The black Christians in white churches were cramped by the churches' style and stifled by the requirements of racial conformity. Though they were finally "in church," it was demonstrably not "their" church, a message that spoke pointedly and consistently through the sermons, the prayers, the spiritual suppression, and the absence of fellowship. In the white churches the Africans were offered a God who had cursed them and ordained their travail and debasement in perpetuity. When faith falters, idols tumble down and false gods flee for cover, but truth is its own best witness and will ultimately be manifest in the scheme of things. It became clear to black and white Christians alike that there were serious incongruities in the White Church's faith and practice which could not be reconciled short of exhaustive spiritual and moral overhaul and reconstruction. Although there were individuals and even some churches who recognized the depravity of Christian racism, so drastic a reform was nowhere on the agenda of the White Church. Hence, it was inevitable that black Christians would heed the call to "come ye out from among them." South Carolina and Georgia were the early incubators of black churches, and the first viable black denomination was that established by Richard Allen in Philadelphia in 1815.

The Black Church *came into existence* fully committed to the private or spiritual aspects of religion—as *yin* to the *yang* of public religious concern. Like all other religions, the Black Church has leaned syncretistically upon the forms and formulas of preexisting religious norms. But the Black Church itself is a precipitate of its *own* culture, developed from, and in response to, its own experience and need. The black experience and the white experience in America may be parallel in history, and they may share a common demography, but they are no more interchangeable than, say, the Mormon Church and that of the Southern Baptists. Religion presupposes self-awareness, human vulnerability, and the availability of help from God. It is the uniqueness of the collective response to the experience of the Holy in response to human need that determines the structure of faith and the practice by which particular ways of faith are identified.

Freedom Is the Principal Thing

The Black Church knew from the beginning what its problems were—and they were many; but it also knew that, in the (ironic) words of Thomas Jefferson (who allowed himself to be a major aspect of the problem), "God's justice [would] not sleep forever." The Black Church knew, too, that its paramount mission was freedom. All other beneficial changes it might garner along the way were only preparatory to *true* freedom—the pearl of great price. Because the Black Church was born in a time and place of human bondage, it is generally "understood"—though incorrectly so—that the Church's emphasis on freedom was limited to liberation from the political encagement which made personal property of black men and women. It is easy and convenient to make this assumption because now that political freedom has been "achieved," and personal liberation is a "fact," freedom cannot possibly be a serious issue of consequence in or out of the Black Church—or any church. But in the Black Church, despite the millions of sermons preached, the prayers prayed, the solemn spiritual songs lifted up to heaven, freedom is as burning an issue today as it was when God first revealed Himself and His true relationship to His black children in America. The freedom the Black Church has been after transcends all of the petty impediments human caprice can assemble. It is the freedom to belong to God, to worship God exclusively; and it is the freedom to participate in the divine agenda without selective hindrance from other human beings. Translated into practical terminology, this means that since God made humankind the apex of His creative work on earth (and gave humans dominion over all else), it follows that God's expectations for human development and human behavior are not maudlin. In the Black Church it was recognized quite early that the Divine Expectation could scarcely be fulfilled in the absence of full freedom. Responsibility is not responsible when it is conditional. The concern was not just for physical or political freedom, although such an achievement was a necessary first step. True freedom meant the absence of *any* inhibiting factors or conditions which could disrupt the Divine Agenda by arbitrarily conditioning the lives of selected human beings who are still held accountable to God and the community. Mankind was created with the powers of reason and creativity; hence, the absence of educational opportunity is a formidable assault on freedom. Hunger, improper health care, joblessness, drug addiction, debasement, and denigration all inhibit the full flowering of the human potential to belong wholly to God.

In the early Black Sacred Cosmos, the first emphasis was on getting to know God more intimately and getting used to the idea that black people were not "cursed of God" or condemned by God to be "hewers of wood and drawers of water" for the white people who called themselves "masters." The Church brought the comfort and the security of God's love and redemption into the hopelessness of abject dereliction. The black response—the prayer and the preaching, the singing, the moaning, the shouting, (or as Du Bois put it, "the frenzy")—kept the human spirit alive and the presence of God an assured consolation.

A second urgent concern was to destroy the evil slave system by refusing to cooperate with it. Personal escape represented the ultimate act of noncooperation. Punishment for "running away" or for assisting those who did was severe, but the Black Church was the travel agency which sent or led tens of thousands of slaves to new freedom via the Underground Railroad. When the slave era was finally ended by the Civil War, there was still much to be done to prepare the ex-bondsmen for full participation in the Divine Agenda and in the body politic. And so the Black Church sponsored schools, savings societies, insurance companies, banks, improvement clubs, and a variety of social services to speed the day when full freedom would come to a cadre of people who were among America's oldest residents but her newest and least recognized citizens.

The struggle for full freedom has kept the Black Church in dialectical tension from its inception, and it continues as we move on into the twenty-first century. To cope with the formidable exigencies presently stalking this civilization, the pendulum of religious responsibility will (and indeed must) continue to move in measured cadence between its traditional practices and its communal responsibilities. Spiritual nurture and social reform are productive of freedom at its best, but the challenges of today and tomorrow will put the Black Church and its mission to the test of relevance and even survival.

The Black Church Shaped a Culture

The Black Church is one of the most remarkable institutions ever to originate in America. Born of the harsh travail of slavery, it has shaped a culture, blessed a people with refuge and hope and dignity, and given to America a new beacon for God and Country. And to those most in need of it, it has given power—the power of self-affirmation. Out of nothing but faith, the Black Church created its own literature, established its own publishing houses, elected its own bishops and other administrators, founded its own colleges and seminaries, and developed its own unique style of worship. Because black individuals themselves have frequently been unsure of their identity, and because the Black Church is itself a feature of the countercurrents of American racial proclivities, the Black Church has not always been without ambivalence in its understanding of what it is and why. At times it has seen itself as a less perfect counterpart of the White Church, striving for white approval. This self-undervaluation made some black churches more "white" in their ritual behavior and their social attitudes than many of the white churches they sought to emulate. Black ministers with Scottish or British accents, the distribution of church offices on the basis of skin color, and the effort to exclude from the worship services every vestige of "Negro music" or "emotionalism" have at times illustrated the uncertainty the Black Church has had about its role and its function in definition and service.

To be or not to be is not always the whole question. Considering the available alternatives in America two centuries ago, the Black Church had to be. Just what and how, that was the question! In the course of time, a small candle lit in the darkness of slavery has become a trusted beacon for the faith.

The Black Church as the Black Community

To understand the power of the Black Church, it must first be understood that until quite recently there was no disjunction between the Black Church and the black community. The church is the spiritual face of the black community; whether one is a "church member" or not is beside the point. That is the tradition for both spiritual and physical survival. Because of the peculiar nature of the black experience and the centrality of institutionalized religion in the development of that experience, the time was when the personal identity of the black individual was communicated almost entirely through this church affiliation. To be able to say "I belong to Mt. Nebo Baptist" or "We go to Mason's Chapel Methodist" was the accepted way of establishing identity and status when there were few other criteria by means of which a sense of self or a communication of place could be projected. While this has been modified in recent times as education, vocational diversification, and new opportunities for secular association have increased, the social identity of the African American as well as his self-perception are still, to an important degree, refracted through the prism of religious identity. *Her pastor, his church, his office in the church,* or merely *her denomination* are important indices of who *he* or *she* is. The Black Church, then, is in some sense a "universal church," claiming and representing all Blacks out of a long tradition that looks back to the time when there was *only* the Black Church to bear witness to "who" or "what" a person was as he or she stood at the bar of community confidence. The church still accepts a broad-gauge responsibility for the black community inside and outside its formal communion. No black person can die "outside" the Black Church. No matter how notorious one's life on earth, the church claims its own at death (though not always in life)—and with appropriate ceremony. The most colorful and protracted funerals in the black community are often those of non-church figures who, by the standards of some other communions, might be questionable candidates for the unrestricted attention of the church.

Looking In from the Outside

The Church often serves as one of the few stable centers of morals and values in our hectic lives. As African Americans try to grapple with the impact of America's scrambled values, most of them live with the painful discomfort of personal values which reflect the unresolved duality of the society to which they are trying to respond. It is like having "two minds in one dark body," as W.E.B. Du Bois described it, each mind trying to cover a part of the self left exposed by the other. Black people are painfully aware that to talk about America is not necessarily to talk about the sum total of all that is American, for the cultural network which holds this country together does not vibrate uniformly in all of its parts. Every black citizen knows by experience that while the part is inevitably a segment of the whole, the whole is not necessarily reflected in the part. That is the condition of his duality, being *in* but not necessarily *of.* For an example, let us return to the idea that war is a catalyst of change. The American response to war and its aftermath is of course shared by the black community, for that community is by definition "American." But it is also black, and the lenses through which experience is refracted may well be different for black and white perceivers. In fact, the very meaning of being black in America is, first of all, to be barred from certain significant experiences available to all other Americans, and to have those selected experiences that are available filtered through an alternative set of screens. The reasons for this should by now have been made clear, and need not be belabored. It is sufficient to be reminded that the distinction persists and that it is a distinction which makes a difference in analysis and understanding.

That African Americans may perceive differently is in no small part because they are differently perceived. Indeed, perhaps the principal inconvenience of belonging to a minority culture is the inevitability of appraisal by others whose judgments are critical in the determination of who and what you are. The ramifications of such conclusions are far-reaching, for it usually means that the significant institutions which undergird the subculture are either devalued, ignored, or assumed to be consistent with those of the overculture. This is, of course, the supreme expression of ethnic or racial arrogance, for the evaluator is seldom prepared to concede legitimacy to any values in conflict with his own. It is like saying, "You're an apple, and I'm a peach, but if you don't have fuzz on the outside and a pit in the middle you must be a freak fruit, or you wouldn't be that way!" This is the characteristic experience of the black subculture in America, and it is particularly ironic that so many of the deficits charged to Blacks have their origin in the conventions and the conveniences of their principal critics. The distortion of the black family is the classical case in point. The Black Church is another.

The institutionalized structure of black–white relationships has produced over the centuries patterns of behavior and perceptions which make it impossible for the most earnest white critics to have a legitimate experience of blackness. Sympathy is not readily translated into empathy by good intentions, and if empathic understanding between Blacks and whites is difficult or rare at the secular level, in the religious sphere, where values are rooted deeply in the common experiences of humanity in the presence of the Ultimate, it is not substantially improved. In short, despite significant experiences common to black and white Americans, there are important cultural reserves with little or no overlap, even in religion, and the signals relied upon for the perception of reality are not the same. It is important to remember that religion is an empirical event, occurring in time and space and involving human interaction at many levels, and while the principal references of religion may well be beyond the limitations of time and space, religion itself is earthbound. It is subject to the configurations of history and the impress of human proclivity. Whatever else it may be, it is a social phenomenon, and precisely because it is social, religion is impinged upon and conditioned by other forces at work in the society.

Worldviews in Conflict

Perceptions of the inherent value of racial distinctiveness have been a feature of American culture for more than three hundred and fifty years, ever since Africans were first introduced into the English colonies. Inevitably, these perceptions were expressed in terms of racial prerogative. And just as inevitably, black appeals to other standards of human valuation were ignored, and black protest was suppressed. Experience soon made it clear that only in their in-group anecdotes and folklore and in their private religion could black people safely give honest expression to attitudes markedly at odds with the role and the image assigned them by the white majority. The prevailing white expectation was that Blacks would always be distinct but could never attain distinction. They would always be unique but never original. Those stereotypes still shape much of our thinking and determine to a large degree the nature of our attitudes and responses. Yet it is still inconceivable to many white Americans that most black Christians think of themselves as having a distinctive religious heritage, and that fully eighty-five percent of America's black Christians belong to black denominations. Blacks have a worldview different from and independent of the traditional concepts of American Christianity, just as their secular lives often take on distinctive patterns of behavior in the unending struggle for creative survival.

Black religion presupposes a God who identifies in a personal way with black people in a society where such human relationships are uncommon. Some black communities outside the conventional church even refer to a "black God." The practicality of having a God who is self-consciously black is, of course, the promotion of group solidarity, intragroup and spiritual.[5] It is also the implicit denial that God is *white*, which is to be inferred from all of the cultural presumptions and behavior which identify themselves as "American." Divine leadership that is identified with the people has been a historically effective strategy for keeping the people identified with one another. Moses knew this. So did Muhammad. To ask "If God is for you, who can be against you?" is but half the question. The other half is rhetorical: "If God is for you, must you not be for yourselves?"—that is, *for one another?* The promotion of ethnicity, or group solidarity, is a function religion has performed for countless peoples, ancient and contemporary, and it is a salient aspect of black religion. Black ethnicity itself is the self-conscious celebration of black identity, but without any felt necessity to deny the larger and more inclusive identity implied in being "American." If our society ever reaches the maturity of a truly democratic pluralism, where all ethnic distinctions are only ceremonial rather than valuational, the Du Boisian cleavage, so common and so painful to the black experience, will be resolved. In the meantime, it must be clear that in spite of earnest goodwill and the most benign intentions, empathy in the absence of experience—whether within religion or without—is difficult to achieve. Sympathy is much less demanding, because it is conditional to the values of the sympathizer peculiar to the community with which he or she identifies. We see what we are equipped to see, and sympathy often takes on ephemerality when perception is refracted through new prisms of law, propaganda, fear, or personal inconvenience. Sympathy alone will not resolve the American dilemma, a point that is ponderously belabored in the contemporary conservative attack against the "white liberals" who have been the traditional "friend" of selective African-American aspirations.

The Search for Confirmation

The roots of the problem are deep. From the very beginning of the black presence in America, every activity involving the visible interaction of Blacks drew curious, and usually hostile, attention. Perhaps it was partially the fascination with the exotic, but it was also a persistent search for confirmation of the prevailing belief that black people were of a different species. Conventional wisdom, with some support from the literati and researchers of the day, made the African a member of the genus *Homo*, but one necessarily *different* in the significant expressions of social existence. Slavery, that peculiar malignancy on the moral pretensions of American civilization, came and went, but the residual mythology, the rationale for black bondage, persists with an amazing obstinacy in contemporary conventions, almost two hundred years since the abominable slave trade was ended.

For example, in spite of the extraordinary American preoccupation with sex, black sexuality, which for more than two centuries was considered only from the practical aspects of slave breeding, still surfaces in modern times as taboo and somehow unrespectable. Indeed, the prejudice, the fear, the ignorance, and the guilt concerning black sexuality have been so profound and deep-rooted in the crevices of American fantasy that, until very recent times, even so innocent an act as kissing was absolutely forbidden to Blacks performing on television or on the screen—even if they were married! Whites could kiss horses, dogs, cobras, or each other, but kissing between Blacks was considered offensive, vulgar, and a serious breach of social propriety. In short, it was a violation of the conventions designed to keep the human acceptability of black people in perpetual doubt by denying them the normal passions and behaviors of white people. A similar, though much more subtle, set of convictions may well be operative in American religion, where the exclusion of African Americans from local white churches functions to protect the racial integrity of the White Church and to keep alive reservations about the moral fitness of black believers. On the other hand, the mainline churches inspire little confidence and less conviction in the black community because they seem too eager to patronize the popular interest, no matter how clearly at odds that interest may be with traditional Christian understanding. The uncomfortable feeling that the conscience of the American church is not seriously troubled by the past, and that it is inordinately preoccupied with matters which do not address seriously the present condition in the United States, is troublesome and disconcerting. But change may be on the way.

What Price the Dream?

The evolving ethnic consciousness first stirred by Marcus Garvey in the 1920s was insufficiently understood and grossly undervalued by civil rights strategists in recent times, but it still persists in African-American skepticism about the prospects of being lost in the undertow of American culture. This ambivalence is a frequent source of frustration and embarrassment for traditional black leaders, who have generally interpreted the Black Dream as the desire for unconditional inclusion and participation in the whole range of values envisioned by the American Dream. But there may be a problem implicit in the unconditional acceptance of or immersion in any culture for those who have had conflicting experiences. An absolute commitment leaves no room for assessment and improvement should the realities beyond the Dream prove less enchanting than its promise. Even dreams have a price. The operating assumption of black leadership has more often than not been that, whatever the cost, it has long since been paid in advance by generations of black exploitation. This logic is mostly sound, but is it functional in the real world of sharply competing personal and group interests? A society is not static, and the demands it makes on its constituents are continuous and varied. We have already learned by painful experience that moral sensibility is seldom retroactive, even in the face of tacit agreement that there are skeletons in the closet. This society is quite willing to let the dead past bury its dead, so long as the future continues to profit from the way things used to be.

More than that, the price of effective belonging includes identification with those cardinal values that make the society what it is, and those struggling for full membership and participation do not want to risk seeming ungrateful by looking too closely at what they hope will be offered them. Nevertheless, now that the walls of racial exclusion have been breached to some degree, there is occasion for reflection and for a less frenetic evaluation of what the struggle has been about. But the road since freedom has been long and arduous, and for many, just getting to the tollgate is one of life's major accomplishments, not to mention the challenge of cruising the road in the terrifying traffic set by others who are more secure, better protected, and far more experienced.

The most obvious task of the African-American community is to strengthen the conviction that its own institutions are worth preserving. Black people are not necessarily immune to any of the by-products of our urban technocracy, nor can the black subculture merely by definition escape the moral and ethical backwash of an ethos defined by war, personal gratification, and the anxiety and disorder that have resulted. The strength and hope of the black subculture lie in the meaning and the nurture of its own institutions, which sheltered and illuminated the long pilgrimage from slavery to freedom to true participation. The black experience is a legitimate and heroic part of the American experience. It is there for all Americans to recognize, honor, and be a part of. It is not a worn-out carapace to be abandoned.

Soul and Creative Survival

The essential condition of any culture is the creative distinctiveness through which meaningful survival is accomplished, and the peculiar endowment that constitutes the black will to creative survival is sometimes called _soul._ Soul is a metaphysical property. It is popularized in such usages as "soul music" or "soul brother"; and there is of course the "soul" of theological reference. But none of these conveys precisely what is involved in soul as an ethnic concept, although there is probably a point at which all these perspectives come together in mutual reinforcement. Whatever else it is, soul is the essence of the black experience—the distillate of that whole body of events and occurrences, primary and derivative, which went into the shaping of reality as black people live it and understand it. It is the connective thread that runs through the totality of the black experience, weaving it together, making it intelligible, and giving it meaning. It is the sustaining force that motivated black survival in the face of the presumptive absurdity of innate racial inferiority.

Soul is a kind of cultural _élan vital_ developed through the experience of living and performing constantly on the margins of human society, under conditions of physical and psychological stress beyond the boundaries of ordinary human endurance. It is a quality and an art developed in the matrix of the African-American experience. It includes the sense of kinship and empathy and understanding that comes from the brutalizing denigration of sustained oppression and alienation. It is the black ego which refused to let go or to self-destruct in a protracted, monstrous historical encounter aimed at its destruction. Soul is expedience in survival—in the absence of which all other values must be abandoned. Soul is the reaffirmation of the black self-estimate, the medium through which the dignity, the genius, and the unity of African Americans are most naturally communicated. It is the enduring ego of the race. Perhaps it is also nature's most superlative defense against the painful depersonalization of the individual and the disintegration of his innate capacity for peer participation in the reconstruction America still has to undergo.

Soul is an ethnic concept, a product and a creator of black culture. It is the art, the music, the religion, and the style of black people. It is the peculiar language of the black experience because it is the embodiment of that experience. Soul is not religion, but it cannot be separated from religion because the whole black experience assumes the character of a religious odyssey. It is black people celebrating their own experiences and achievements. Soul is black folk being themselves without apology, or the felt need for one. It is the triumph of black survival and the readiness to become full partners with the rest of America, which has long claimed its produce without public recognition of its logo.

Freedom and Responsibility, and Liberation

Responsible freedom is the authentication of personhood. It is that condition which permits maximum communication between God and mankind, and mankind with itself. The image of God is reflected in the human individual: *a person with dignity.* Dignity is an attainment, most Christians believe, impossible to realize when the free expression of the human will is denied or made conditional. Hence, the tradition of struggle against un-freedom is probably as old as religion. Yet the expectation that the Black Church should bear the prime responsibility for the full freedom and dignity of African Americans is deeply rooted in the black psyche, for that is the record of the black experience. The larger issue all Christians are called to address is whether the Church Universal represents the liberating activity of God and, if so, should provide an impetus for all men to liberate themselves. The answer from black religion is that God wants man free as God is free, and that God and mankind must work together to accomplish full freedom for all God's children. It is little wonder, then, that the ideal black church quickly established itself as one in which the spiritual commitments of the congregation were made manifest in their efforts to "advance the race," or to recover the inherent dignity of a people cast in the image of God.

Shaped as they were by the circumstances of the black experience, the critical values of black religion were predestined to be both spiritual and para-spiritual. Spiritual for all of the reasons that human contingency needs divine reassurance and support; para-spiritual because African Americans recognized quite early that only the most qualified spiritual commitment was possible so long as their bodies, their wills, and their behavior in this world were not theirs to command or commit. As a result, black religion has at times meant escape, insurrection, rebellion, sabotage, civil disobedience, political partisanship, economic withdrawal, and similar struggles against the un-freedom which qualified their commitment to God. No religion can be responsible without freedom, and the dignity of the God-created person is not to be compromised by any human will or caprice.

A Destiny to Fulfill

The overwhelming majority of the Blacks in this country were slaves when the first black denomination was founded, and prospects for any significant change in their status at that time were hardly anticipated. Yet today the Black Church represents an investment of hundreds of millions of dollars. Countless thousands of black men and women have been graduated from schools and colleges founded and supported by the Black Church. Black Church leaders are highly visible on the world scene as Christians everywhere explore ways of promoting their common interests and resolving their common problems. A black preacher has been a serious candidate for President of the United States. Looked at objectively, that is a long way from the segregated galleries black Christians renounced two hundred years ago. But the question the Black Church always has to face is: "Is that enough?" Black disabilities are still many, and the need for even more critical involvement seems greater than ever.

The Black Church is frequently chided for being preoccupied with building more churches and burning more mortgages when too many black people are hungry and homeless, an indictment often summed up as "elegance without relevance." Others dismiss it as an essentially cultic enterprise whose principal commitment is to the aggrandizement of its visible leadership. While such views may reflect the aberrations of particular churches, not excluding white churches, such conclusions are more reflective of our institutionalized prejudices than they are of our critical, impartial judgment. The Black Church is more than America has been willing to concede it to be. The Church as an institution is by heritage a conservator of existing values. As such, it does not characteristically rush into a full-blown response to every bubble that appears in the social flux. The Black Church responds to its own reading of history, born of a very painful experience. The Black Church has developed its own traditions to meet the strange imponderables of the black experience in America. One of those traditions is a concern with the human situation on both sides, a concern which in recent years has been institutionalized in important programs of social action. It was in this tradition that Martin Luther King, Jr., and the members of the black churches of Montgomery offered prayers for Rosa Parks and those who debased her humanity, and then got out and walked for dignity and self-respect for all African Americans. It was also in this tradition that Leon Sullivan and the black congregations of Philadelphia kept right on singing and praying while they avoided the goods and services of those merchants who refused to hire Blacks to share the thousands of jobs their patronage supported.

The Black Church is equally "at home" whether it is praising the Lord or resisting the devil—the historic formula for the salvation of the soul and the liberation of the body.

The 1960s were a momentous decade in the history of social change. They were a unique occasion for America to free herself from some of the chauvinism that shackles us all to a past misadventure from which we have yet to recover fully. The 1960s were also the occasion for the modern Black Church to demonstrate its relevance and maturity. While America faltered, Martin Luther King, Jr., and his followers did more to embellish the name of Western Christianity than has been done since the original Martin Luther tacked his challenge of corruptions on the door of the church at Wittenberg in the sixteenth century. More than that, the high moral challenge of King's crusade and his inevitable martyrdom did more to reestablish conscience and credibility in religious America than all the conferences and pronouncements the American church has addressed to human rights and human dignity in many a day. King was a living example of what the faith claimed to be about; and King was, by ironic necessity, a product of the Black Church, an institution which owed its existence to a very uncharitable appraisal of the spiritual and moral sufficiency of African-American Christians.

Looking Back

When, a hundred years ago, W.E.B. Du Bois predicted that the twentieth century would be "the century of the color line," Du Bois was more right than even his clairvoyant intellect could have foreseen. This has indeed been the century of the color line—the century in which America has tried to sort out and define its values by sorting out and defining its citizens by race and place. A hundred years of strident, schizophrenic, and sometimes sanguinary effort, and the color line is still with us; the American dilemma has not gone away. Why *hasn't* it gone away? Why *hasn't* it been resolved? In the favorite fantasies of our self-perception, we are a God-fearing, democratic, justice-oriented, caring people who make the critical decisions for the rest of the world to accept and be judged by. But at home we fumble and stumble and fail over the meaninglessness of color. The "Second Reconstruction," a euphemism often used for the civil rights movement that shook the country at mid-century, has been over now for more than a generation. A lot of Americans died in that effort to make their country "right," and a lot of Americans discovered themselves and their potential to make contributions to God and country, which would never have been possible under the limiting covenants of racial repression that have for so long made America hostage to a schedule of values it disavows. The civil rights movement produced a new class of patriots and *héros sans couleur.* Their slogan was, "We shall overcome!" But they did not overcome. And now the color line of the twentieth century threatens to be the "center line" of the twenty-first.

Assessing the import of the civil rights movement at the behest of President Lyndon Johnson, the foreboding candor of the Kerner Report informed us that America was being divided into two parts: "one black and one white, separate and unequal." The dilemma persists. In confirmation of its persistent, pervasive presence, the Milton Eisenhower Foundation issued a carefully documented report of its research on racism in America. The Eisenhower Report proved even more chilling than Kerner. Under the dour title *The Millennium Breach,* the Eisenhower Report advised America that "people need to become aware that things are getting worse again. . . . While leaders and presidents talk of full employment, inner city unemployment is at crisis levels . . . the rich are getting richer, the poor are getting poorer, and minorities are suffering disproportionately."

At the time *The Millennium Breach* was made public in the late winter of 1998, black unemployment in selected areas like South Central Los Angeles was above thirty percent, compared to the national average of less than five percent. Nevertheless, while the economic factor is crucial to the index of the quality of life for African Americans, it is by no means the sum of the onus of racism. The awesome penalties and inconveniences of racism affect every interest and every level of human life and experience for those at whom it is directed. It is not merely a matter of employment, or opportunities for employment, but of the quality of health care, education, justice in the courts, respect for the individual, and so on, ad infinitum. Once again, the basic issue is *people*—what it means to be human in a human society, and to be so recognized.

The Century of Freedom

In a special edition in the spring of 1998, *Time* magazine devoted itself to celebrating the signal accomplishments of the twentieth century. The list was extensive, ranging all the way from flight to cyberspace. America became the unquestioned leader of the political world, "[where] the ideals of . . . individual rights and civil liberties, personal freedom and democratic participation finally held sway over more than half the world's population." The twentieth-century Pax Romana *Time* lifts up for our reflection is studded with wonders, and it labors the human imagination even to grasp some of them in concept. Even more difficult to conceive is how all this could be accomplished with such world import, but hardly a rustle in the tall, dry grass of racial insensitivity and repression. *There has been change*—significant change for selected fragments of America's disinherited. The answer to the question politicians like to ask—"Do you consider yourself better or worse off since our party took over?"—would probably be a resounding affirmative if put to African Americans measuring the twentieth century against any other. Yes, things *are* better. Things are *worse*, too. There is no orderly or logical relationship in the equation which holds access and opportunity, merit and capacity, respect and expectation in proper balance and alignment. If you insist on treating a person like a slave, he will act like one. Treat him as half-human and he will never rest until he finds the other half of himself. Only then will his soul be "rested."

The *Time* essay concludes with an interesting prediction for the next century:

> We will no longer be able to permit unequal educational opportunities. Schools will need to be open to competition and subjected to standards so that we avoid creating a two-tiered society. The ultimate goal of democracy and freedom, after all, is not to pursue material abundance, but to nurture the dignity and the value of each individual. That is the fundamental story of this century.[6]

Time is certainly right in part. All people everywhere want the human recognition from significant others that permits them the dignity and the respect that is part of the package of humanity. In the absence of this very fundamental understanding, none of the lesser values can ever be "satisfying" or "enough" for those who want true freedom.

The Children of Hope

Contemporary studies show that the color line becomes far less flexible among mature adults than among children and younger adults of both races—whites and Blacks. So does the hope for a more equitable future. Whether youthful tolerance is merely a phase in the process of coming of age and the resistance of the mature adult is a bow to conformity or some other security coding is not clear. What is indisputable is that while children do get themselves involved in racial slurs and other antisocial behavior, it is far more likely to be individualistic than generic. It is the individual himself, not his class or his race, that makes him unacceptable—a bit of wisdom that unreconciled "mature" adults might well learn from their children of the cyber-age.

The most challenging problem ahead of us may well be the task of providing the children of America with an environment that is as nearly race-free as possible for as long as it is possible to do so. Adults entering the next century will take their accumulated baggage of bias along with them, of course, but they can extend the protection and the security of their children by permitting them to truly experience the world in transition rather than forcing their commitment to a world that was never quite clear about just *what* it was, or what it wanted. Or why. Today's children are smarter than their counterparts in the generation before, and they have more information immediately available which will not be filtered through the dubious charcoal of convention. If there is true hope for the resolution of the American dilemma, it lies with our children. That hope deserves the best encouragement and protection we can provide for it.

This is an assignment for a society which has convinced itself that it *cares* about youth, and has then proceeded to consign them to the care and nurture of strangers. Apparently, through some privileged logic known only to us, the expectation is that our children will grow up "sound" in the values their parents never taught them. But to negotiate successfully the youth culture which pervades our schools and their collateral institutions today is an enormous accomplishment in and of itself. To have to do so alone in such a vast wilderness of undiscovered knowledge and unrefined information would put even Hercules to the test. Small wonder that teenage suicide is soaring, and murder *in the schools* (of all places!) has become commonplace. These strange pathologies are not *necessarily* race-related, but they *may* be the bizarre signals of our children's rejection of the social confusion which makes life in America the Beautiful considerably less so. The American norm appears to be a way of life that leaves our children feeling ambivalent about who they are and who they want to be in a culture which has been dangling between the horns of a dilemma for three hundred years.

Assault on the Black Churches

Mainline denominations in general, including Catholicism, have had a continuous decline in membership for at least three decades. During the same period, the Mormon Church has made extraordinary progress in its determination to become truly international, and the Black Church, despite its losses to the Black Muslim Movement, continues stable in its membership and increasingly aggressive in its social outreach and community involvement. Once the Mormons, or Latter-Day Saints, faced realistically the implicit dangers of isolating themselves with a theologically based racial polity, they set out, in characteristic Mormon fashion, to mend it with new revelations, and then they moved on with zeal and determination to recover lost ground. But in typical American fashion, their initial emphasis after being freed of racial constraints by official revelation was to focus on the perceived spiritual needs of and benefits of Mormonism to dark-skinned people outside the United States. Their successful recruitments in Asia and Africa soon gave the Mormons claim to be the fastest-growing religion in America and, except for Islam, in the world.

The general decline of religion in America has been associated with the constant bombardment of new ways of thinking and behaving which are in real or imagined conflict with "old-time religion"—that encodement of Christian values we were all expected to know almost intuitively, and to practice as public policy. However, in the extraordinary century just ending, the explosion of information deluged society with new questions, new answers, and new ways of living and of looking at life. To many, the "old-time" church became obsolete. To some others, the Church represented just another pseudo-secular institution with unearned exemption from the annealing fires of a society in charge. Much of the traditional respect and reverence for the Church was dissipated in theological arguments about sex and gender. Personal impropriety and scandal in office moved the decline along. Suddenly, "sacred persons" in or out of religious garb were viewed through public eyes which were jaundiced by the excesses they thought they saw. Assaults on church personnel, robbery and violation of church premises, and the wanton destruction of church icons and artifacts seemed to mark growing disillusionment about the integrity and the social usefulness of organized religion.

A more direct attack on the churches—if not on religion itself— has been the criminal destruction of churches by arson. In a period of only two years during the last decade of the retiring twentieth century, about 165 black churches were put to the torch. Almost all of them were in the South, and the prevailing presumption was that the fires were racially motivated. Official investigations appeared sluggish until President Clinton himself visited the site of a burned-out African Methodist Church in Greenfield, South Carolina. There was a measured reluctance in the media and among political interests to interpret the burnings as hate crimes, or as a racist conspiracy. Much was made of the fact that some white churches had also been firebombed, and that in at least one case the arsonists who burned a black church were themselves black—and intended to profit from the fire. But the argument that the burning of all these churches across the South was merely the work of teenage vandals or rapacious opportunists was unconvincing and uncomforting. It had all happened before.

Black churches and black schools have been burned throughout American history. For all the spiritual inconvenience and economic deprivation that a cherished house of worship reduced to ashes must symbolize today, it has all happened before. The ambivalence toward African Americans and their religious interests has sometimes taken extraordinary turns. During the slave era, when black churches—where they were permitted to exist at all—were strictly monitored and regulated, it was not unusual for white planters to be converted by black slave preachers. Occasionally a slave preacher with unusual "spiritual gifts" would be purchased specifically to pastor a white congregation.

The Reverand John Chavis of Raleigh was sent to Princeton as a slave to study theology. Upon his return to North Carolina, he traveled widely to preach to Presbyterian congregations, both black and white, and he was headmaster of an elite school for the sons of the planters and the political aristocracy.

Joseph Evans, a black Methodist preacher, was whipped repeatedly for trying to establish a black church in Fayetteville, North Carolina, at the end of the eighteenth century. But Evans's faith was so compelling that three times he broke the ice in the Cape Fear River to swim to his underground church, which met secretly in the swamps and sand hills of eastern North Carolina. In the face of such compelling spiritual tenacity, Evans was finally permitted to build a small church that was soon taken over by whites, who retained him as their pastor until he died in 1812. Black members were required to sit under a shed outside the church they had built. After the Civil War, the church reverted to black membership and has remained black to this day.

Throughout our history, white Christians and black Christians have devised some extraordinary arrangements for sharing the faith, but there was never a time when the independent black churches were not under threat—overt or implied—of destruction. In Charleston, South Carolina, in 1822, the 4,000-member African Methodist Episcopal Church pastored by Morris Brown was destroyed because it was suspected of being involved in an insurrectionist plot. In North Carolina, even the venerable Reverend John Chavis was "suppressed," although his congregations were mostly white. During Reconstruction, many black churches and schools were burned whenever they became a "nuisance" beyond the toleration of conventional boundaries.

During the civil rights struggle, scores of African-American churches, businesses, and homes were burned. Indeed, bombings and burnings became so routine that many Americans accepted them as the inevitable price of progress, the "carrying charge" for black freedom. But four little girls in Sunday school at Birmingham's Sixteenth Street Baptist Church never had a chance to confront so puzzling an explanation: Addie, Carole, Cynthia, and Denise were literally blown to heaven when their church was bombed on September 15, 1963.

The Sixteenth Street Baptist Church was rebuilt, as most of the recently burned churches will be rebuilt, and this time with substantial help from white Americans whose spiritual commitments and racial practices are at odds with each other.

As happened during the civil rights crusade, small groups of white Americans have traveled hundreds of miles to offer their labor, their skills, and their encouragement in the rebuilding of some of the burned-out churches. They come at their own expense and work without charge—black and white together. Local building-supply houses sometimes make limited donations of building materials to the churches in their trading area. In a syndicated story, William Raspberry reports that International Paper Corporation has promised to supply the burned-out churches collectively with "$16 million worth of building supplies." Free.[7]

Justice in the Courts and on the Street

The savage beating of Rodney King on the streets of Los Angeles happened to be caught on camera by an amateur photographer. It was fortunate for America that the atrocity was filmed, for it would have been extraordinarily difficult for King to have convinced the justice system before which he had to stand trial that his rights had been abused to the very door of death. The abusive "whipping" of

African Americans who for whatever reason find themselves in the hands of the minions of the law is routine, often conspiratorial or presumptive, and always triggered with an unspoken understanding on the part of many white police officers that any black person is a criminal, caught or uncaught. Such notions are deeply rooted in the psychological contusions which discolor our culture and mark the spot where the pain is.

Many police agencies across the country issue so-called profiles of *potential* criminals. Anyone who seems to fit the "profile" in terms of the kind of car he or she may drive, *the color of the skin,* "body language," etc., becomes an automatic candidate for arrest. The overwhelming number of these selective arrests are of African Americans, men and women who elect to travel the streets and highways of America. Such searches and seizures are not only of doubtful legality, they are dangerous in that they set the stage for deadly confrontation between "the law" and private citizens who are not always willing to be run through a demeaning criminal procedure for the victimless crime of DWB—Driving While Black.

In the beating of Rodney King, America caught an unasked-for look at police behavior with very deep racial overtones. But during the celebrated trial of O. J. Simpson in Los Angeles in 1995, the taped remarks of Mark Fuhrman spelled out the sordidness of police abuse of black citizens with all of the excitement of sharing a favorite experience. Fuhrman, who was a veteran detective in the Los Angeles Police Department, spoke for several hours in a taped interview with Laura McKinney, a screenwriter. The sum of what he had to say detailed the routine falsification of evidence, the destruction of evidence, deliberate false arrest, the beating and torture of prisoners, police collusion in a "code of silence" designed to obstruct justice, and other strategies commonly used to deprive African Americans (Mr. Fuhrman insisted on calling them "niggers") of equal justice before the law.[8]

If the country was revulsed by the Fuhrman tapes, that revulsion was possibly premature, for shortly afterward, white policemen whipped a black motorist to death in Detroit. And in New York City, an innocent black bystander was hauled to the precinct station by white officers who beat him into helplessness and then sodomized him with a plunger handle.

The police are not alone, of course, in their willingness to target and to punish black Americans before any crime has been proven, but the ferocity of police attacks upon the psyche and the *soma* of African-American citizens is ominous in its prospect for the days ahead. The *Fuhrmanization of justice* cannot be vaunted in a democratic society without threat to the general tranquillity and the moral sensitivities of a free citizenry, no matter what their race. Mark Fuhrman made it clear, however, that the police tactics he describes and apparently embraces are not only common strategy in the apprehension of criminals, but are particularly useful in bringing black criminals to justice with efficiency and expedition. His thesis seems to be that after all is said and done, in pursuing black suspects as opposed to white suspects, the black suspects are probably guilty anyway, so why waste time or money or bother with legal protocol? Concoct your best case and arrest them!

Unfortunately, such Fuhrmanized justice is well understood and covertly endorsed by many outside the ranks of the police. So pervasive is the general acceptance of the Fuhrman dogma that some criminals routinely stake their freedom (and sometimes their lives) on it. A common defense in criminal court is referring to some anonymous "black man" allegedly seen at or near the scene of the crime. Hunting down the fictive "black man" can buy time. And if he can be caught and properly run through the horrors of the racial labyrinth, his freedom or his life may be the price he has to pay for being who he isn't. In Massachusetts, a white man murders his wife and arranges for the body to be discovered in a black neighborhood. In South Carolina, a white mother hoping to marry a prominent local citizen drowns her two young sons in a lake and claims that "a black man" kidnapped them. Black people, anonymous and otherwise, have been the nation's scapegoats and the culture's psychological prop for as long as they have been in America. In the century ahead, the challenges will be so persistent and of such magnitude for all of us that familiar scapegoats may be unable to carry the traditional overload that black toleration seems to demand.

The police are not alone in trying black America, but the blatant ferociousness of their "official" behavior seems a deliberate appeal to the passions and policies of former times, and there is little evidence that it has peaked or is declining. It is often alleged that "the police act for the people," but if this is true, it is time for "the people" to redefine themselves and to issue new guidelines for the very important jobs with which the dedicated men in blue have been entrusted. Unfortunately, some of "the people" prefer to act for themselves, not as models for police behavior, but confident in the expectation that in any racial confrontation, police bias will give them a certain protective edge. In consequence, hate crimes become increasingly bizarre as the perceived risk seems to diminish.

In 1997, in Fayetteville, North Carolina, a black man and a black woman walking home along a country road at night were randomly selected for murder by two skinheads simply because they were black. In Clavendon County, South Carolina, an African-American boy of nine ventured across the road to play with some white children he saw there. He was viciously whipped by the white parents, who roped him to a tree and fired guns in his direction. In Jasper, Texas, a black man walking home from a visit with nearby relatives was chained by his ankles to a pickup truck and dragged until his blood, his head, and pieces of his torso littered the roadway. It is no longer necessary to have a lynch mob to have a lynching. Two or three conspirators can produce the same results without the conventional crowd who turned out in the old days to share support and to witness for themselves the favorite strategy for "keeping the nigger in his place." Today, the six o'clock news will bring the sordid details into the comfort of the living room.

Other Concerns

There are other race-related concerns which are less dramatic than confrontation with the law or the lawless. One of them is being a perpetual scapegoat for a society which does not seem to care where the onus of responsibility or the burden of inconvenience falls, so long as it is racially selective. But society loses in the short run and in the long run whenever large numbers of less-favored individuals struggle for meaningful survival. Society reaps enormous dividends when people are too responsible to be reckless, too fairly treated to hate, too well educated to be burdensome, too satisfactorily employed to be idle, too healthy to live in despair, and too valued to be abused. Suicide among black teenagers is now the third leading cause of death, up from nothing just a few years ago. Young black males are forced into a kind of floating mass of TNT, a scandalous waste of human potential. The poverty rate among blacks is three times that of whites. Whites live several years longer, have much lower infant mortality rates, and can afford and get much better health care. Racism may not be the sole cause of any of these disparities, but it is the common denominator that holds them in a constant relationship and that must be broken in the common interest.

And we are left with one fewer tool for the fight now. By 1998, the California voters' approval of a referendum to dismantle the state's affirmative-action programs had produced a somber outlook for the future for the minorities who had seen affirmative action as a ray of hope in a canyon of hopelessness. The passage of Proposition 209 had an immediate and chilling effect on black and Spanish enrollment at the state's frontline colleges and universities. Of the 8,000 students granted freshman admission to Berkeley for the fall of 1998, only 255 were black—less than half of the 598 admitted under the affirmative-action formula in 1997. The African-American admissions rate was similarly depressed at UCLA, where it plunged to almost half of the 280 admitted in 1997.

"Copycat" bills of the pattern of California's controversial Proposition 209 have been introduced in the legislatures of at least thirteen other states, and while none of them has become law, minorities must live with the fear that they may be out of school, out of a job, or out of a contract because the belated efforts to help them with opportunities to become a contributing part of productive society have been withdrawn. There is an ancient adage that warns about "cutting off the nose to spite the face." Another tells about "throwing out the baby with the bathwater." The national interest would be well served if people gave fresh consideration to both.

Conclusion

WHEN the full story of Martin Luther King, Jr., is written, it
*The Black Sacred Cosmos and
Martin Luther King, Jr.*

will be in the form of a commentary on a culture rather than the
biography of an individual; for the enduring significance of Martin
Luther King has far less to do with the life of an individual than
with the times and the circumstances against which that life was
played out. Martin Luther King is the tragic hero by whose lumen
the profile of Western culture, American-style, was projected on
the conscience of the nation for one brief moment of history. The
significance of King is measured not so much by the nature of his
accomplishments or the realization of his dreams as by the power
of the paradox he created for America by being who he was and doing what he did. Martin Luther King was never on trial at all.
America was on trial, self-consciously on trial, and America developed a defensive psychosis which inevitably led to the removal of
Dr. King. He was the symbol—the unbearable symbol—of what is
wrong with ourselves and our culture.

Because Martin Luther king was a black man, and because he ar-
ticulated so clearly and expressed so perfectly the central message
of Christian doctrine, he was for white-oriented America the negation of negation: a contradiction in terms, a paradox *par excellence.*
He could not be dismissed as a fool, or as a quack, or as a "Negro
cultist," because his credentials in faith and learning were of the
highest order, coming as they did from some of white America's
most respected institutions. But how do you deal with the negation
of a negation? How do you deal with a black man who does not

259

hate, but who knows he is hated; who loves when he knows he is not loved; who wants to live, but whose life is a constant challenge to death; who prays for his abusers; who says to a society which had consigned him to oblivion, "Is this what you meant by the faith?"

One response to the paradox created by King is that we contrived to see ourselves in him—"our better selves," we said hopefully and often, and *sotto voce*; and that is symptomatic of our tragedy, for what we saw was fantasy. Neither the real Martin Luther King nor the impossible *ignis fatuus* we sought to make of his love, his courage, and his dignity said much about our efforts except that they were poor.

It was inevitable that we would have to kill Martin Luther King, and it was just as inevitable that we would make of him a myth and a legend in preparation. *Whom the gods would destroy, they first make mad.* Since Dr. King successfully resisted madness, human society, which is often more subtle and more pragmatic than the gods, began assembling an anecdotal vita. It was imperative that we create *King, the Myth,* because we were unprepared to deal with *King, the Man* in any way different from our traditional ways of dealing with men who are black. So we created an elaborate mythology to justify an enlarged perspective, without realizing that since no African American other than Dr. King could fit that perspective, it was no less sterile and unenlightened than our traditional views about the sources of value in being human.

We were right back where we started, but the process of myth-making is itself vital to the way racial accommodation works in this society. It makes possible a kind of ritual participation—a ritual sharing in which Blacks and whites together create the social truths they agree to live by. Societies do this without respect to racial accommodation, of course, as in the naming of heroes, the interpretation of significant events, the sanctification of dogma, etc.; but the American racial rapprochement, where it has existed at all, has traditionally depended upon the mutual acceptance of an inordinate body of deliberate, contrived mythology about everything from sex to salvation. As a consequence, white people and their black counterparts seldom touched base in the common realities of their mutual existence. Myth has been the language with which we talk past each other and avoid confrontation. When the mythology is about a person—Martin Luther King, for example—it is used as a vehicle for the displacement of emphasis and the distortion of values. Society may avoid, if it chooses, confronting what is truly significant about what a man is and what he does, by addressing itself to the mythological screen which diffuses the impact of his personality. We do not have to be serious about a myth, and if the myth obscures the reality behind it, or in some way qualifies that reality, we do not have to be serious about the reality either. The best of all possible postures is to be able to look over the man *and* the myth with the privilege of delay.

In the case of Martin Luther King, the chief mythmakers have been the Blacks who knew him before the live coal touched his lips and the whites who heard him prophesy thereafter. It was the Blacks—the friends, the relatives, the teachers, the biographers, the classmates, the casual acquaintances—who supplied the anecdotal data (sometimes with the proper local-boy-made-good embellishment); but it was influential white America that put the peculiar construction on the data supplied, and gave it the meaning and analysis that shaped the mythological prism through which America was willing to contemplate Martin Luther King. Together, the Blacks and the whites created something. An understanding. A rapprochement. In the age-old tradition, but with new consequences. King's boyhood antics became the clues to a singular destiny (after the fact), and his ordinary collegiate experiences became the sure sign of divine intention. Even his ancestors had to be purified by myth back to the threshold of slavery to make them acceptable progenitors of a unique African American with which America had somehow to come to terms. How important is it that King's paternal grandfather was "part Negro, part Irish" in a society which for three hundred years defined as "Negro" anyone having one drop of African blood! Perhaps that was an anticipation of the Tiger Woods phenomenon (Woods is repeatedly identified as black, although his mother is Asian). But what is the significance of being born into a family of "black Puritans"[1] when black religion takes its departure from the black experience in encounter with God? Our society gives such accidents an inordinate significance, and that significance has something to do with the credibility of a man who is

The notion that black constituencies were disdainful of black leadership was rooted in a complex mythology that had to do with the black leader's inevitable vulnerability when faced with the awesome reality of white power. Martin Luther King demonstrated that determined togetherness *creates* power *ex nihilo*, as it were, and in the face of this power, the systems which protected the white mystique proved both vulnerable and corrupt. The stage was set for the ultimate liberation of all African Americans by freeing them from the paralysis induced by accepting at face value the conventions of white-over-black as a final principle of reality.

The black people had to relearn how to believe strongly in themselves and one another. When we consider the awesome weight of tradition implacably enforced by every stratagem of social policy, we need not wonder why. Black people have always had an unwavering religious faith, and the peculiar genius of Martin Luther King lay in his ability to transform religious fervor into concerted social action, and to offer political leadership under the rubric of his religious calling. The effort had been made before, but never for so sustained a period under conditions of such extreme danger and liability. It may well be the final judgment of history that Martin Luther King's greatest contribution to black freedom was made in Montgomery when he helped black people free themselves from self-doubt and self-abasement. Perhaps his greatest mission was simply to teach people to talk together, pray together, walk together, and stay together. Once they had learned to do that, the ensuing course of events was predictable. No chains can hold a people who believe in God, themselves, and one another.

The Southern Christian Leadership movement, or something like it, was the inevitable precipitate of the Montgomery experience. From that experience, King emerged the leader of a successful local confrontation with institutionalized racism. But racism was also regional, national, worldwide. It was but one aspect of the wider convolutions of man's inhumanity to man. Montgomery gave Martin Luther King a broader vision of responsibility—and larger ambitions to match his vision. The Southern Christian Leader Conference was the logical step in a progression which would ultimately lead King to see the world as his parish. The 1963 March on

Washington (which drew 250,000 Blacks and whites together), the Nobel Peace Prize, King's eventual leadership in the anti–Vietnam War crusade, and the projected Poor People's Campaign were all confirmations and evidences of King's growing concept of a larger calling than he first accepted when he assumed the pulpit at Dexter Avenue Church, or when he led the walk for dignity in Montgomery.

King's understanding of his mission was not shared by some segments of the black community. From the very beginning, traditional black leadership looked askance at the young minister, and at his methods. In the first place, he was a preacher, and while clerical leadership was more solidly established in the black community than in any other, it had at times been indifferent, at times self-aggrandizing, and at other times altogether dysfunctional in its accommodation to white paternalism. King was not only a Christian humanitarian involved in a cause, he was also a man, and, as such, subject to the loyalties, the analyses, and the criticisms of men. In the role he assigned himself, or was assigned by fate or Providence, many would applaud him, fear him, honor him, love him, misunderstand him, hate him, and idolize him. Some would agree with him; some would not. But few could ignore him, and few did.

Nevertheless, a developing class of non–clerically oriented leaders feared the emergence of another black preacher who might be coopted by the white moderates as an instrument for maintaining the *status quo ante* while giving the illusion of moderation, which was conceived as a synonym for as little change as possible over as long a period as could be managed. So while "Montgomery" was applauded by the black rank and file, the implied threat to established civil rights leadership, and to emergent forms then still in the stage of debate or limited experimentation, produced a wariness on the part of traditional black leadership, and new leadership alike. The quiet hope was that Martin Luther King and his impractical campaign would soon spend its energy. But Martin Luther King had seen the mountaintop, and he fully intended to plant his pennant of nonviolent leadership at the summit.

New Day, New Challenge

The Black Church played a principal role in the desegregation of America. The Southern Christian Leadership Conference represented the formal commitment of the churches to the elimination of racial injustice, but the involvement of the Black Church as an institution was considerably deeper than could be indicated by that organization alone. Hundreds of otherwise anonymous black preachers, fired by the opportunity of serving both God and society in the risky drama of reclaiming the soul of Christian America, joined the marches and the sit-ins and the boycotts which eventually discredited American apartheid. Sometimes these nameless clergymen were successful in involving their congregations and in helping them to see a dimension of the faith stressed in the Invisible Church of the slave era but often neglected in the qualified freedom Blacks have since enjoyed. At other times the inertia of satisfaction which often besets those who expect little, and who settle too readily for even less, becalmed the best efforts to push for new horizons. This is a malady common to the oppressed, and African Americans are no exception. When things are bad, the realization that they could be worse is a powerful argument for doing nothing. When things are better, the memory of when they were worse is an implicit warning against rocking the boat. The Black Revolution had waned and faded by the mid-1970s, and the willingness of the Black Church to let other organizations carry on the unfinished struggle for black liberation was increasingly apparent. What had happened? Had the Black Church abandoned its historic mission to rescue man as the image of God, and to restore the integrity of the faith by demonstrating its consistence with the morality of God?

There were those, to be sure, who were quite satisfied with what had already been won in the struggle. And there were others who were convinced that the struggle was in fact over and that the processes which had been set in motion to win civil and economic relief for Blacks would continue of their own momentum. But there were other, less obvious factors at work. The Black Church had not in fact withdrawn from the fray, but it had modified its perspectives and thereby changed its pace. The desegregation of schools, particularly at the college and university level, opened new doors of opportunity to African Americans. A veneer of desegregation in selected job markets meant new but limited economic advancement for some. A small, highly visible black middle class emerged, tacitly conscious of its distance from the black masses from which it was so recently rescued. The Black Church was directly affected by these events.

The revolutionary ethos had produced a school of black theological revisionists whose reinterpretation of the faith allowed black Christians for the first time to find a place in the divine scheme of things other than on the periphery of the white man's private spiritual cosmos. At the same time, the leadership potential in the black community was increased sharply by the sudden expansion of the small pool of well-educated blacks, and there was a dramatic increase in the numbers of Blacks elected to political office. This political breakthrough brought some relief from the age-old dependence on white representation in positions sensitive to the welfare and interests of black people. Black men and women were suddenly visible in the political process. But African Americans are still very far from having anything like proportionate representation, and their impact on the political process, while increasing, has yet to mature. The Black Church, then, has remained a preeminent resource—for the black constituency and for America as a whole—for addressing our continuing dilemma, which enervates the American psyche and postpones the American Dream.

The Black Church of the Future: Will It Be Ready?

For two hundred years, spanning the most critical periods of our spiritual and political history, the Black Church has been a major contributor to the development of the black subculture and to the general welfare of the American enterprise. Yet at the very moment that it might well be celebrating its remarkable accomplishments on behalf of a civilization that has at times seemed oblivious of its existence, the Black Church has certain anxieties of its own. This apprehensiveness is not new, but is as old as the Black Church itself. It is the persistent nemesis which plagued the Black Church fathers even as they launched the course of black independence from the spiritual and ecclesiastical supervision of the White Church two centuries ago.

To put it another way, it is the uncomfortable suspicion that whatever is of intrinsic value to black people must find its legitimation elsewhere if it is to be respectable. We have seen black music appropriated, "rehabilitated," and sold back to its origins. Among the most prominent features of integration have been the sudden obsolescence of black schools, the wholesale retirement or downgrading of black adminstrators, and an instant surplus of black teachers. Since higher education discovered a certain expedience in admitting black students, the historic black colleges, second only to the Black Church in their cultural and historical significance, have been forced against the wall because Americans think it absurd that anyone would want to preserve black colleges when white colleges are "integrated." It is little wonder, then, that there is paranoia in the Black Church, for the Black Church sees itself in the ominous shadow of the conventional experience in integration.

There are some who would dismiss the Black Church as schismatic in origin—an illegitimate separation from the "true" (i.e., white) body of Christ. This grotesque vision of Church history is patently in contradiction to the reality of Pentecost, when the church was born.

In the first place, the White Church in America is not the "true" church, of course, if "true" is intended to mean exclusively legitimate. Nor would many white Christians seriously entertain such a claim. Whatever else it may be, the White Church in America is itself a fragment of fragments. And while some American denominations have sought earnestly to heal their historic separateness, others feel no strong compulsion to modify their distinctions in the interest of Christian togetherness. Even more obvious is the fact that since schism implies a preexisting unity, it could hardly have been a feature of importance in the rise of black communions. Some Blacks did worship in segregated churches with whites, but their relationships were hardly graced by a degree of interpersonal respect and communion that could be called unity. That a segregated church cannot be a Christian unity would seem to require no argument.

In the second place, while it is true that race was certainly a factor in the peculiar circumstances under which the Black Church did in fact develop in America, it was a problem originating in the White Church, from which black Christians finally felt compelled to withdraw if their faith and their humanity were not to be forever compromised. Racial exclusiveness has never been a factor of consequence in the Black Church. It was not the motivating impetus, nor is it the sustaining principle on which the Black Church rests and pursues its calling. The original invitation to believe and to be a community in Christ was not addressed to any particular race, but "to devout men, out of every nation under heaven." So reads the second chapter of the Book of Acts. Of those devout men, some were undoubtedly black, for the scripture goes on to list, among the nations represented, nations from the continent of Africa. It was the Day of Pentecost, the day the church was born, and black people were there among the rest. Hence, it is from black participation in the faith from day one that the Black Church derives its legitimacy.

When the Black Church in America emerged as an independent entity, it leaned heavily on rituals and polity while avoiding the ideology of the existing churches. The familiar ways and means of churchmanship a few black retainers had internalized during their servile membership in the white churches were adapted to become the structural eclectic of the Black Cosmos. Black Methodist ritual remained Methodist; black Baptist polity remained Baptist. And the Protestant ethic was left intact with the expectation that new interpretation would give it new meaning. There was no need for change. The fundamentals of the faith did not turn on race or ethnicity, but on spiritual essence. Thus did the Black Church achieve its own identity and conceive its own mission. In the pursuit of that mission, the Black Church can say of itself, in contrast to other communions, that at no time in its history has the Black Church closed its doors or denied its fellowship to people who were not black. Nor has it ever limited its concern to people who are.

Pedes Terra Cotta

It is the enduring fragility of the human spirit that assures the Black Church of its continuing mission. Even though we are in the image of God, our vision, or the lack of it, holds us earthbound. Image is not essence, and there may be disjunction between how we are perceived and what we are. The image in which we are cast—the first incentive to spiritual and moral achievement—takes substance from where the image was created.

Pedes terra cotta, feet of clay, is the celebrated phenomenon of our times. It is the recognition that we are human, without proper appreciation for the potential of our humanity. We are considerably less interested these days in the challenge to be better than we are, and to disengage our feet from the muck which holds us captive, than in a license to abort the worrisome spark that tells us we ought to resist. It is easier to wallow where we are than to struggle toward where we ought to be. To make the choice less onerous, we have developed a new and confidential language cleverly designed to insulate us from the moral static of our new abandonment. Behind the gossamer screen of our wanton self-indulgence there exists a world in counterpoint with an awesome schedule of heartache, misery, dehumanization, and death. When every act of human depravity can be legitimized, and when there is no distinction between creativity and destruction, the costs of survival go up and the probabilities of survival go down. The reason for and the meaning of survival, if any, become more obscure and less compelling. As long as there is hatred and evil in the world, as long as there are the poor in spirit and those who need to be comforted, and until there is a voice in every place to speak the truth to the disinherited of whatever race, the whole Church has a future because its larger ministry is to the world. Self-knowledge breeds self-confidence, and self-confidence is the courage of the convictions we claim to hold. A church that is confused about its identity is more confused about its mission. That is the occasion for the American dilemma and the compromise of the great promise of a fresh new civilization laying claim to the right to call itself a nation "under God." Only the concerted will of the American people can resolve the dilemma, but the Black Church, like the White Church, has a role and a responsibility to be seriously involved in that resolution while religious involvement may still make a difference.

The whole Church needs to reconsider the range of its opportunities and responsibilities to God and to humankind. The legal color line is dead. Forever. It was a painful and unfortunate experiment in the idolatrous attempt to be more than human at the expense of being less than humane. It failed because there is only one order of humanity, and whatever the range of human aptitude and capability, it is neither more nor less than what it is. Human. The Church needs the means to deal with this elementary principle far more effectively than it has in the context of spiritual and practical ministry. The legal color line is dead, the color code is not—but once again, that is our dilemma. The American dilemma continues. Our principal sensitivities and commitments remain captive to a schedule of values which magnify our differences rather than celebrate what we have in common. Although our work and our play are sometimes "racially inclusive" (by law!), we have not learned to think inclusively, and the resulting social chaos continues to exact its relentless toll on us all.

Among the great nations of the world, we are privately more sensitive to right and responsibility in human affairs than most, and we have a covert national conscience which gives us private consolation. But conscience is only the *potential* to do something. *It has to be effective!* The road to national devolution is paved with warm thoughts and good intentions that have withered in the fire of nonperformance.

Where do we go from here? A more sensitive question is, "Where is there left to go?" History is closing our options with an implacable determination. What can we do? Are there resources beyond the "civil rights" previously hatched out of the American Dream?

What Road to Remedy and Reconciliation?

In 1995, the Southern Baptist Church (the largest denomination in America, and one of the most conservative) startled the country by admitting its participatory role in American slavery and segregation and offering a formal apology. The Baptist gesture was matched a year later by (Baptist) President Clinton, who apologized for the country's involvement in the notorious Tuskegee Experiment in Alabama, which treated selected members of a pool of four hundred black males with testicular syphilis by giving them placebos, permitting the destructive venereal disease to run its course and take its toll in blindness, disability, and death. The President gave strong consideration to a national apology for slavery, but apparently cooled on that idea when his advisors pointed out the political deficits it would likely incur. Instead, he established an "Initiative on Race," appointing historian John Hope Franklin to chair a seven-member panel to hold "dialogues and consultations" and "town meetings" on our racial problems and report back to the President in late 1998.

Apologies for collective wrongs pose problems for many Americans. Some see no logic in apologizing for what other individuals of their race may have done. For others, an apology which carries no restitution for the abuses recognized in the apology, and no promise of discontinuing the offensive behavior, seems to add insult to the injury. It may also be interpreted as a distraction from a more serious intent to get at the problem. The President's Initiative on Race was launched under circumstances not favorable to its relevance or success. Despite the personal integrity of Dr. Franklin, the public was suspicious that the Initiative was just another "racial study" to excuse or delay remedial action. The Initiative could offer no relief, and consulting with like-minded people was not an impressive way to bring change.

Civil Rights—and More

The most spectacular gains in African-American participation in a more complete spectrum of American values have come with civil rights. "Civil rights" are the legal endowments which inure to, or are vested in, the individual person as a recognized member of a designated human community. Such a community is committed by consensus to the rule of law, which protects its members from excesses against one another so that the creative development of the individual and the community alike are not held hostage to security and other visceral needs, and which regulates and humanizes the competition for scarce resources.

Civil rights presuppose human rights, of course. And human rights derive not from human investment or human consensus, but from the very fact of being human. They are intrinsic to human identity. They are inherent, and inalienable—perhaps because "man" bears the image of God, or perhaps because *Homo sapiens* is, at this writing, the superlative expression of an unfolding universe.

It is critical at this point in our history that these distinctions be clearly understood. It was the protracted distortion and abuse of human rights, and the willful obliviousness to the consequences of such behavior, that made the civil rights revolution of the 1950s and 1960s necessary at such a horrible cost to the nation. Thinking man will not accept indefinitely conditions of existence which deny the intellectual and creative experiences by which human beings are defined. Sooner or later, the vision of freedom seeps through the harshest granite of repression and becomes the obsession which alone sustains survival. Sooner or later, human self-awareness and the struggle for human dignity reject the doubtful securities of accommodation to a plane that is less than human, thereby affirming the universal human need for full human self-expression. Such was the autobiography of the civil rights movement, a painful, heroic segment of American history we must not be called upon to repeat.

The civil rights movement is history, but the social traumas it sought to heal still linger. The old polarity between Blacks and whites has now become multi-focal and cross-indexed. The many false starts toward a solution of this most persistent national dilemma have in every case underestimated its virulence and its viciousness, and we have elected to patch up only the most obvious deterioration of the national commitment rather than to invest in the total renovation dry rot demands. Moreover, we have deferred paying effective national attention to our racial discord, leaving it to bedevil some future generation while we buy time with public placebos and political rhetoric, which do nothing to heal the place where it hurts. The time we buy today will have to be paid for at premium prices tomorrow by the children we claim to love and protect by living on *their* credit and postdating the bill.

It is getting late, and as we march at the head of the great nations of the world toward the threshold of the twenty-first century, the cadence is offbeat and tentative because our own house is in grave disorder. The quality of life in many of the countries we profess to lead is better than it is at home for many Americans of whatever race. There is no longer "a chicken in every pot," but there are multiple locks on every door, and we are deathly afraid of one another.

The world has changed more since World War II than it did in the preceding three centuries. We have changed with it, but our changes have been more selective because we control more of the resources upon which changes depend. Yet the quality of life for millions of Americans has either not improved, or has deteriorated, and in consequence the index of social irritability is higher than ever before in our history. We would like to dismiss the gang murders, the drive-by shootings, and the turf wars as the incidental phenomena of a pervasive criminal element preying on itself. But there is dramatic evidence of a more pervasive irritability, such as road rage, serial killings, workplace massacres, church bombings, schoolhouse bloodfests, and death-dealing assaults on public institutions. Parents kill their children, and children kill their parents and each other, with scarcely a shadow of remorse—right here in America. The dramatic escalation of such behavior suggests a level of tension and irascibility in the American community that requires a fresh approach for achieving the social change we must have in order to survive as a democratic society. When life itself is so expendable, the cardinal values command less urgency and appreciation.

The ideal change, and the change most likely to endure, must involve reconciliation. Reconciliation may be the most painful act to make, because it calls upon all parties to make real sacrifices rather than gestures of goodwill or cosmetic blandishments. Something has to give, and something has to be given up—including some very cherished conventional notions about ourselves and about others. The statute of limitations has run out on some ideas, long held sacred, which have divided us into separate, hostile camps. Effective racial reconciliation will require the sacrificial spirit of Abraham, the tenacity of Moses, the wisdom of Solomon, and the unshakable faith that being American is worth what it takes to save America from itself.

The best strategy is to approach racism, not as the *minority grievance* it once was, but as a national problem in which we are all implicated, whether willfully, involuntarily, reluctantly, or by default. The issue was addressed as a minority grievance against America in the civil rights revolution of the 1950s and 1960s. That grievance grew out of an illegal national consensus to arbitrarily withhold from one-tenth of all citizens a broad spectrum of civil rights and their endowments, solely on the basis of race. The struggle in the streets, backed by the struggle in the courts, brought significant relief, but the process languished long before the movement had accomplished its mandates. A counter-process of reductionism has since been relentlessly stalking the gains that were wrung from a bitter and recalcitrant opposition that held us all hostage to the false notion of racial preference and superiority.

The issue was addressed, but it has not been resolved. The problem we are left with is to identify, understand, and eliminate the remaining vestiges of racial discrimination. It is in the national interest to do this because racism wastes the human potential, endangers the public tranquillity, compromises the national integrity, and burdens the economy of the nation, to the detriment of everyone. We are no longer dealing with a factional grievance, but with a national problem. A grievance presupposes an adversarial relationship. A problem recognizes the need for a solution that welcomes and requires a common commitment from all those affected by it and all those who have a feeling for rectitude and reconciliation. Recrimination and vilification are not effective instruments of reconciliation, but the pain, the suffering, and the inconvenience deriving from the unresolved problem of racism must be made clear so as to avoid the risk of confirming the fantasy that all is well, when all is not well at all. There must be candor in disclosure, honesty in inquiry, and resolute determination in attack, or we will fail again, as we have so often failed before.

We cannot afford another aborted attempt to resolve our racial dilemma. The social greening of America cannot be accomplished in a nation divided by race. If we have such formidable problems being comfortable sharing the national manor with an ethnic minority which labored to build it from scratch, the prognosis for the multicultural society now a-building is dour indeed. A 1997 report from the Census Bureau reveals that one out of every ten Americans is foreign-born. Of this number, only one in five comes from Europe. Most of the others come from Latin America. In less than fifty years, Americans of European descent may well be America's largest *minority!*

President Clinton has set the tone for honest inquiry by establishing an "Initiative on Race." But the commission can do no more than its mandate permits. The real work of reconciliation will have to be done by the American people. It is we who will have to bite the bullet of transformation if we want the bullet that is poisoning our national innards removed.

Epilogue: Reconciliation

Give me your hand, my brother
Give me your hand
Divided we fall, my brother
Together we stand.
Come, let the night be past
Walk in the light at last
Now is the time to cast
Our lot as one.

Give me your hand, it's white
And mine is black.
Together lift high the light
That must guide back
America, adrift at sea
Lost in the fog that slavery
Cast over you and me
Let's find the sun.

C. ERIC LINCOLN
This poem originally appeared
in a slightly different version
in: *This Road Since Freedom*
(Carolina Wren Press, 1990).

Notes

Prologue

1. "Ex Libris," *The Journal of Higher Education,* May 17, 1996, as quoted in C. Eric Lincoln, *Coming Through the Fire: Surviving Race and Place in America* (Durham, N.C.: Duke University Press, 1996).

Introduction

1. W.E.B. Du Bois, *The Souls of Black Folk* (Nashville: Fisk University Press, 1979), pp. 6 and 13. W.E.B. Du Bois, "The Negro Church," *The Atlanta University Publications* (New York: Arno Press/The New York Times, 1968), p. 208.
2. Gunnar Myrdal, *The American Dilemma* (New York: Harper, 1944).

2: The Racial Factor in the Shaping of Religion in America

1. All biblical quotes are from the King James version.
2. Cf. Frederick Perry Noble, *The Redemption of Africa* (Chicago: Fleming H. Revell, 1899), Vol. 1, p. 7. Says Noble: "In the Egyptians we have a dark race originating from the mingling of black and white races. If these blacks were Negroes or like Negroes—and the best authorities regard this as the case . . . the civilization of Egypt is only less Negro than [Caucasian]." Obviously, the present writer accepts the dictum of the best authorities.
3. Saunders Redding, *They Came in Chains* (Philadelphia: Lippincott, 1950).
4. Noble, pp. 134–5.
5. Winthrop D. Jordan, *White Over Black* (Chapel Hill: University of North Carolina Press, 1968), p. 24.
6. Ibid., p. 27.

7. W.E.B. Du Bois, ed., "The Negro Church," p. 27.

8. Kelly Miller, *Radicals and Conservatives and Other Essays on the Negro for America* (New York: Saborken Books, 1968), p. 193.

9. Du Bois, *The Negro Church*, p. 30.

10. Gilbert Osofsky, *The Burden of Race* (New York: Harper & Row, 1967), p. 40.

11. Jordan, p. 183.

12. H. Shelton Smith, *In His Image, But* . . . (Durham: Duke University Press, 1972), p. 11.

13. Jordan, p. 186.

14. Lorenzo J. Greene, *The Negro in Colonial New England* (New York: Atheneum, 1968), p. 257.

15. Jordan, p. 93.

16. Ibid., p. 260.

17. Osofsky, p. 35.

18. Greene, pp. 271–2.

19. Ibid., pp. 259, 260.

20. Jordan, p. 179.

21. Greene, p. 261.

22. Du Bois, p. 11.

23. Ibid., p. 22.

24. Greene, p. 288.

25. Smith, p. 53. See also Carter G. Woodson and Charles H. Wesley, *The Negro in Our History* (Washington, D.C.: Associated Publishers, 1922), for a discussion of the failure of the Catholics, Episcopalians, Quakers, and Presbyterians to attract substantial numbers of black converts.

26. Greene, p. 276.

27. Benjamin Brawley, *A Social History of the American Negro* (London: Collier-Macmillan, 1970), pp. 140ff.

28. Kenneth M. Stampp, *The Peculiar Institution* (New York: Alfred A. Knopf, 1956), p. 158.

29. Ibid., p. 159.

3: The Black Response

1. Benjamin Mays, *The Negro's God* (Boston: Chapman and Grimes, 1938), pp. 43–4.

2. "David Walker's Appeal," Bradford Chambers, ed., *Chronicles of Negro Protest* (New York: Parents Magazine Press, 1968), p. 69.

3. Charles H. Wesley, *Richard Allen, Apostle of Freedom* (Washington, D.C.: Associated Publishers, 1969), pp. 52–3.

4. Gayraud Wilmore, Jr., *Black Religion and Black Radicalism* (New York: Anchor/Doubleday, 1973), pp. 113, 114.

5. Charles H. Wesley, *The Negro in Our History* (Washington, D.C.: Associated Publishers, 1966), pp. 79–80.

6. William J. Walls, *The African Methodist Episcopal Zion Church* (Charlotte, N.C.: AME Zion Publishing House, 1974), p. 94. Cf. Harry V. Richardson, *Dark Salvation* (New York: Anchor/Doubleday, 1976), p. 135, which reports that "the annual meeting of the group of churches in 1828 is regarded by some as the first General Conference" of the AME Zion Convention.

7. B. F. Wheeler, *The Varick Family* (Mobile, 1906), p. 607.

8. Walls, p. 44.

9. Ibid., p. 141.

10. Wesley, p. 70.

11. Ibid.

4: Black Ethnicity and Religious Nationalism

1. For a discussion of black cults, the reader is referred to C. Eric Lincoln and Lawrence H. Mamiya, "Daddy Jones and Father Divine: The Cult as Political Religion," *Religion in Life*, Spring 1980.

2. Lerone Bennett, Jr., *What Manner of Man?* (Chicago: Johnson Publishing Co., 1968), p. 80.

3. Ibid., p. 66.

4. Ibid., p. 82.

5. David Lewis, *King: A Biography* (Champaign: University of Illinois Press, 1970), p. 158.

6. Leon H. Sullivan, *Build Brother Build* (Philadelphia: Macrae Smith, 1969), p. 70.

7. Ibid., p. 67.

8. C. Nathan Wright, Jr., *Black Power and Urban Unrest* (New York: Hawthorne, 1967), cover flap.

9. Martin Luther King, Jr., *Where Do We Go from Here: Chaos or Community?* (New York: Harper & Row, 1967), p. 30.

10. Wright, pp. 2–3.

11. Gayraud Wilmore, Jr., *Black Religion and Black Radicalism* (New York: Anchor/Doubleday, 1973), p. 248.

12. Ibid., p. 267.

13. Arnold Schuster, *Reparations* (Philadelphia: Lippincott, 1970), p. 6.
14. Ibid., p. 14.
15. *An Introduction to CNBC* (Washington, D.C.: The Congress of National Black Churches, undated).

5: The Face of American Pluralism

1. "Pluralism and Sectarianism," in Elwyn W. Smith, *The Religion of the Republic* (Philadelphia: Fortress, 1968).
2. Wilbur G. Katz and Harold P. Southerland, "Religious Pluralism and the Supreme Court," in W. G. McLoughlin and Robert N. Bellah, eds., *Religion in America* (Boston: Beacon Press, 1968), p. 269.
3. Smith, p. 268.
4. Ibid., p. 268.
5. McLoughlin and Bellah, pp. 52, 65, 66.
6. Will Herberg, *Protestant–Catholic–Jew* (New York: Doubleday, 1955), p. 274.
7. "The Third Force's Lesson for Others," *Life,* June 9, 1958.
8. James H. Cone, *A Theology of Black Liberation* (Philadelphia: Lippincott, 1970), p. 23.
9. James H. Cone, *Black Theology and Black Power* (New York: Seabury, 1969), p. 118.

6: The View from the Narthex

1. *Time,* June 19, 1978.
2. *The Christian Century,* October 16, 1964.
3. Jeff Nye, "Memo from a Mormon," *Look,* October 22, 1963.
4. Wallace Turner, *The Mormon Establishment* (Boston: Houghton Mifflin, 1966), p. 244.
5. O. Kendall White, "Mormonism's Anti-Black Policy and Prospects for Change," *Journal of Religious Thought,* Autumn–Winter, 1972, p. 43.
6. *Look,* December 3, 1963.
7. *The Christian Century,* September 29, 1965.
8. Ibid.
9. O. Kendall White, p. 39. See also *The Christian Century,* October 16, 1974, and Wallace Turner, pp. 218–66.
10. T. S. Eliot, "We Are the Hollow Men."
11. *The Logan Herald Journal* (Logan, Utah), November 5, 1974.
12. *The New York Times,* June 10, 1978.

13. John J. Stewart, *Mormonism and the Negro* (Orem, Utah: Book Division of Community Press Publishing Company, 1960), pp. 48, 49.
14. *The Christian Century*, October 16, 1974.
15. Quoted in "The Struggle for Black Ordination in the Mormon Church," by Jeff Levin (Duke University, unpublished paper), p. 43. Cf. Molly Ivins, "Mormon Decisions on Blacks Promises Impact on Utah," *The New York Times*, June 18, 1978.
16. For a discussion of Spanish (Catholic) precautions against the threat of the spread of Islam among the American Indians through black proselytization and intermarriage with Blacks, see Clyde-Ahmad Winters, "Afro-American Muslims from Slavery to Freedom," *Islamic Studies*, Vol. XVII, no. 4, 1978, pp. 187–90.
17. *Mr. Muhammad Speaks*, May 1960.
18. Malcolm X, quoted in C. Eric Lincoln, *The Black Muslims in America* (Boston: Beacon Press, 1961).
19. From a personal interview with Warith Deen Muhammad, April 9, 1980.
20. *Mr. Muhammad Speaks*, May 1960.
21. C. Eric Lincoln, "Retrospection," in *This Road Since Freedom* (Durham, N.C.: Carolina Wren Press, 1990).
22. Jacob Rader Marcus, *Early American Jewry* (Philadelphia: Jewish Publications Society, 1961), Vol. II, p. 526.
23. Louis Finkelstein, ed., *The Jews: Their History* (New York: Schocken, 1970), p. 521.
24. R. G. Weisbord and Arthur Stein, *Bittersweet Encounter* (Westport: Greenwood, 1972), p. 14.
25. Lenora E. Berson, *The Negroes and the Jews* (New York: Random House, 1971), p. 17.
26. Weisbord and Stein, p. 32.
27. Ibid., p. 126.
28. Earl Raab, "The Black Revolution and the Jewish Question," *Commentary*, January 1969.
29. Nat Hentoff, ed., *Black Anti-Semitism and Jewish Racism* (New York: Schocken, 1970), pp. 207, 209, 208.

7: The Legal Route to Remediation

1. A catalogue of important rulings on bias from *Brown* to *Bakke* would include at least the following cases: *Brown vs. Board of Education*, 347 U.S. 483 (1954); *United States vs. Montgomery County Board of Edu-*

cation, 395 U.S. 225 (1969); *Swann vs. Charlotte-Mecklenburg Board of Education*, 402 U.S. 1, 16 (1971); *North Carolina State Board of Education vs. Swann*, 402 U.S. 43, 45–46 (1971); *Griggs vs. Duke Power Co.*, 401 U.S. 421 (1971); *Defanis vs. Odegaard*, 416 U.S. 312 (1974); *Washington vs. Davis*, 426 U.S. 229 (1976); *Franks vs. Bowman Transportation Co., Inc.*, 424 U.S. 747 (1976); *United Jewish Organizations of Williamsburg, Inc. vs. Carey*, 430 U.S. 144 (1977). Cf. *The Chronicle of Higher Education*, Vol. XVI, no. 17, July 3, 1978.

2. *The Bakke Case Primer*, Institute for the Study of Educational Policy, Howard University, undated.
3. *Time*, July 10, 1978.
4. The Constitution of the United States, Art. I, Sec. 2, par. 3.
5. Oscar Handlin, *Race and Nationality in American Life* (Boston: Little, Brown, 1957), pp. 136, 137–8.
6. *Dred Scott vs. Sanford*, 1857.
7. A. J. Toynbee, *A Study of History*, 2nd ed. (New York: Oxford University Press, 1954), Vol. I, p. 224.
8. "The Opinion of Thurgood Marshall," *The Chronicle of Higher Education*, Vol. XVI, no. 18, July 10, 1978, p. 13.
9. *Time*, March 12, 1984.
10. "The Opinion of Thurgood Marshall," p. 13.
11. *The New York Times*, July 3, 1980.

8: Principles, Problems, and Prospects

1. Martin E. Marty and Edith I. Blumhofer, *Public Religion in America Today* (Chicago: The Public Religion Project).
2. C. Eric Lincoln and Lawrence H. Mamiya, *The Black Church in the African American Experience* (Durham, N.C.: Duke University Press, 1990), Chapter 1, passim.
3. This has long been the interpretation of the "established" church, and it functions as a beachhead for much academic investigation and publication within and outside the Black Sacred Cosmos itself. Cf. Joseph Washington, *Black Religion*; E. Franklin Frazier, *The Negro Church*; etc.
4. The missionary agency of the Church of England.
5. This is a prime function, indeed the obvious pragmatic function, of all true black ideology—i.e., to sharpen the awareness of the group as legitimate and valuable, and to underscore this with divine attention and concern.

6. *Time,* April 13, 1998, pp. 70ff.
7. *Durham* (N.C.) *Herald,* June 10, 1997.
8. See C. Eric Lincoln, *Coming Through the Fire: Surviving Race and Place in America* (Durham, N.C.: Duke University Press, 1996).

Conclusion

1. Lerone Bennett, Jr., *What Manner of Man?* (Chicago: Johnson Publishing Co., 1968), p. 16.
2. Broken homes, absent fathers, slum tenements, narcotic addiction, illegitimacy, etc., etc., etc., as depicted in Claude Brown's *Manchild in the Promised Land.*

Bibliography

Abrahamse, A. F., P. A. Morrison, and L. J. Waite. *Beyond Stereotypes: Who Becomes a Single Teenage Mother?* Santa Monica, Calif.: Rand Corporation, 1988.

Adams, John A., Jr. *The Black Pulpit Revolution in the United Methodist Church and Other Denominations.* Chicago: Strugglers' Community Press, 1985.

Albanese, Catherine L. *America: Religions and Religion.* Belmont, Calif.: Wadsworth, 1981.

Alexander, Thomas G. *Mormonism in Transition: A History of the Latter-Day Saints, 1890–1930.* Urbana: University of Illinois Press, 1986.

Allen, James B. "Would-Be Saints: West Africa Before the 1978 Priesthood Revelation," *Journal of Mormon History* 17 (1991): 207–47.

Allen, Walter. "The Search for Applicable Theories of Black Family Life," *Journal of Marriage and the Family* 40 (1978): 111–129.

Anderson, Elijah. "Some Observations on Youth Employment." In Bernard E. Anderson and Isabel V. Sawhill, eds., *Youth Employment and Public Policy.* Englewood Cliffs, N.J.: Prentice-Hall, 1978.

———. "The Social Context of Youth Employment Programs." In Charles L. Betsey, Robinson G. Hollister, Jr., and Mary R. Papageorgiou, eds., *Youth Employment and Training Logjams: The YEDPA Years.* Washington, D.C.: National Academy Press, 1985.

Austin, Allan D. *African Muslims in Antebellum America: A Sourcebook.* New York: Garland, 1984.

Baer, Hans A. *The Black Spiritual Movement: A Religious Response to Racism.* Knoxville: University of Tennessee Press, 1984.

Baer, Hans A., and Merrill Singer. "Toward a Typology of Black Sectarianism as a Response to Racial Stratification." *Anthropological Quarterly* 54 (Winter 1981).

Bane, Mary Jo. "Household Composition and Poverty." In Sheldon Danziger and Daniel Weinberg, eds., *Fighting Poverty: What Works and What Doesn't.* Cambridge, Mass.: Harvard University Press, 1986.

Banks, James A., and J. D. Grambs. _Black Self-Concept_. New York: McGraw-Hill, 1972.

Barrett, Leonard E. _Soul-Force: African Heritage in Afro-American Religion_. Garden City, N.Y.: Anchor/Doubleday, 1974.

Bennett, Wallace R. "The Legal Status of the Negro in Utah." Paper delivered at Symposium on the Negro held by the Utah Academy of Sciences, Arts, and Letters at Weber College, Ogden, Utah, November 20, 1954.

Benson, Ezra Taft. _Civil Rights: Tool of Communist Deception_. Salt Lake City: Deseret Books, 1968.

Berenson, William M., Kirk W. Elifson, and Tandy Tollerson III. "Preachers in Politics: A Study of Political Activism Among the Black Ministry," _Journal of Black Studies 24_ (June 1976).

Berson, Leonora E. _The Negro and the Jews_. New York: Random House, 1971.

Book of Mormon, The. Salt Lake City: Church of Jesus Christ of Latter-Day Saints, 1981. (orig. ed., 1830).

Bowles, Carey C. _A Mormon Negro Views the Church_. Maplewood, N.J.: Author, 1968.

Boyd, Malcolm. "A White Minister Looks at the Black Church," _The Crisis 89_ (November 1982).

Bradbury, Katharine, and Lynne Brown. "Black Men in the Labor Market," _New England Economic Review_ (March/April, 1986): 32–42.

Brewer, David L. "Religious Resistance to Changing Beliefs About Race," _Pacific Sociological Review 13_ (Summer 1970): 163–70.

———. "Utah Elites and Utah Racial Norms." Ph.D. dissertation, University of Utah, 1966.

Brigham, Janet. "Nigeria and Ghana: A Miracle Precedes the Messengers," _Ensign 10_ (February 1980): 73–76.

Bringhurst, Newell G. "An Ambiguous Decision: The Implementation of Mormon Priesthood Denial for the Black Man—A Re-examination," _Utah Historical Quarterly 46_ (Winter 1978): 45–64.

———. "Charles B. Thompson and the Issues of Slavery and Race," _Journal of Mormon History 8_ (1981): 37–47.

———. "Elijah Abel and the Changing Status of Blacks Within Mormonism," _Dialogue 12_ (Summer 1979): 22–36.

———. "The Mormons and Black Slavery—A Closer Look," _Pacific Historical Review 50_ (November 1981): 329–38.

———. _Saints, Slaves, and Blacks: The Changing Place of Black People Within Mormonism_. Westport, Conn.: Greenwood Press, 1981.

————. "'A Servant of Servants . . . Cursed as Pertaining to the Priesthood': Mormon Attitudes Toward Slavery and the Black Man, 1830–1880." Ph.D. dissertation, University of California, Davis, 1975.

Brisbane, Robert H. *The Black Vanguard.* Valley Forge, Pa.: Judson Press, 1970.

Brock, William. "Slavery Not a Misfortune but a Crime." In Julia Griffiths, ed., *Autographs for Freedom,* Vol. 2. Auburn, N.Y.: Alden, Beardsley, 1854.

Brodie, Fawn M. *No Man Knows My History: The Life of Joseph Smith.* New York: Alfred A Knopf, 1945.

Brotz, Howard. *The Black Jews of Harlem.* New York: Schocken, 1970.

Browne, Robert S. *Race Relations in International Affairs.* Washington, D.C.: Public Affairs Press, 1961.

Bush, Lester E., Jr. "Mormonism's Negro Doctrine: An Historical Overview," *Dialogue* 8 (Spring 1973): 11–68.

Caldwell, Gaylon L. "Moral and Religious Aspects of the Status of the Negro in Utah," *Western Humanities Review* 13 (1959): 102–6.

Carroll, Jackson W., Douglas W. Johnson, and Martin E. Marty. *Religion in America, 1950 to the Present.* San Francisco: Harper & Row, 1979.

Carter, Kate B. *The Negro Pioneer.* Salt Lake City: Daughters of the Utah Pioneers, 1965.

Carter, Robert T. "Cultural Value Differences Between African Americans and White Americans," *Journal of College Student Development* 31 (January 1990): 71–79.

Childs, John Brown. *The Political Black Minister: A Study in Afro-American Politics and Religion.* Boston: G. K. Hall, 1980.

Christenson, J. B. "Negro Slavery in the Utah Territory," *Phylon Quarterly* 13 (October 1957): 298–305.

Clark, Michael J. "Improbable Ambassadors: Black Soldiers at Fort Douglas, 1896–99," *Utah Historical Quarterly* 46 (Summer 1978): 282–301.

Clark, Wynetta Martin. *I Am a Negro Mormon.* Ogden, Utah: Author, 1970.

Clemmons, Ithiel. "Racial and Spiritual Unity in the Body of Christ." *A/G Advance/Enrichment* 31 (8) (Fall 1995): 66–88.

Clowes, William Laird. "Miscegenation and the Race Problem, 1890." In Lenworth Gunther, ed., *Black Image: European Eyewitness Accounts of Afro-American Life.* Port Washington, N.Y.: Kennikat/National University Publications, 1978.

Cogley, John, ed. *Religion in America.* New York: Meridian, 1958.

Coleman, Ronald G. "Blacks in Utah History: An Unknown Legacy." In

Helen Z. Papanikolas, ed., *The Peoples of Utah*. Salt Lake City: Utah State Historical Society, 1976.

————. "Utah's Black Pioneers: 1847–1869." *UMOJA: A Scholarly Journal of Black Studies*, new series *11* (Summer 1978): 95–110.

Collins, Sheila. *The Rainbow Challenge: The Jackson Campaign and the Future of U.S. Politics*. New York: Monthly Review Press, 1985.

Cone, James H. *For My People: Black Theology and the Black Church: Where Have We Been and Where Are We Going?* Maryknoll, N.Y.: Orbis, 1984.

Cose, Ellis. "Counting Up Human Cost." *Newsweek* (May 18, 1992), p. 47.

————. "One Drop of Bloody History," *Newsweek* (February 13, 1995), p. 70.

Davis, Frank G. *The Economics of Black Community Development*. Washington, D.C.: University Press of America, 1978.

Davis, George, and Gregg Watson. *Black Life in Corporate America: Swimming in the Mainstream*. New York: Doubleday, 1985.

Davis, James, and Woodie White. *Racial Transition in the Church*. Nashville, Tenn.: Abingdon Press, 1980.

DeLameter, John. "The Social Control of Sexuality." In Ralph H. Turner and James F. Short, Jr., eds., *Annual Review of Sociology*, Vol. 7. Palo Alto, Calif.: Annual Reviews Inc., 1981.

"Demography of the Marriage Market in the United States," *Population Index 50*(1) (Spring 1984): 5–25.

"Discrimination Against Blacks Along the Shifting Mormon Frontier, 1830–1920," *Nevada Historical Quarterly 24* (Winter 1981): 298–318.

Douglas, Norman. "The Sons of Lei and the Seed of Cain: Racial Myths in the Mormon Scriptures and Their Relevance to the Pacific Islands," *Journal of Religious History 8* (June 1974): 90–104.

Drake, St. Clair, and Horace R. Cayton. *Black Metropolis*, Vol. II. New York: Harcourt, Brace, 1970.

Du Bois, W.E.B. "The Function of the Negro Church," in *The Philadelphia Negro*. Philadelphia: University of Pennyslvania, 1899.

————. "The Gift of the Spirit," in *The Gift of Black Folk*. New York: Washington Square Press, 1970.

————. *Prayers for Dark People*. Edited by Herbert Aptheker. Amherst: University of Massachusetts Press, 1980.

Duncan, Adam M. "Civil Rights in Utah: A Concept of Race and an Attitude." Paper delivered at symposium held by Utah Academy of Sciences, Art, and Letters, Utah State University, Logan, Utah, November 9, 1963.

Dutson, Roldo Van Leuven. "A Study of the Attitude of the Latter-Day Saint Church, in the Territory of Utah, Toward Slavery As It Pertained to the Indian as well as the Negro from 1847 to 1865." Ph.D. dissertation, Brigham Young University, 1964.

Dybiec, David, ed. *Slippin' Away: The Loss of Black-Owned Farms.* Atlanta: Glenmary Research Center, 1988.

Eastmond, J. Nicholls, Jr. "The New Revelation: A Personal View," *Dialogue* 12 (Summer 1979): 50–53.

Embry, Jessie L. "Ethnic Groups in the LDS Church," *Dialogue: A Journal of Mormon Thought* 25 (Winter 1992).

————. "Separate But Equal? Black Branches, Genesis Groups, or Integrated Wards?" *Dialogue: A Journal of Mormon Thought* 23 (Spring 1990).

Espenshade, Thomas J. "Marriage Trends in America: Estimates, Implications, and Underlying Causes," *Population and Development Review* 11(2) (June 1985): 193–245.

Esplin, Ronald K. "Brigham Young and Priesthood Denial to the Blacks: An Alternate View," *BYU Studies* 19 (Spring 1979): 394–402.

Farley, Reynolds. *Blacks and Whites: Narrowing the Gap!* Cambridge, Mass.: Harvard University Press, 1984.

————. "Changes in the Status and Characteristics of Blacks: 1940 to Mid-1980s." Paper prepared for the Committee on the Status of Black Americans, National Research Council, Washington, D.C., 1987.

Farley, Reynolds, and Walter Allen. *The Color Line and the Quality of Life in America.* New York: Russell Sage Foundation, 1987.

Farley, Reynolds, and Suzanne Bianchi. "The Growing Racial Difference in Marriage and Family Patterns." Paper presented at meeting of the American Statistical Association, Statistics Section, Chicago, 1986.

Farrakhan, Louis. *A Torchlight for America.* Chicago: FCN Publishing, 1993.

Featherman, David L. *Opportunity and Change.* New York: Academic Press, 1978.

Foster, Donald L. "Unique Gospel in Utah." *Christian Century* 82 (July 14, 1965): 890–92.

Franklin, John Hope. *From Slavery to Freedom.* New York: Alfred A. Knopf, 1967.

Freeman, Richard B., and Harry J. Holzer, eds. *The Black Youth Employment Crisis.* Chicago: University of Chicago Press, 1986.

Gager, John G. *The Origins of Anti-Semitism: Attitudes Toward Judaism in Pagan and Christian Antiquity.* New York: Oxford University Press, 1983.

Garibaldi, Antoine, ed. *Black Colleges and Universities: Challenges for the Future*. New York: Praeger, 1984.

Gary, Lawrence E., ed. *Black Men*. Beverly Hills, Calif.: Sage, 1981.

Gaustad, Edwin Scott. *A Religious History of America*. New York: Harper & Row, 1974.

Gavins, Raymond. *The Perils and Prospects of Southern Black Leadership*. Durham, N.C.: Duke University Press, 1977.

Geltman, Max. *The Confrontation*. Englewood Cliffs, N.J.: Prentice-Hall,1970.

George, Carol V. R. *Segregated Sabbaths*. New York: Oxford University Press, 1973.

Gerber, Israel J. *The Heritage Seekers: American Blacks in Search of Jewish Identity*. Middle Village, N.Y.: Jonathan David, 1977.

Gerlach, Larry R. *Blazing Crosses in Zion: The Ku Klux Klan in Utah*. Logan: Utah State University Press, 1982.

Gilmore, Al-Tony. "The Black Southerner's Response to the Southern System of Race Relations: 1900 to Post–World War II." In Robert Haws, ed., *The Age of Segregation: Race Relations in the South, 1890–1945*. Jackson: University Press of Mississippi, 1978.

Glasgow, Douglas. *The Black Underclass: Poverty, Unemployment, and Entrapment of Ghetto Youth*. New York: Vintage, 1981.

Glenn, Norval D., and Erin Gotard. "The Religion of Blacks in the United States: Some Recent Trends and Current Characteristics," *American Journal of Sociology 83* (September 1977).

Graham, Billy. "Racism and the Evangelical Church," *Christianity Today* (October 4, 1993), p. 27.

Grover, Mark L. "The Lineage of Cain in the Land of Racial Democracy: The Mormon Priesthood and the Brazilian of African Descent." Paper presented at the annual meeting of the Mormon History Association, Omaha, Nebr., May 5–8, 1983.

Harding, Vincent. "Religion and Resistance among Antebellum Negroes, 1800–1860." In August Meier and Elliott Rudwick, eds., *The Making of Black America*. New York: Atheneum, 1969.

———. *There Is a River: The Black Struggle for Freedom in America*. New York: Harcourt Brace Jovanovich, 1981.

Haroldsen, E. O., and K. Harvey. "Diffusion of Shocking Good News," *Journalism Quarterly 56* (Winter 1979): 771–75.

Haselden, Kyle. *The Racial Problem in Christian Perspective*. New York: Harper, 1959.

Hentoff, Nat. *Black Anti-Semitism and Jewish Racism* (New York: Schocken, 1970).

Herberg, Will. *Protestant—Catholic—Jew* (New York: Doubleday, 1955).

Herskovits, Melville J. *The Myth of the Negro Past.* Boston: Beacon Press, 1958, 1990 (orig. ed., Harper & Bros., 1941).

Heywood, Yates. *The Negro Question Resolved.* Salt Lake City: Paragon Press, 1964.

Hicks, H. Beecher, Jr. *Images of the Black Preacher.* Valley Forge, Pa.: Judson Press, 1977.

Higgins, Chester A. "Leadership Change . . . New Man Heads Six Million Baptists," *The Crisis 80* (November 1982).

Hill, Donna. *Joseph Smith: The First Mormon.* Garden City, N.Y.: Doubleday, 1977 [esp. ch. 12, "Blacks in the Early Church," pp. 379–94].

Hill, Samuel S., Jr. "The South's Two Cultures." In Samuel S. Hill, ed., *Religion and the Solid South.* Nashville, Tenn.: Abingdon Press, 1972.

Hillman, Eugene. *Toward an African Christianity: Inculturation Applied.* New York: Paulist Press, 1993.

Hoge, Dean R., and David A. Roozen, eds. *Understanding Church Growth and Decline, 1950–1978.* New York: Pilgrim Press, 1970.

Hull, Gloria T., Patricia Bell Scott, and Barbara Smith, eds. *But Some of Us Are Brave: Black Women's Studies.* Old Westbury, N.Y.: Feminist Press, 1981.

Hunt, L. L. and J. G. "Black Religion as Both Opiate and Inspiration of Civil Rights Militance: Putting Marx's Data to the Test," *Social Forces* 56 (September 1977).

Isaacs, Harold R. *Idols of the Tribe.* New York: Harper & Row, 1975.

Jackson, J., II. *A Story of Christian Activism: The History of the National Baptist Convention, U.S.A., Inc.* Nashville, Tenn.: Townsend, 1980.

Johnston, Rubye F. *The Development of Negro Religion.* New York: Philosophical Library, 1954.

———. *The Religion of Negro Protestants: Changing Religious Attitudes and Practices.* New York: Philosophical Library, 1956.

Jones, Lawrence N. "The Black Churches in Historical Perspective," *The Crisis 89* (November 1982).

Jones, William R. *God in the Ghetto.* Elgin, Ill.: Progressive Baptist Publishing House, 1979.

———. *Is God a White Racist?* Garden City, N.Y.: Doubleday/Anchor, 1973.

Jordan, Winthrop. *White over Black* (Chapel Hill: University of North Carolina Press, 1968).

Katz, Phyllis A. "The Acquisition of Racial Attitudes in Children." In Phyllis A. Katz, ed., *Towards the Elimination of Racism* New York: Pergamon, 1976.

Kohn, Marek. "Science and Race Matters," *World Press Review* (December 1995), p. 48.

Kunjufu, Jawanza. *Black Economics: Solutions for Economic and Community Empowerment.* Chicago: African American Images, 1991.

Kunz, Phillip R. "Blacks and Mormonism: A Social Distance Change," *Psychological Reports* 45 (August 1979): 81–82.

Lacy, Daniel. *The White Use of Blacks in America.* New York: McGraw-Hill, 1972.

Lee, Carlton L. "Religious Roots of the Negro Protest." In Arnold Rose, ed., *Assuring Freedom to the Free.* Detroit: Wayne State University, 1964.

Lerner, Gerda, ed. *Black Women in White America: A Documentary History.* New York: Vintage, 1972.

Levine, Lawrence. *Black Culture and Black Consciousness.* New York: Oxford University Press, 1978.

Lincoln, C. Eric. *The Black Church Since Frazier.* New York: Schocken, 1974.

———. *The Black Experience in Religion.* Garden City, N.Y.: Anchor/Doubleday, 1974.

———. "Black Methodists and the Middle-Class Mentality," In James S. Gadsden, ed., *Experiences, Struggles, and Hopes of the Black Church.* Nashville, Tenn.: Tidings, 1975.

———. *The Black Muslims in America.* Boston: Beacon Press, 1961.

———. *Coming Through the Fire: Surviving Race and Place in America.* Durham, N.C.: Duke University Press, 1996.

———. "Contemporary Black Religion: In Search of a Sociology," *Journal of the Interdenominational Theology Center* V (Spring 1978).

———. "The Social Cosmos of Black Ecumenism," *The Journal of the ITC* 7 (Fall 1979).

———. *Sounds of the Struggle: Persons and Perspectives in Civil Rights.* New York: William Morrow, 1967.

Lincoln, C. Eric, and Lawrence H. Mamiya. *The Black Church in the African American Experience.* Durham, N.C.: Duke University Press, 1990.

Lye, William. "From Burundi to Zaire: Taking the Gospel to Africa," *Ensign 10* (March 1980): 10–15.

Lythgoe, Dennis L. "Negro Slavery in Utah." M.A. thesis, University of Utah, 1966.

Mack, Raymond W. *Race, Class, and Power,* 2nd ed. New York: Van Nostrand/Reinhold, 1968.

Madron, Thomas William, Hart M. Nelsen, and Raytha L. Yokley. "Religion as a Determinant of Militancy and Political Participation Among Black Americans," *American Behavioral Scientist* 17 (July–August 1974).

Mamiya, Lawrence H. "From Black Muslims to Bilalian: The Evolution of a Movement," *Journal for the Study of Religion* 21 (June 1982).

Marden, Charles E., and Gladys Meyer. *Minorities in American Society*, 2nd ed. New York: American Book, 1962.

Marty, Martin E. *Righteous Empire: The Protestant Experience in America*. New York: Dial, 1970.

Marx, Gary T. *Protest and Prejudice*. New York: Harper & Row, 1969.

Mauss, Armand L. "Comments: White on Black Among the Mormons: A Critique of White and White," *Sociological Analysis* 42 (Fall 1981): 277–83.

——. "The Fading of the Pharaoh's Curse: The Decline and Fall of the Priesthood Ban Against Blacks in the Mormon Church," *Dialogue* 14 (Fall 1981): 10–45.

——. "Mormonism and Secular Attitudes Toward Negroes," *Pacific Sociological Review* 9 (Fall 1966): 91–99.

Mays, Benjamin E. *Seeking to Be Christian in Race Relations*. Study and Action Pamphlets on Race Relations. New York: Friendship, 1964.

Mays, Benjamin E., and Joseph W. Nicholson. *The Negro's Church*. New York: Russell & Russell, 1969 (reissue orig. ed., *Religions Research*, 1933).

McClain, William B. "What Is Authentic Black Worship?" In James S. Gadsen, ed., *Experiences, Struggles, and Hopes of the Black Church*. Nashville, Tenn.: Tidings, 1975.

——. *Whither Thou Goest* (Boston: Schenkman, 1984).

McConkie, Bruce R. *Mormon Doctrine*. Salt Lake City: Bookcraft, 1958 [esp. entries on "Negroes," "Cain," "Ham," "Pre-existence," "Priesthood," and "Races of Men"].

McMinn, Lisa Graham, and Mark R. McMinn. "For Whom the Bell Curves," *Christianity Today* (December 12, 1994), p. 19.

McMurrin, Sterling M. "The Negroes Among the Mormons." Address to the Annual Banquet of the Salt Lake City Chapter of the NAACP, June 21, 1968.

McNamara, Patrick H. *Religion, American Style*. New York: Harper & Row, 1974.

McPherson, James B., et al. *Blacks in America*. New York: Doubleday, 1972.

Meltzer, Milton. *Slavery: From the Rise of Western Civilization to the Renaissance*. New York: Cowles, 1971.

Mitchell, Henry H. *Black Preaching.* New York: Harper & Row, 1979.

Monson, Farrell Ray. "History of the South African Mission of the Church of Jesus Christ of Latter-Day Saints, 1853–1970." M.A. thesis, Brigham Young University, 1971.

Montagu, Ashley. *Man's Most Dangerous Myth.* New York: Harper Bros., 1942.

Morgan, Timothy C. "Racist No More? Black Leaders Ask," *Christianity Today* (August 14, 1995), p. 53.

Morganthau, Tom. "What Color Is Black?" *Newsweek* (February 13, 1995), pp. 62–65.

Morris, Aldon. *The Origins of the Civil Rights Movement: Black Communities Organizing for Change.* New York: Free Press, 1984.

Mukenge, Ida Rousseau. *The Black Church in Urban America: A Case Study in Political Economy.* Lanham, Md.: University Press of America, 1983.

Murray, Charles. *Losing Ground: American Social Policy, 1950–1980.* New York: Basic Books, 1984.

Myers, Gustavus. *History of Bigotry in the United States.* New York: Random House, 1960.

Myrdal, Gunnar. *An American Dilemma: The Negro Problem and Modern Democracy.* New York: Harper & Row, 1962 (orig. ed., 1944).

Nelsen, Hart M., Thomas W. Madron, and Raytha L. Yokley. "Black Religion's Promethean Motif: Orthodoxy and Militancy," *American Journal of Sociology 81* (July 1975).

Nelsen, Hart M., and Anne K. Nelsen. *Black Church in the Sixties.* Lexington: University of Kentucky Press, 1975.

Nelsen, Hart M., Raytha L. Yokley, and Anne K. Nelsen, eds. *The Black Church in America.* New York: Basic Books, 1971.

Nelson, Lowry. "Mormons and the Negro," *The Nation 174* (May 24, 1952): 448.

Newell, Linda King, and Valeen Tippetts Avery. "Jane Manning James: Black Saint, 1847 Pioneer," *Ensign* 9 (August 1979): 26–29.

Nobel, Lowell. "Blacks and Whites: Who's Inferior?" *Urban Family* (Winter 1995), p. 34.

Ochs, Stephen J. *Desegregating the Altar: The Josephites and the Struggle for Black Priests, 1871–1960.* Baton Rouge: Louisiana State University Press, 1990.

Oliver, David H. *A Negro on Mormonism.* Salt Lake City: D. H. Oliver, 1963.

Olsen, Peggy. "Ruffin Bridgeforth: Leader and Father to Mormon Blacks," *This People* (Winter 1980): 15–16.

Ottley, Roi, and William J. Weatherly. *The Negro in New York*. New York: Praeger, 1967.

Palmer, Spencer J. "Mormons in West Africa: New Terrain for the Sesquicentennial Church." Annual Religion Faculty Lecture, Brigham Young University, September 27, 1979.

Pannell, William. *The Coming of Race Wars? A Cry for Reconciliation*. Grand Rapids, Mich.: Zondervan, 1993.

Paris, Peter. "The Social World of the Black Church," *The Drew Gateway* (Spring 1983).

Parsons, Talcott, and Kenneth B. Clark, eds. *The Negro American*. Boston: Houghton Mifflin, 1966.

Perkins, Spencer. "Can Blacks and Whites Be Neighbors?" *Urban Family* (Winter 1992), pp. 21–23.

Perkins, Spencer, and Chris Rice. *More Than Equals: Racial Healing for the Sake of the Gospel*. Downers Grove, Ill.: InterVarsity Press, 1993.

Peterson, Mark E. "Race Problems—As They Affect the Church." Address at Brigham Young University, August 27, 1954. LDS Church Archives.

Raboteau, Albert, Jr. *Slave Religion: The Invisible Institution in the Antebellum South*. New York: Oxford University Press, 1980.

Redding, J. Saunders. *They Came in Chains*. Philadelphia: Lippincott, 1950.

Reed, Adolph L., Jr. *The Jesse Jackson Phenomenon*. New Haven, Conn.: Yale University Press, 1986.

Reimers, David M. *White Protestantism and the Negro*. New York: Oxford University Press, 1965.

Reuter, Edward B. *The American Race Problem*. New York: Crowell, 1970.

Richardson, Harry V. *Dark Salvation: The Story of Methodism As It Developed Among Blacks in America*. Garden City, N.Y. Anchor/Doubleday, 1976.

Riggs, Marcia Y. *Awake, Arise and Act: A Womanist Call for Black Liberation*. Cleveland: Pilgrim, 1994.

Roberts, J. Deotis. "The Impact of the Black Church: Sole Surviving Black Institution," *Journal of the Interdenominational Theological Center VI* (Spring 1979).

Robinson, Frank. "C. H. Mason and the White COGIC." Los Angeles: West Angeles Church of God in Christ Tape Ministry, n.d.

Rohyer, Wayne C. *Black Profiles of White Americans*. Philadelphia: F. A. Davis, 1970.

Roof, Wade Clark. *Race and Residence in American Cities*. Philadelphia: American Academy of Political and Social Science, 1979.

Roof, Wade Clark, and William McKinney. *American Mainline Religion: Its Changing Shape and Future.* New Brunswick, N.J.: Rutgers University Press, 1987.

Rosenberg, Morris, and Roberta Simmons. *Black and White Self-Esteem: The Urban School Child.* Washington, D.C.: American Sociological Association, 1971.

Salisbury, W. Seward. *Religion in American Culture.* Homewood. Ill.: Dorsey Press, 1964.

Sanders, Cheryl Jeanne. *Empowerment Ethics for a Liberated People: A Path to African American Social Transformation.* Minneapolis: Fortress Press, 1995.

Scherer, Lester B. *Slavery and the Churches in Early America, 1619–1819.* Grand Rapids, Mich.: William B. Eerdmans, 1975.

Scott-Jones, Diane. *Black Families and the Education of Black Children: Current Issues.* Paper commissioned by the Committee on the Status of Black Americans, National Research Council, Washington, D.C., 1987.

Sernett, Milton C. *Black Religion and American Evangelicalism: White Protestants, Plantation Missions, and the Flowering of Negro Christianity, 1787–1865.* Metuchen, N.J.: Scarecrow Press, 1975.

Simpson, George E., and J. Milton Yinger. *Racial and Cultural Minorities,* 5th ed. New York: Plenum, 1985.

Smart, M. Neff. "The Challenge of Africa," *Dialogue 12* (Summer 1979): 54–57.

Smith, George D., Jr. "The Negro Doctrine—An Afterview," *Dialogue 12* (Summer 1979): 64–67.

Smith, H. Shelton. *In His Image, But . . .* Durham, N.C.; Duke University Press, 1972.

Smith, Joseph Fielding, Jr. "The Negro and the Priesthood," *Improvement Era 27* (April 1924): 564–65.

———. *The Way to Perfection.* Salt Lake City: Deseret Books, 1931 [esp. chs. 7 ("Appointment of Lineage"), 15 ("The Seed of Cain"), and 16 ("The Seed of Cain After the Flood")].

Smith, Kelly Miller. *Social Crisis Preaching.* Macon, Ga.: Mercer University Press, 1984.

Smith, Wilfred Cantwell. *Islam in Modern History.* New York: New American Library, 1959.

Spanier, Graham B., and Paul C. Glick. "Mate Selection Differentials Between Whites and Blacks in the United States," *Social Forces 58* (3) (March 1986): 707–725.

Stack, Carol. *All Our Kin: Strategies for Survival in a Black Community.* New York: Harper & Row, 1974.

Stanley, A, Knighton. *The Children Is Crying: Congregationalism Among Black People.* New York: Pilgrim Press, 1979.

Stark, Rodney, and Charles Y. Glock. *American Piety: The Nature of Religious Commitment.* Berkeley: University of California Press, 1970.

Steinberg, Stephen. *The Ethnic Myth: Race, Ethnicity, and Class in America.* New York: Atheneum Publishers, 1981.

Stewart, John J. *Mormonism and the Negro.* Orem, Utah: Community Press, 1960.

Stokes, Catherine M. " 'Plenty Good Room' in Relief Society," *Dialogue: A Journal of Mormon Thought 21* (Winter 1988).

Sudarkasa, Niara. "Interpreting the African Heritage in Afro-American Family Organization." In Harriet Pipes McAdoo, ed., *Black Families.* Beverly Hills, Calif.: Sage Publications, 1981.

Taggart, Stephen G. *Mormonism's Negro Policy: Social and Historical Origins.* Salt Lake City: University of Utah Press, 1970.

Tanner, Jerald, and Sandra Tanner. *The Negro in Mormon Theology.* Salt Lake City: Modern Microfilm Co., 1963.

Thurman, Howard. *Jesus and the Disinherited.* New York: Abingden-Cokesburg Press, 1949.

Turner, Ronny E. "The Black Minister: Uncle Tom or Abolitionist?" *Phylon 34* (March 1973).

Turner, Wallace. *The Mormon Establishment* (Boston: Houghton Mifflin, 1966).

Tuttle, William M., Jr. *Race Riot.* New York: Antheneum, 1970.

Walker, Clarence E. *A Rock in a Weary Land: The African Methodist Episcopal Church During the Civil War and Reconstruction.* Baton Rouge: Louisiana State University Press, 1982.

Wallace, Turner. *The Mormon Establishment.* New York: Houghton Mifflin, 1966.

Walton, Brian. "A University's Dilemma: B.Y.U. and Blacks," *Dialogue 6* (Spring 1971): 31–36.

Washington, James M. *The Origins and Emergence of Black Baptist Separatism, 1863–1897.* Ann Arbor, Mich.: University Microfilms International, 1983.

Washington, James Melvin, ed. *Conversations with God: Two Centuries of Prayers by African Americans.* New York: HarperCollins, 1994.

Washington, Joseph R., Jr. *Black Religion.* Boston: Beacon Press, 1964.

————. *Black Sects and Cults: The Power Axis in an Ethnic Ethic.* C. Eric Lincoln Series on Black Religion. Garden City, N.Y.: Anchor/Doubleday, 1973.

Weatherford, W. D. *American Churches and the Negro.* North Quincy, Mass.: Christopher Publishing House, 1957.

Weisbord, R. G., and Arthur Stein. *Bittersweet Encounter.* Westport, Conn.: Greenwood Press, 1972.

West, Cornell. *Race Matters.* Boston: Beacon Press, 1993.

White, O. Kendall, Jr. "Boundary Maintenance, Blacks, and the Mormon Priesthood," *Journal of Religious Thought 37* (Fall/Winter 1980): 30–44.

White, O. Kendell, Jr., and Daryl White. "Abandoning an Unpopular Policy: An Analysis of the Decision Granting the Mormon Priesthood to Blacks," *Sociological Analysis 41* (Fall 1980): 231–45.

"White Pieties and Black Reality." In James C. Stone and Frederick W. Schneider, eds., *Teaching in the Inner City, Vol. 3: Commitment to Teaching.* New York: Crowell, 1970.

Wilmore, Gayraud S. *Black and Presbyterian: The Heritage and the Hope.* Philadelphia: Geneva Press, 1983.

————. *Black Religion and Black Radicalism: An Interpretation of the Religious History of Afro-American People,* 2nd ed. Maryknoll, N.Y.: Orbis, 1983.

Wilson, William Julius. *The Declining Significance of Race: Blacks and Changing American Institutions.* Chicago: University of Chicago Press, 1978; 2nd ed., 1980.

————. *The Truly Disadvantaged: The Inner City, the Underclass, and Public Policy.* Chicago: University of Chicago Press, 1987.

Wiltse, Charles M., ed. *David Walker's Appeal.* New York: Hill and Wang, 1965.

Woodson, Carter G. *The History of the Negro Church.* Washington, D.C.: Associated Publishers, 1921.

Yette, Samuel F. *The Choice: The Issue of Black Survival in America.* New York: Putnam, 1971.

Yin, Robert K. *Race, Creed, Color, or National Origin.* Atarsca, Ill.: F. T. Peacock, 1973.

Index

301